A Billion Blue Wildebeest

A Memoir of an African Childhood, some Animal Rescues, and One Disabled Cat

Catherine MacLaine

ALKIRA
PUBLISHING

A Billion Blue Wildebeest
Catherine MacLaine
Copyright © 2025
Published by Alkira Publishing, Australia
ABN: 32736122056
http://www.alkirapublishing.com

This is a work of nonfiction; all the events in this book happened. To the best of my ability, I have related events, places, animals and people, and recreated conversations, from my memories, my journals, family home videos, letters, emails, and aerograms, as faithfully as possible.

In order to protect the privacy of some individuals, certain biographical details and names have been changed and some locations changed to maintain narrative flow or protect privacy. Pseudonyms were used throughout (Fire, Joan, Neema, Leopard Lodge, David, Matthew, Luke, Saul, Ahmed, Sister Maria, and the Queen of Diamonds), but the following individuals have been represented with their true names: Dr. Thomas Kahema, Jacob, Pravin, Afwene, Ms. Voss, all of the Tingatinga artists, George and Joy Adamson, Boy, Alex, all the Von Nagy family, Dr. Sekidio and all my family members and pets. Any mistakes found in this book are my responsibility alone.

All illustrations from the author. All photographs by the author unless otherwise stated

Paperback ISBN: 978-1-922329-87-5
Hardback ISBN: 978-1-922329-90-5

For the child who stands

amongst the ancestors.

Contents

Chapter 1	Not Enough Salaams	1
Chapter 2	The Announcement	4
Chapter 3	Pierced and Punctured for Africa	8
Chapter 4	Africa, the Dawn Continent	13
Chapter 5	Pole Pole	17
Chapter 6	Dead Caterpillars & Disabled Cats	22
Chapter 7	Home Amidst Sisal	26
Chapter 8	Nonna and the Mongrel	30
Chapter 9	Putzi Flies and Plenty, Plenty Candles	35
Chapter 10	He Staggers	41
Chapter 11	Mongooses Make Dreadful Pets	49
Chapter 12	Did You Not Ask for a Snake?	54
Chapter 13	All We Ever See Are Wildebeest	59
Chapter 14	He Eats Funny Too	64
Chapter 15	The Word for Ten	71
Chapter 16	Only A Mock Charge	78
Chapter 17	Eponymous Animals	90
Chapter 18	African Cat on A Dutch Airline	97
Chapter 19	Tingatinga	102
Chapter 20	Her Mother Bought Your Painting	110
Chapter 21	A Brown Dog	115
Chapter 22	A Present for Mother	120
Chapter 23	Hello Mr. Africa	126
Chapter 24	School	133
Chapter 25	Just Keep Going, Mr. Nyoka	140
Chapter 26	Halcyon Days at the Zebra Park	147
Chapter 27	An Original Animal, & the Empty Water Bucket	153
Chapter 28	A Graceless Cat	164
Chapter 29	Creeping Thieves	171

Chapter 30 Uncoated and Incomparable	177
Chapter 31 Not a Mistake in My Chart	182
Chapter 32 Not A Bad Nyoka	186
Chapter 33 African Jollification	190
Chapter 34 Implacable Foes	194
Chapter 35 Cathyfromafrica	200
Chapter 36 The Lion King	203
Chapter 37 Cin's Dinner Guest	208
Chapter 38 FOMO Cat	215
Chapter 39 Fupi and Fupi and Fupi	220
Chapter 40 Man-Eater	225
Chapter 41 Swept by the Roar	232
Chapter 42 A Movie Star	236
Chapter 43 Limpy Lou	242
Chapter 44 Feeder Fish and Donkey Hides	247
Chapter 45 Seven Stumped Vets	252
Chapter 46 La Luna	259
Chapter 47 Regrets and Mongooses	266
Chapter 48 Two Empty Cages	273
Chapter 49 Rearing Queen of Diamonds	280
Chapter 50 The Magic Circle	287
Chapter 51 Animal Communicator	294
Chapter 52 The Tragedy	299
Chapter 53 The Basking Platform	305
Chapter 54 Baby Birds	310
Chapter 55 All Three Chambers	314
Chapter 56 Wildebeest Trophy	329
Epilogue	333
About the Author	339
A Note from the Author	340
Acknowledgments	341

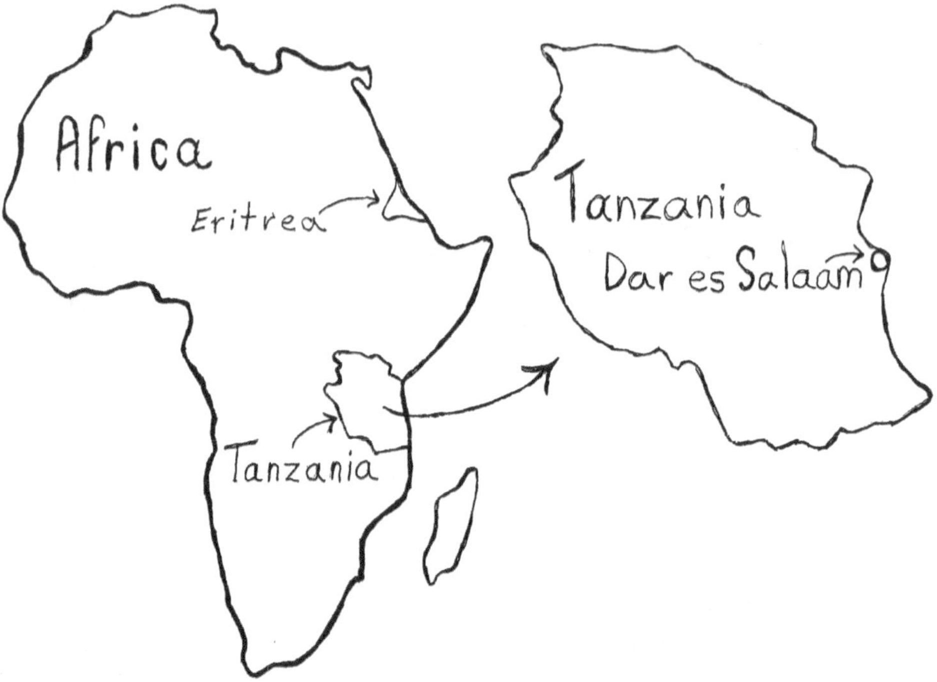
Africa
Eritrea
Tanzania
Tanzania
Dar es Salaam

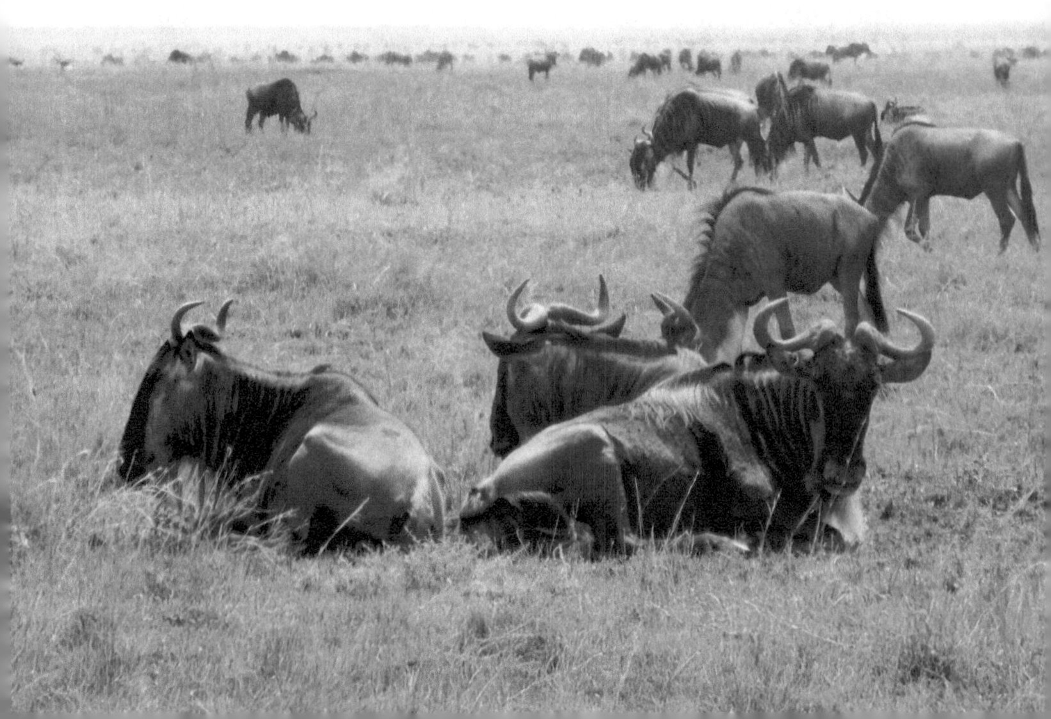

Chapter 1
Not Enough Salaams

There are as many Africas as there are books about Africa.
—Beryl Markham

Virginia, February 2017

A brown tabby street cat, born in Tanzania, East Africa, sat on a hotel bathroom floor in the United States of America. I, a Canadian citizen, who now lived in America but had grown up in Africa, was down there with him, fighting back tears of relief and feeding him from my cupped hands. For whatever reason, this cat was now happily wolfing down all the same food he had previously declined for the last thirty or so hours. The feeding had to be done by hand. His flailing head tremors were still there, in full force, but at least I could help his aim as the poor wretch stuffed his face.

I raised my bleary eyes from the ravenous cat and cast a longing glance at my hotel bed, visible from the bathroom doorway. A faint whiff of bleach and detergent had wafted up from that oh-so-tempting bed when I had dropped my suitcase onto it so wearily a short while ago.

To finally stretch out in an actual bed again after a day and a half of overseas travel—I couldn't wait! I was returning from my first trip back to Tanzania in forty-two years, a country in which I had spent several years of my childhood. It had been a bucket list trip to my old hometown of Dar es Salaam, as well as various Tanzanian wildlife parks. I had returned from my far-too-short trip laden with over a thousand photographs.

And one particular treasure: Stanley.

Tearing my eyes away from the enticing bed, I turned my attention once more to my new cat. I had adopted Stanley from Dar days ago. On the day we met, he had bitten me.

"*Salaam, salaam, tulia,*"[1] I had murmured in Kiswahili and Arabic to him throughout our long trip to America, hoping to stave off another panic attack (my bites were only half healed, after all) and not sure yet how many English words this African cat knew. From his prior life as a *taka taka paka*,[2] Kiswahili may well have been the only language he'd heard. And about a third of Swahili comes from Arabic words anyway.

Now, probably more due to sheer exhaustion than my *salaams*, Stanley was meek as a lamb here on the bathroom floor. He lay stretched out and still to be cleaned from where he had soiled his fur while in his traveling carrier all those arduous hours. From wheels up in Tanzania to wheels down here in America, more than a full day had already passed. The wretched cat guzzled syringe after syringe of water. The syringes were an easier way to keep him hydrated rather than leaving him to try to lap water from a bowl, given those head tremors. I blinked hard and tried to refocus multiple times, bringing the syringe to his mouth, but eventually his thirst was satisfied. Attempting to rally my disrupted circadian

---

1   peace, calm
2   garbage cat/street cat

rhythms once more, I clumsily applied a wet washcloth to his odorous coat. In due course, his feces-encrusted, urine-soaked fur was cleaned and dried. He stretched his legs, staggering around the bathroom with his characteristic wobble.

Now—at long last—the two of us could finally get some sleep. Feebly stripping every last towel off the racks with leaden hands, I left him ensconced in his own impromptu terry cloth nest and tottered off to my own bed, with almost a knuckle-dragging simian gait. I was just grateful not to have been bitten again.

It soon dawned on Stanley that I was on the other side of the bathroom door and that he was now separated from me for the first time during our entire withering, harrowing, thirty-hour journey.

This would not do.

I was loath to try fishing an escaped, disoriented African cat out from underneath an American hotel bed. The structure of my thoughts, gossamer at best after this much traveling, had now dissipated. My slushy brain, however, clung to one resolve: that cat *has* to stay in the bathroom tonight.

Stanley redoubled his efforts to convey to me just how very, *very* anxious he felt at being separated from me in this manner. The heart-rending yowling rose in pitch. Flailing, grasping tabby paws, with little, white-tipped toes, reached desperately for me from under the bathroom door.

How can one sleep in a comfortable bed when one's cat is crying so pitifully?

There are simply not enough *salaams*.

Dawn found the two of us groggily rousing from sleep, having passed the night curled up together on the bathroom floor.

Chapter 2
The Announcement

Dear Dad,
I will say goodbye to you in Kiswahili: Kwaheri.
Love, Cathy

Montreal, November 1970

The day I was informed that our family would soon be catapulted overseas, I was outside, digging out happily hibernating caterpillars that I had found. Caterpillars who, I adamantly concluded, needed to be rescued. My mother had called me indoors on that day in early November 1970, a month shy of my eighth birthday, for the announcement that we would be moving.

Again.

But this time we would be moving outside Montreal, outside Canada, outside North America. We were going to cross the Atlantic Ocean and, and we were—

We were moving to Africa.

I stared down at the kitchen floor, still spotless from its thrice daily mopping.

Puddles formed from the snow melting off the boots I had

forgotten to remove, and the familiar scent of pine-scented floor cleaning solution now wafted up to my nose, which was still a little runny from the winter gusts outside.

"Will there be any caterpillars that I can play with, in Africa?"

Mother followed my gaze to the jam jar of caterpillars I clutched in my small hands. I looked back up at her beseechingly.

My brother, Craig, a pensive teenager, stayed silent and contemplative, his hands shoved deep in his pockets. Dad, who was actually my stepfather, gave me a warm smile as he too glanced at my caterpillars.

Mother exchanged a sharp look with Dad, then crouched down to look me in the eye and reassured me that there would be ample caterpillars in Africa with which I could play. "And countless other animals too."

"I needn't bring these?"

"No, my darling, you needn't." She stroked the hair off my forehead. "I think Canadian caterpillars would be happier staying here in Canada, don't you?"

Mother's seismic news continued. Our departure was in five weeks, she said. Which meant I would not be here to see these little creatures (rescued from certain death, after all) change into butterflies in the coming months.

Seeing her little girl still somewhat dubious, Mother sweetened the deal. "And there will be snails in Africa!" she went on, tapping into my affinity for all animals. "And we can visit the national parks, and you'll see all sorts of wild animals there!"

Mother watched my freckled face, noting my wavering smile as I swallowed hard and my eyes went back to observing my caterpillars. I had three woolly worm caterpillars and a garden snail—a veritable embarrassment of riches. My brow furrowed, and I wiggled my loose front tooth with my tongue as I pondered this whole Africa thing.

"And don't worry about the tooth fairy."

My loose tooth had not escaped Mother's notice. She continued, "The tooth fairy will be well able to find you there!" She shot Dad a meaningful glance. "Isn't that right?" Mother widened her eyes at Dad and cleared her throat.

"Why, yes! Oh, certainly!" Craig and Dad together rallied to the cause, seeking in bright and cheerful tones to reassure me that the tooth fairy would be well able to find me, whether here in Montreal, Canada, or far across the ocean in Africa.

The subject of Africa had been discussed before in my childhood, due to the somewhat odd fact that my mother had been born there. By a twist of fate, my maternal Italian grandparents happened to have been in Eritrea, East Africa, firmly planning to get back to Italy in plenty of time for the birth of the baby, but my blue-eyed Caucasian mother had been born on African soil instead. Eritrea had been an Italian colony back then, and my grandfather was there with the colonial Italian Cavalry, a military occupation but not quite a war zone at that time. Also on the East Africa coast, but further south, was the country to which we would be moving: Tanzania.

Later that day, Dad and I settled down with our *Encyclopedia Britannica*.

"Sweetheart, let's start with T for Tanzania."

He must have been gamely hiding his own mixed feelings about Africa. It is, undeniably, at least a trifle daunting to be told you are to relocate your family halfway across the world, seven time zones ahead, and that you are being posted to a country you've never seen.

The State Trading Corporation, STC, working with the Tanzanian government on their export and import operations, needed a financial comptroller with experience in a large corporation. My stepfather had applied and was hired for the job.

He had very recently married my mother after her amicable divorce from my father, Bob MacLaine, so really each one of us was still adjusting to these life changes. After the Ts had been sufficiently pored over, we consulted the As for Africa, after which I wanted to look up, one by one, each of the wild animals found in East Africa. Regrettably, that night I was shooed off to bed, after "elephant," "giraffe," and "lion" had been studied but before we could get to "zebra."

I was beginning to get the impression that Africa was a land where animals with paws chased after animals with hooves. And ate them.

Chapter 3
Pierced and Punctured for Africa

Yes, we had three rounds of injections. No, you didn't like them.
—Craig

Montreal, November 1970

Big puffy folds of my eiderdown bedspread covered my seven-year-old little body, curled up fetus-tight, down at the foot of my bed—strategically positioned, for good measure, under a large pile of my stuffed animal toys. Because of my brilliant stealth, I was now confident that I had quite definitely avoided any possibility of being discovered and hauled into any stupid vaccine clinic. The previous night, Mother had informed me, as gently as possible, that we were all going to receive immunizations in preparation to go live in Africa. My response could not have been more horrorstricken had Mother warned me of an impending amputation. Still, none of that mattered now, because they'd never find me. The three of them would just have to go without me. And that was final.

Two hours later the four of us were queued up at the Westmount Municipal Clinic on Stanton Street in downtown

Montreal, Canada.

"So! Headed to Africa, eh? How exciting!" The doctor greeting us in the examining room was far heartier than any of us felt.

"Let's see, now . . ." he continued. "Let's see . . . Where in Africa, did you say?"

"Tanzania." Dad kept his response minimal, watching my face. The doctor had his back to us as he began searching through his files, so he missed the whole family's nervous glances at me, as they each wondered how much time was left before a certain anguished little girl completely unraveled.

"Tanzania, eh? Let's see which ones you will need for Tanzania." He rifled through pages extracted from his filing cabinet that contained daunting lists of suggested vaccines for Africa. "Hepatitis A, Hepatitis B . . . Oh, yes, definitely those. Polio—you have all had that vaccine already, haven't you, eh? Typhoid, yellow fever . . . Oh, I can give you that one later. Tuberculosis, meningitis, and cholera . . ."

My face was growing paler by the minute.

The nurse explained she would administer two shots in one arm and one in the other. She went on to mention something else, none of which I absorbed. By now I was rocking back and forth in my seat with my arms wrapped around my middle, staring at my parents.

Mother and Dad took their vaccines calmly and sensibly. Craig took his, calmly and sensibly. Now it was my turn.

I was neither calm nor sensible, and the first vaccine had yet to be administered.

"NoPleaseNoPleaseNoPlease!" My babbled bargaining, in which I offered to just forgo Africa entirely, at a steadily ascending volume, was duly noted and declined.

A cool quick swipe from an alcohol swab on my arm.

A piercing wail filled the room, just like the first one emitted by me yesterday after learning I would soon receive shots, and I realized this second piercing wail was emitted by me too.

Before I knew it, the first injection had been administered.

"N-no more shots, please," I whimpered, rubbing the smarting spot on my arm. Noticing my parents' embarrassed faces, I ruefully turned to the nurse. "I'm sorry that I screamed just now, ma'am."

"Oh, sweetie, this won't take long," she replied, sympathetic. "And guess what! I have a heap of Bugs Bunny Band-Aids you can choose from when this is over!"

The anguish and agony of two shots in one arm and one in the other was eventually over, and as promised, she handed over the entire motherlode for my perusal.

"Getting shots isn't much fun, eh, kiddo?" Craig said softly, as he carefully held the box for me. My own hands were still too tremulous to not drop it. I belabored my selection from a wide array featuring not only Bugs Bunny but also Mickey Mouse, Snoopy, and Superman. It had not escaped my notice that my big brother had not flinched in the least while receiving his shots, and in my estimation, he deserved nothing short of the Victoria Cross. He was well known for his long, lanky stride and an uncanny resemblance to Paul McCartney, but to me, his courage eclipsed all these.

Why can't I be brave like you always are? I wanted to say. But I didn't. Three Snoopy Band-Aids were patiently applied to each site where my skinny arms had been poked and pierced and perforated for Africa, and we all put our coats back on, left the fluorescent-lighted building with the slight antiseptic scent, and headed back out into the bitter Canadian winter, back to the car. Mother and Dad chided me, as we trudged through the parking lot, over my "disgraceful histrionics" having frayed their nerves in the vaccine clinic just now. I sighed and tried to ignore my still-smarting arms.

"Well, anyway," I continued in a small voice, "I'm just glad the shots are over. That was no fun."

Craig looked sharply at me, but we trudged on in silence for a few more minutes. Then: "Say, kiddo?"

We had almost reached the car by now, with Mother and Dad still reproachful but several steps ahead of us.

"Yes?"

Craig met my watery, lopsided attempt at a polite smile with a warm smile of his own. In a conspiratorial whisper, he asked me if Cadbury was still my favorite chocolate bar. I replied that it was.

"Okay . . ." he said, thinking hard. "How about . . ." Still keeping his voice low enough to be out of Mother's earshot. "How about I buy you a chocolate bar, but you mustn't tell Mother. And perhaps that might make you feel better?"

I was genuinely touched that my brother was offering to buy me something, when I knew he was meticulously saving up every penny from his *Montreal Gazette* newspaper delivery route to buy himself his very own motorcycle. However, I was not inclined to turn down his offers to ply me with chocolate.

"Would that make you feel better, kiddo? For next week?"

"Next week? Why? What's happening next week?"

"For our next Africa shots."

I stopped dead in my tracks.

Craig's voice was continuing. "Remember what the nurse just told us? Three rounds of three injections, each round a week apart. Then after that, we still need to get the yellow fever vaccine . . ."

Mother and Dad spun around, hearing my piercing wail

A Billion Blue Wildebeest

of despair, and I was bundled into the car.

Chapter 4
Africa, the Dawn Continent

"The sun, vividly painting the sky with the colours of gold and silver, saffron and opal, when its rays and gorgeous tints were reflected upon the tops of the everlasting forest with the quiet and holy calm of heaven."
—Henry Morton Stanley, 1871, *How I Found Livingstone.*

Dar es Salaam, December 1970

My first African sunrise, seen from the air, rendered me speechless. Stunned, even. Glorious beams of gold, copper and purple transitioned into periwinkle. The splendor was reflected on the clouds and lifted my mood, which had slumped somewhat after hours of monotonous flight. Hope now stirred out of the dormant recesses of my seven-year-old brain and a grin spread across my freckled face. I stole a glance at my brother, seated in the row behind us. He was brightening up too.

The comic book I had been reading, *Tintin in the Congo*, slid off my lap, forgotten.

About thirty thousand feet below me was the continent that I had gazed at in our *Encyclopedia Britannica*, memorizing its shape. By this point, we had traveled for two days, on two flights, with multiple stops. The sheer enormity of Africa was difficult to grasp—the entire continent itself was two-thirds larger than my homeland of Canada. Over three times bigger than the United States, I was told. So far on this journey, I had flown over Canadian snow, over ocean, over mountains and over desert. Now I was seeing snow—*snow?*—once again. In Africa. I didn't expect it. Was this fact in our encyclopedia, and I just missed it?

Mount Kilimanjaro, the tallest peak in Africa, was barely visible off the left wing, very far off in the distance. I only remember a tiny snowcapped peak with nothing around it. Kili, nicknamed "the Roof of Africa," is freestanding, and not part of any mountain range.

I was disappointed to have gotten only the briefest glimpse of Kili, but I was devastated to be told by my parents that despite my best efforts to stay awake, I had slept through my very first crossing of the equator.

It seemed only minutes after breakfast was cleared when I started to notice the familiar pressure in my ears and a change in the angle of the light through the windows.

"Ladies and gentlemen," came the captain's voice over the PA system, "we are beginning our descent into . . ."

I missed what he said next because I was drumming my feet again and clapping my hands in exuberance. Mother and Dad both had to hush me.

"My little sister is such a nut," Craig said to his seatmate, who had asked where "that noise" was coming from.

We descended below the canopy of wispy cirrus clouds, and my future home came into view. From my window this bright morning, I saw the eastern coastal portion of Tanzania for the first time. The land was bathed in the earliest rays of the sunrise, and I could just make out fields in varying shades of green and tan. Thoughts of my new homeland crossed my mind. This was the land, after all, for which I had had to be perforated, pierced, and punctured with all those dreadful vaccinations, week after week after week. Unlike the "once and done" ordinary childhood vaccinations that I had (barely) endured, these "Africa shots" had continued week after week after week. Warranted? I fervently hoped so. I reflexively rubbed my arm as my thoughts turned to the comforting subject of animals.

What if Africa turned out to be bare, with nary an animal to be seen? My family had all promised me, in a body, that I would find no shortage of animals in Africa to delight in.

Even my biological father, back in Montreal, had assured me of a plenitude of animals when I had promised to write to him regularly from Africa. Indeed, the following years involved multiple "Dear Dad" letters, which he and I both enjoyed. My mother, too, sent regular updates to him about "the Craig-O and the Cath," as my brother and I had been nicknamed from infancy. Her "Dear Bob" letters were often combined with mine.

Now, fidgeting in my plane seat, I ruminated over the scarcity of animals I feared in Africa.

The loss of my beloved caterpillars had been no light matter, in my mind, and I was convinced I was due ample recompense. My convictions wavered. What if neither bird nor beast could be found?

Africa had jolly well better be worth it.

Buildings and roads soon came into sharper focus. I could hear the aircraft's wheels lowering for landing. Mother, Dad, and I joyfully held hands, waiting for the familiar rumble.

Then: *Bump-buh-bump.*

A Billion Blue Wildebeest

Wheels down in Tanzania.
The reverse thrust engines roared.
"Ladies and gentlemen, welcome to Dar es Salaam."

CHAPTER 5
Pole Pole

Dear Dad,
So far Dar es Salaam is HOT!
Love, Cathy

Dar es Salaam, December, 1970

We learned about *pole pole* in our very first week in Dar es Salaam.

The Kiswahili phrase covers the concept of going slowly, or gently. This was not to be confused, we learned, with the solitary word *pole*.[3] We learned about *pole pole* because we were, initially, really taken aback by the heat and humidity.

Mother typically moved with characteristic unhurried decorum, but this humidity made her more languid still. During our first week, her indefatigable cheer (as characteristic as her unhurried decorum) remained intact, though she could often be found having a short afternoon nap.

"I've been encouraged," she would explain, while readjusting the fan, and lying down, "to take things *pole pole*."

Before Mother recovered her usual vim and vigor around

---

3   an apology, or expression of sympathy

the end of our first week, it would just be Dad and me venturing out under the equatorial sun, into the sweltering streets of Dar es Salaam for errands. Dad, having shepherded his kith and kin to the land of leopard and lion, adapted to the heat quite well, and the two of us learned a brachiating pattern of going from one air-conditioned building to the next. When such buildings could be found, that is. Small roadside *dukas*[4] usually only had a single fan to combat the withering heat, but the banks and chemists had blessed, blessed, air conditioning. Outdoor errands were to be undertaken little by little, we learned (*kidogo kidogo* soon joined *pole pole* in our vocabulary), until we acclimated.

For most of our family, December 1970 was our first time on African soil. Some might argue whether Africa is actually "the Cradle of Humankind," but it did serve as the cradle for my own African mother. For her, born in Eritrea and having lived in Morocco also, this was a return to a familiar continent. Or perhaps not so familiar. We had arrived in anglophone Africa, where the languages spoken were, I came to learn, quite different from the arabophone regions of Africa like Egypt and Morocco, or the francophone parts of West Africa. Dar es Salaam was the largest Kiswahili-speaking city in the world. I soon learned *Swahili* referred to the people themselves, whereas *Kiswahili* meant "the language of *Swahili*." However, after hearing many other people use the word *Swahili* to refer to the language, I too slipped into the habit. Unbeknownst to me, at first, I was picking up Arabic too, since many Swahili words come from Arabic. There were variations of Swahili spoken in the neighboring countries, as illustrated in the saying "Swahili was born in Tanzania, got sick in Kenya, died in Uganda, and was buried in the Congo."

---

4   shops outside the city

Dad was vastly relieved to find that many Tanzanians spoke basic English or better, all the better to hide one of his few weaknesses: his abysmal grasp of any foreign language.

Mother had a fair knowledge of German, Spanish, and Arabic, but complete mastery of French and English as well as her native Italian. To no one's surprise, she picked up Kiswahili with equal ease.

Craig and I had grown accustomed to our African, polylingual mother forgetting which language it was that she was thinking in.

"*Laisse-lui tranquille!*"[5] was her spontaneous outburst to me one day, as she saw me trying to catch a lizard during one of our walks downtown. Then, blinking hard and switching back from French to English, she muttered, "I mean, that one doesn't need rescuing," and dragged me away.

Mother knew all too well my impulse to rescue untold numbers of animals. Perhaps it was even predictable, considering she had named me after two maternal aunts who had, multiple times, rescued marginalized, persecuted people during the Second World War in Europe. Nonetheless, she wisely and lovingly reined in my "open door" plans regarding animal rescue. Doubtless she knew that otherwise that open door would have been most certainly removed from its hinges and simply leaned up against the wall, to gather dust indefinitely.

"But Mother, you said we were put—"

"I know. But no," she answered quickly, before I could finish quoting back to her the philosophy with which she had raised Craig and me: "We were put on Earth to help others." I had firmly concluded that "others" encompassed animals too.

Pouting, now that my lizard rescue attempt had been

---

5   Leave that one alone!

thwarted, I trudged along with her and muttered about how vulnerable that lizard would be to being killed by snakes or cars, if not safely brought indoors.

She missed what I was muttering, but she did not fail to notice that I had forcefully kicked a pebble.

I kept my head down.

Mother sighed heavily.

I had known almost nothing about Dar es Salaam (previously Mzizima) before we arrived, only that the name came from Arabic, meaning *abode of peace*, and that it was a coastal city. Hence the humidity. We soon noticed that the full name was not often used, and we fell into the habit of calling the city "Dar," as all our friends did.

It was the largest city in Tanzania, with a population then of around thirteen thousand, with Tanzania being amongst the largest countries on the continent of Africa. There were few sightseeing spots in Dar, and the city was mostly used by tourists as a layover on their way to Zanzibar and other African destinations.

When we arrived, it was already a busy, rapidly developing city, and all African wildlife stayed well away. Unlike seventeen years ago, in 1953, I was told that a pair of hippos had sauntered into Dar from a creek near the airport. They were none too welcome and retreated hastily.

In those first few weeks, as our family was still adjusting to being a new family (my stepfather and my mother were arguably still newlyweds), we drew a collective breath and began to adjust to our new home. Meanwhile, Tanzania itself was adjusting to its own new independence.

It was a profound experience to arrive in a country newly free from colonial rule. About ninety years earlier, the scramble for Africa had begun. Various European powers claimed for themselves parts of African territory, and within about forty years, more than 90 percent of Africa had all been carved up, a continent of more than eleven million square miles, and its peoples colonized. It took many decades for each African country, one by one, to wrest back control of its own land. Around the time of my mother's birth in the late 1920s, only three out of Africa's fifty-odd countries had regained their independence, and by the time I was born, it was slightly more than half. It was not until I was in my early thirties that, at long last, all African countries, every last one of them, were formally free and independent.

We arrived exactly nine years after Tanzanian Independence, to the month. Admirably, independence had been regained without a bloody conflict in this case. Every Tanzanian who was older than nine, to a man, had until recently lived under colonial rule. And anyone younger than nine had heard the stories from their elders. Independence was such a seismic event that I found it was common to hear dates identified as "Oh, that was five years before Independence" or "That was two years after Independence."

Soon after arriving in Tanzania, I was enrolled in the international school in Dar es Salaam. From time to time during our school days, especially in music class, I duly sang the Tanzanian national anthem, *"Mungu Ibariki Africa,"*[6] along with my classmates, little realizing its importance to Tanzanians.

"We used to have to sing 'God Save the Queen,'" came the blunt explanation from a Tanzanian friend. It was only in the last nine years that Tanzania had adopted their own national anthem.

---

6 "God Bless Africa," Swahili translation of Enoch Sontonga's "Nkosi Sikelel' iAfrika."

CHAPTER 6
Dead Caterpillars & Disabled Cats

Dear Catherine MacLaine,
Can you let us know at least two to three months before you come, so we can start working on the paperwork, especially the international movement permit from the Ministry of Agriculture, Livestock, and Fisheries, and the Veterinary export certificate issued by the Director of veterinary services.
   —Dr. Thomas W. Kahema, Executive Director of Tanzania Animal Welfare Society (TAWESO)

USA, circa 2016

I have no memory of a time when I didn't love animals. Nor have I any memory of the times I must have disappointed my mother because I *only* loved animals. It was only later in life that she recounted to me how consistently, throughout my entire childhood, I declined to play with any doll. Stuffed toy animals were the mainstay of my early years instead. My nonna,[7] Laura Malingri Bagnolo DeRege, from the Piemonte region of Italy, had planned to give me a particularly beautiful and expensive doll ("With a porcelain face and an exquisite

---
7   Maternal grandmother.

dress!" as Mother later told me) for my sixth birthday. The plan, predictably, had to be hastily aborted. I had thrown a petulant fit when offered a doll in previous years, and Mother was not about to make that mortifying mistake again. So my birthday arrived with not any expensive doll but a simple dime store stuffed toy animal instead. This filled me with the utmost delight. Nonna was not offended in the least and instead declared that it was "a very DeRege family trait to love animals. Clever girl!"

"Still," said Mother ruefully, "that one had a porcelain face . . ."

Well-intentioned attempts to help animals, albeit with occasional mishaps, started as a theme early in my life. Amongst my earliest memories (age four, perhaps?) is when I brought caterpillars into bed with me, convinced they would thrive, having been rescued from certain peril. Here in my warm and cozy bed, they would surely flourish. Upon awakening, I found the hapless creatures dead. I had inadvertently rolled over on them in my sleep. The deaths of those caterpillars upset me so greatly that I never brought caterpillars to bed again. This was perhaps one of the earliest examples where I saw a well-intentioned rescue plan have an unexpected outcome.

Before coming to Africa, my most recent rescue attempt had been three more little caterpillars. This time, instead of taking them to bed, I had put them in a warm and safe jam jar. Now, with the utmost reluctance—and a tear or two—I set them free in a nearby park. Canadian caterpillars would be happier, I was told, if they stayed there in Montreal and did not accompany me to Africa. Nor had they needed rescuing, I was also told, since they were perfectly capable of hibernating safely through winter. Each insect was given one last kiss on their short, bristly, black and orange fur, then painstakingly and tenderly placed under the biggest log I could find to resume their winter hibernation.

These were farewell kisses that I no longer disclosed to Craig, who would have only said, "Kiddo, it is never a good idea to kiss larva."

Because of my love for the beasts and the birds, any stories about cruelty to animals particularly wounded me. When I began planning my first trip back to Tanzania in my mid-fifties, I was not surprised to learn that the street cats there, as in many developing countries, led miserable lives with little hope or help. In general, starvation was frequent, rescue was rare, and death came early.

From my childhood attempts to rescue caterpillars, the urge to help animals, this warp and woof of my soul's fabric, was always core to my being.

Alas, I could not save all the street cats in Tanzania. I did, however, arrive at the resolve to get at least one of them out of the country, so I proceeded to explore what arrangements were necessary to export one cat from Tanzania to America. Already living with me in America at that time were some disabled cats, and so it seemed a reasonable conclusion to seek out and adopt a disabled African one also. Regardless of whether it would be perceived as bizarre to send an inquiry to an African animal shelter about adopting one of their disabled cats, I carried on.

After an online search for any animal shelter in Dar, I was delighted to receive a prompt response from the Tanzania Animal Welfare Society (TAWESO), run by Dr. Thomas Kahema. I came to learn this animal shelter had been officially opened in 2015 by the world-renowned primatologist Dr. Jane Goodall, resident of Dar, who turned out to be a friend of Dr. Thomas.

The website confirmed my suspicion about the plight of street animals: *The brutal killing of dogs and cats is common.* So I typed in my request for a disabled one and hit Send.

In my mind's eye, I saw Dr. Thomas, far across the ocean, over in Tanzania, staring at his computer screen dumbfounded. My inquiry was on his screen. He was still dumbfounded. He called his friends from the next room to come read my message too.

"Am I reading this correctly? She wants a what?"

Chapter 7
Home Amidst Sisal

Dear Dad,
There are monkeys in the trees near our house. Sometimes they can be heard at night. Mother is terrified of the lizards we have in the house.

—Craig

Dar es Salaam, 1971

Our house had a view of the sea. Truth be told, it was a small view of the sea. As the African pied crow flies, our house was perhaps a fifth of a mile away from low cliffs overlooking the Indian Ocean. The small stretch of ocean that we could see from the second floor, through one small break in the heavy tree line, was a mesmerizing sapphire stretch whose salty scent would waft all the way over to us when the wind was just right. If we craned our necks from our upstairs terrace and looked through binoculars, during those days in early 1971, we would see dhows gliding along from time to time.

Our street, Mahando Drive, ran along the eastern part of the Masaki neighborhood, on the horse-ear-shaped Msasani peninsula. We soon drifted into the habit of referring to it as "the peninsula" like everybody else did. This outcropping of land, jutting into the Indian Ocean, was about three-quarters of a mile wide and maybe slightly longer than a mile long, and it was nicknamed *Uzunguni*,[8] though by the early 1970s, many different nationalities lived there. Amongst the few buildings on the peninsula was an archipelago of homes encircled by vast swathes of sisal fields. Years earlier, the entire Msasani peninsula had been a sisal plantation. When I revisited Dar in 2017, it was still being called "the peninsula," but every square inch of land had been fully developed into residential or commercial property. Long gone were the hyenas that my brother had seen at night on Toure Drive. Indeed, no wildlife at all, not even the monkeys, was left.

Kwaheri[9] sisal.

The peninsula was no longer recognizable in the least.

But for now, sisal, with its long, pointy leaves, was a daily part of my childhood days.

I wondered if it would hurt to be poked by those pointy ends. It did.

There were multiple flowering bushes in our garden, and I would trail my open palm against their soft leaves as I walked past, a gesture not to be done with spiky sisal fronds. The sisal plant grows about four feet high and has long, lance-shaped leaves, which can be processed into a fiber used to create rope and twine. Sisal rope was probably in my hands, in one form or another, every day that I was in Africa, most especially because I spent many happy hours playing on our sisal rope swing that hung from a flame tree in our backyard. Area rugs here were made of sisal, as were bags and baskets. I saw sisal on sandals and in hats. Sisal baskets were in my treehouse and

---

8   Where the Europeans live.
9   Goodbye.

in my bedroom. Prior to Africa, I only remember sisal on cat scratching posts sold in pet stores.

Sisal had once been Tanzania's main export. Nowadays, it seems to me to remain only in Tanga, in Morogoro, and up around Kili, but this "green gold" brought massive flows of cash into the coffers of Tanzania for centuries.

Until nylon came along.

When synthetic substitutes for rope and twine were developed, the sisal industry went into sharp decline, with plantations all over central and southern Tanzania going out of business. Amongst them, this abandoned one on the Msasani peninsula. By the time our family arrived in Tanzania, the bottom half of the peninsula was already being somewhat developed for residential purposes, with a few houses on its coast facing the Indian Ocean. The remaining sisal fields became one of my main play areas, and I spent countless hours outdoors, searching for geckos amid the spear-shaped leaves.

I had better luck finding gecko nests in our own front garden, where they nested in the frangipani trees. I often found gecko eggs attached together in tiny pairs. It might be argued that one ought never disturb nests, but just like my Canadian caterpillars, I remained convinced that these precious eggs would surely be imperiled without my rescuing hand. I gathered every gecko egg clutch I could find. These I would *pole pole* smuggle into my bedroom—Mother took a dim view of anything remotely reptilian—and carefully place on the highest shelf of my room. The rescued hatchlings, now safe from snakes, would soon be wandering throughout my room, scaling vertical walls with their little adhesive feet. *Kidogo, kidogo*, adult geckos and lizards too became part of my smuggling operation.

There was a reason for this: Mother had forbidden me to

have a mosquito repellent coil burning in my room.

"Quite right," Dad agreed. "Dreadful fire hazard, those things, to say nothing about the poisonous fumes indoors."

And so the mosquitoes had at first romped freely in my bedroom, biting me with impunity. But when I brought in the geckos, who love when their dinner has six legs, they obligingly obliterated all insects.

Mother shrieked.

"Well, you forbade me a mosquito coil in here," I said. But when Mother complained about this in her letters written to her own mother, Nonna supported my mosquito eradication method. After all, the irrefutable fact remained that of all the bedrooms, mine alone was blessedly devoid of mosquitoes.

Chapter 8
Nonna and the Mongrel

Dear Bob,
Her dog, Alice, is awful, but she loves it.

—Mother

Mother went to the local SPCA and came home with Alice.

—Craig

"There is no twilight in East Africa. Night tramps on the heels of Day with little gallantry and takes the place she recently held, in severe and humourless silence."

—Beryl Markham, *West with the Night*

Dar es Salaam, circa 1971

"Ciao, Cathy dearest!" My grandmother kissed me on the cheek. Although Nonna was no stranger to Africa, this was her first visit to us here in Tanzania in early 1971.

"Do you know"—another kiss on the other cheek—"you have no twilight here in Tanzania? The sun drops like a stone here!" She set her purse down to free up both slender hands, the better for gesturing to demonstrate a rapidly falling object. "*Ecco!*[10] The sun is down! *Ecco*, the sun is up! In Eritrea, we

---
10   There!

had *at least* twenty minutes before it was completely dark."

Nonna's previous years of living in Asmara, Eritrea, on the Horn of Africa (or "the Horn," as she called it), had positioned her about a thousand miles north of the equator, whereas here in Dar, she found herself only about four hundred miles south of it. In sentences fragmented with Italian, German, French, and English, her conversation went on, as she delighted in the similarities she did find.

"You have bougainvillea and jacaranda here! *Just* like Asmara!" The fact that Africa had very few carpets was noted ("Asmara too!") and that we had rather more sisal than she had ever seen anywhere in Africa.

By now Nonna was all the way through the front door. She turned to my mother. "My only two grandchildren living below the equator! How Craig has grown! So tall is he now! And Cathy, is she—is she still getting—how you call it—*mal di orecchio*?"[11]

"Yes. Alas, *Mutter*," my mother answered, toggling between English, Italian, and German with equal ease, "Cathy is still getting those from time to time but"—she waggled her hand with open palm facing the floor—"*ma meno*."[12]

"Hello, Nonna!" I said, when I could get a word in. "Yes, just about no twilight here!" I kept my reply all in one language because I was too tired to toggle.

Nonna had turned back to Craig with intense concern in her eyes. "But so tall and *troppo magro*!"[13]

Craig replied, chuckling, that he had indeed just gone through a growth spurt and had grown six inches in six months. He, too, made the choice to keep it all in one language.

Mother and Nonna continued their chatter as they headed

---

11 earaches
12 not as frequently
13 too thin

down the uncarpeted hall, with me following behind from a distance. I felt validated that Nonna had mentioned how few carpets tended to be on this continent. I had been wondering if it was only Tanzania.

The conversation had moved on from the subject of the equatorial twilight and had subsequently drifted into complete Italian sentences, other than Mother's German term of endearment, "*meine mutter.*"[14] The three of us began unpacking Nonna's suitcase, laid out on the bed. Her flight from Italy had been uneventful until the annoying turbulence.

"But alas, there is always turbulence when you cross the equator, you know," Mother said in Italian.

"I had forgotten all about that," Nonna said. She lamented that celebratory pastries were no longer given out to passengers as they crossed over the equator, and how she had wanted to see Mount Kilimanjaro as her plane entered Tanzanian airspace but had only the briefest of glimpses as fellow passengers similarly strained and mostly blocked her view.

"I'll take you to a game park." Mother smiled. "Plenty of wildlife to see."

"But the roads are terrible," I warned, remembering our previous visit to a park. I carefully did not mention the disproportionate number of wildebeest in the game parks here. Vast. This, just like the astonishingly short twilight here, had to be seen to be believed.

By now Alice had entered the room, curious about the newcomer. She was a street dog from the local animal shelter, about the size of a spaniel, with rather ordinary tricolor markings. Some of my relatives had impressed me very early in life with their compassion in rescuing mongrels instead of

---

14   mother of mine

purchasing beautiful pedigree dogs, and I'd resolved to follow their example. Mother had resigned herself to the fact that my birthday wish for a mongrel dog had ossified, so her offer of a purebred Rhodesian Ridgeback evaporated.

This little brown mongrel puppy was instead small and simple, sometimes squirmy, and occasionally smelly. I loved her immediately.

As Nonna brought my mother up to date on news from our assorted Italian relatives, Alice padded about, sniffing and exploring. Her ears tilted this way and that with the ebb and flow of the conversation, and she evidently decided that the bed needed to be explored next. All conversation was interrupted as she jumped onto the bed, adorning the eiderdown bedspread with dusty paw prints.

"*Aah! Cane orribile!*"[15] Mother's outburst caught my attention from the closet, where I'd been helping to hang up Nonna's clothes. It was followed by her loud entreaties for me to remove my not-horrible-to-me dog. Alice had already jumped off the bed, and now stood in the middle of the room, glancing back and forth between the two adult women with a feebly wagging tail, not quite certain what to do next.

"Oh!" said Nonna, casting a reproachful glance at Mother and a warm glance at Alice. "Is not *cane orribile*." Before I could whisk my pet away, as per Mother's bidding, Nonna had dropped to her knees and was stroking the confused little dog, lovingly murmuring Italian endearments to her. Alice didn't care what language this was. She panted happily, gazing raptly back into Nonna's warm brown eyes.

"Is your dog, Cathy dearest?" Nonna wanted to know, switching back to English, still caressing the little brown mongrel. My mother held her tongue and didn't speak in any

---

15 horrible dog!

language, knowing she had absolutely no hope of the dog being removed now. Nonna was an extremely keen animal lover and was besotted by Alice.

"Yes, Nonna." I joined her on the floor, where she had settled herself to spend several long minutes patting my dog. "Alice was a present to me for my birthday. Mother chose her for me from the local animal shelter."

By now Alice was basking in caresses from the two of us seated on the floor, and it was Mother who was left standing alone with uncertainty. "I shall, um . . . I shall just go make a pot of tea, perhaps, shall I, *meine mutter*?" She edged toward the door.

I strongly suspected that besides tea, Mother would also find some sort of little tasty treat to slip to Alice, as she did so often, since kindness always was core to her being. She regularly oscillated between mild distaste for my "horrible" dog and begrudging affection because Alice was—undeniably—very sweet.

"Tea? Yes, that's fine, Anna," said Nonna, her eyes never leaving Alice. Nonna's half-unpacked suitcase was quite forgotten. "Ah, your little dog is quite lovely, Cathy. How do you call her?"

I replied that her name was Alice, and then added the qualifier that Alice was just a mongrel.

"Ah, my darling, but do you not know? It is the mongrels who are the most intelligent of all the dogs."

Chapter 9
Putzi Flies and Plenty, Plenty Candles

Dear Bob,
The other night it rained. Apparently, the rainy season is near. I've never seen anything like it. My bed is in the middle of a huge room, far from two windows. I woke up all wet, soaking, exactly. The winds are so strong (monsoons) that they carry the rain with such power that unless you close everything, you've had it.

—Mother

Dear Dad,
It's just been raining a lot, and right now Craig is doing a jigsaw. Lots of bugs here. My nose is bleeding.

—Me

Dear Dad,
It gets very hot all day, and then it gets quite cool at around 7 p.m.

—Craig

A Billion Blue Wildebeest

Tanzania, early 1970s

I left a country with four seasons for a country with two: the dry season and the rainy season. The rainy season was in turn divided into the long rains and the short rains, I soon learned. The long rains were followed by the long dry season, which then gave way to the short rains. Then comes January and February.

So I eventually arrived at the conclusion that Tanzania did have four separate seasons after all.

But the monsoons . . .

One underestimates an African monsoon at one's own peril. I abruptly found out that rain can blow horizontally. We soon learned to hastily close all windows during the rainy seasons.

Although the rains would come and go, the one factor that remained constant in the cauldron that was Dar was the soup of humidity.

Our fresh laundry would be hung to dry on clotheslines, but drying would take twice as long due to the humidity. And then every stitch of our laundry, including socks and undergarments, had to be carefully ironed, due to the fly larvae.

Dad's calm demeanor cracked. "What fly larvae?"

We had been gathered at the dining room table writing letters when Mother casually discussed the fly larvae as our houseboy, Afwene, passed through the room.[16]

"Fly lar—" Dad seemed dumbfounded.

---

16   "Houseboys" and "servants" were other new concepts we had to learn, coming to Africa. It was understood that *wazungu* would offer employment to Africans and, as our Tanzanian friends told us in no uncertain terms, it was frowned upon to do otherwise. The term "house boy," rather than being derogatory, was used by the Tanzanians themselves and is still in use today.

This he had not foreseen.

"Yes, *Bwana*, flies. *Putzi* flies. Mango flies." Afwene then went on to describe how the larvae can burrow into your skin, rather like a maggot. He included fairly revolting details pertaining to the appearance of the burrowed larvae (rather like a boil) and the resulting discomfort (quite painful, apparently). Throughout his recitation, his "'twas ever thus" look on his face was matched by Mother's similarly resigned expression.

"But when clothing is ironed, that kills any larvae, so don't worry, darling," Mother told Dad, dismissing the trifling matter of larvae-laden laundry.

If I found myself still puzzling over the confusing weather, at least I could ruminate over these imponderables while wearing meticulously ironed underwear.

As rain rinsed the sisal and dripped off the ends of the bougainvillea, I occupied myself mostly indoors. There were fewer options for outdoor amusements, and going to a game park loses its appeal when one must push a vehicle that has gotten bogged down in the mud. Repeatedly. Soggy sisal fields, too, were not optimal playing grounds.

My parents, fully cognizant that both my brother and I were avid readers, went to considerable pains to keep our bookshelves well stocked, especially for rainy days. The rains were crucial to the agricultural industry, and village rainmakers were held in high regard. Indeed the rainmakers had been the authorities in precolonial Tanzania, when it was known as "the Swahili coast."

Our first month in Tanzania was a bit of a crash course in all things African.

"You will need plenty, plenty candles," a *duka* owner told us in our early days. Dad and I had squeezed ourselves into the tiny shop on the outskirts of town while Mother and Craig waited outside. The owner was dressed in an ordinary shirt and trousers, unlike the traditional African tribal clothing featured on so many tourist pamphlets. He rose from his white plastic lawn chair to greet us with a warm smile. These chairs seemed to be everywhere in Dar.

His kind face was almost sympathetic as he continued with his casual warning to us. "And a torch." I was noticing, besides the ubiquitous white plastic chairs, that many Tanzanians used British English terms here. "You will need a torch, as well as candles." Something in his tone made me suspect he wasn't trying to push his wares but truly alerting us of some unpleasantness ahead. He explained that power cuts were common.

"You will find *hakuna umeme*[17] here many times per month," he cheerfully predicted. Something to do with capacity shortages and infrastructure failures.

With a sigh, Dad purchased candles and a flashlight. Then Dad made the *duka* owner yet more cheerful by purchasing batteries for the flashlight. Our assorted flashlights were then strewn throughout our house—and one up in my treehouse, for good measure.

Not only did we encounter *hakuna umeme* just as forewarned, but we came to find that *hakuna maji*[18] was fairly common too.

"Those infrastructure failures again," we were told.

It was in Africa that I first became familiar with jerrycans, large flat-sided containers. These were filled promptly with water at the first warning "*Ebooh!*" along with every bathtub in the house.

---

17   there is no electricity
18   there is no water

The water shortages predictably made it into our aerograms home.

Mother added to one: *We are without water again, which is annoying. I hope the rains come soon.*

In Craig's aerogram, he said, *Right now we go without water a lot. In fact, most of the time.*

Some of my friends merely shrugged at the shortages.

"*Ah, hakuna shida,*"[19] they said, a Swahili phrase I soon realized was a widespread philosophy. During the shortages, my parents encouraged me to remain patient. I remained patient. And I added *hakuna shida* to my vocabulary.

The faucet of the upstairs bathtub dripped slightly, and my little dog, Alice, found this water more to her liking than that in her own water bowl.

Click, click, click, click went her claws as she trotted down the hall, around the corner and into the bathroom. Then a slight thump as she leapt blindly into the tall, deep, and empty tub—a considerable leap for a small dog—and drank her fill directly from that dripping bathtub faucet. Eventually, her thirst quenched, she would duly leap back out, and we would hear the *click, click, click, click* as she departed.

There came one afternoon when we heard the familiar *click, click, click* of a thirsty little dog once again, coming down the hall toward the nice familiar bathtub with the nice familiar dripping faucet.

SPLASH!

Alice spun, splashed, and stumbled around inside the tall, deep, and not empty at all bathtub. Nobody had told her we'd filled it due to an expected water shortage. My now sopping little dog frantically leapt out and skidded back down the hall, pausing only momentarily to shake off the water before

---

19 No problem, no worries

A Billion Blue Wildebeest

resuming her swerving, skittering escape.

My family always tried to make it a point to never laugh at a humiliated dog. None of us was able to hold to our resolve that afternoon, though, and all of us noticed that from that day onward, Alice only drank from her water bowl.

Chapter 10
He Staggers

Dear Catherine,
I hope things are going well. I am introducing you to our special needs cat, as per your request, called Bajaj. He is a neutered (I did his neuter myself) tabby cat with generally healthy condition but got into an accident before he was brought to TAWESO a year ago. All his joints do not work, but he stands and moves, though he staggers.
Kind regards,
Thomas

—Dr. Thomas W. Kahema, TAWESO

"I was a waif, cast into the world, treated as circumstances developed themselves."

—Henry Morton Stanley, 1869

Dar es Salaam, February 2017

Today I was going to meet my chosen cat.

Now in my mid-fifties, I had returned to Dar, this time as a tourist on a bucket list trip. The trip had been inspired after I had gazed once again at some Tanzanian paintings, and several months later, visa in hand, I boarded a flight to come back.

The first part of my trip, the week before, I had visited game parks in the North of Tanzania, and now the last part of my trip was my old hometown of Dar.

The long-awaited day had arrived to meet the cat I had arranged, several months ago, to adopt and bring back home with me to the US.

It turned out that Dr. Thomas had been delighted when I asked specifically for a special needs cat. He suggested one particular brown tabby male.

"He staggers," I was told.

Dr. Thomas explained in his emails to me that this cat had been brought to their shelter (TAWESO) by a rescuer who explained that the cat's staggering gait was the tragic consequence of his legs having never healed properly after surviving being hit by a Bajaj.

"Very popular Indian make and model car here in Tanzania," Dr. Thomas explained. "So that's why we named him Bajaj."

"Well, that dreadful name is the absolute *first* thing I will change," I muttered to myself when I read the email. This was followed by the comforting thought, *And a muscular skeletal issue can easily be improved with surgery.* I'd had another cat whose mobility was improved after multiple surgeries. "This will be all right."

The Tanzanian gentleman's email went on to explain that the animal could function reasonably well. He went on to reassure me that the tabby was using the litter box normally, since I had said that this would otherwise be a deal-breaker for me.

The pitiful-looking African cat in the photo was, undeniably, the picture of pathos, and I readily wired money to the shelter for the various fees that would be involved. Dusting off my Swahili dictionary, I then carefully committed *paka wangu kipenzi*[20] to memory.

On the way to TAWESO, I asked my driver, Luke, to make one stop.

"A fish market, *Mamma*?" he asked me in surprise. Many Tanzanians tended to respectfully address me as *Mamma*, something I was still getting used to on this return trip.

"Yes, Luke, I want to bring some fish to my *paka wangu kipenzi*, please."

He dutifully diverted the car past sisal fields and through busy traffic intersections to a local fish market, and shortly afterward we resumed our journey, now laden down with fish for all the cats at the shelter, especially the cat who had been hit by an Indian car. It had been my suspicion that these cats didn't often get a little extra treat, and it gave me some satisfaction that perhaps I could at least remedy this, at least for these cats, at least for this one day.

On this drive, Luke had a friend with him, Saul, who also worked at the animal shelter and chuckled at my barrage of questions.

"So tell me! Tell me! Tell me all about my *paka wangu kipenzi*! I'm told he staggers?"

"Oh, yes," Saul replied. "He staggers! And he eats funny too!"

That should have been my first clue.

I looked at him sharply, then dismissed his remark, concluding that I had surely misheard. Cats, while known to be finicky eaters, are not known to "eat funny."

The young Tanzanian man's head then wobbled and swayed wildly like a drunken man, as he mimicked for me the

---

[20] my darling cat

motions of a cat struggling to eat from a bowl. Both Tanzanians then laughed and joked about "too much *pombe!*"[21]

"You give *pombe* to the *cats?*" I cried, aghast.

The two men hastily reassured me that no alcohol was ever given to any cats and that my cat just staggers *like* a drunken man.

"But don't worry about it, and oh, here we are at the shelter, *Mamma*."

"*Karibu!*"[22] I was warmly greeted at TAWESO, and the rather pungent bag of fish was taken off my hands with the assurance that its reeking contents would be doled out to all the cats.

Never before have I felt so impatient to get through the lengthy customary preliminary African greetings. "A smile and a nod just won't do," we were told when we first moved to Dar over forty years earlier.

To give the correct Swahili greeting to the correct age group in Tanzania was of paramount importance. I had quickly learned to only greet my elders with "*Shikamoo*," which roughly translates as "I bow before you and touch your feet as a mark of respect." The elder would then respond with "*Marahaba*," a word explained to me as "I acknowledge and accept your respect."

During my first day back in Tanzania, as an adult, it had come as a slight shock to me that Tanzanians were giving *me* the *shikamoo*, not the *marahaba*. Now, in many of the gatherings of people in which I found myself around Dar, I was the elder.

I did still occasionally stumble into my childhood-ingrained pattern of giving the *shikamoo*, but every Tanzanian,

---

21   alcohol
22   Welcome!

without fail, treated my mistake very graciously, to my relief.

Nothing had changed about the sheer length of Tanzanian greetings, however.

"How was your flight?" they wanted to know.

"Are you surprised at how much Dar has changed since you were last here?"

"And your family, they're well?"

"Did you sleep well?"

"What a charming *kanga*!"[23]

"And do you want to wash your hands?"

Well, they did smell rather badly of fish.

Verbally I gave polite answers, but inwardly, impatient thoughts were simmering: *Can you just take me to meet my cat? Now? I've waited weeks and weeks!*

Finally, they politely inquired, "Would you like to meet your cat?"

I nodded mutely, not daring to trust that my impatience might not burst out were I to open my mouth. Dr. Thomas himself was not on the premises just then, but running late and due to arrive at any moment. The staff on-site could see perfectly well, however, that I was longing to meet the cat.

On this bright sunny Dar es Salaam day, I, at long last, stood in front of the cage. All the surrounding cats meowed hopefully. But this one held his tongue.

The brown tabby was lying down. He eyed me warily and became yet more wary as the Tanzanian animal shelter staff lifted him out of the cage and into my waiting arms.

"*Pole! Pole! Pole!*" came the sharp reminder from the senior staff member to the kennel staff picking up the already struggling animal. The mews from the other cats rose and fell along with the words of the surrounding staff dealing with

---

23   wraparound sarong skirt

my cat.

Finally in my arms! I marveled at his size and how his brown tabby stripes immediately reminded me of the banded mongooses I'd had as pets here in Dar long ago.

My very first cuddle with this long, long, *long*-awaited cat soon came to an abrupt end as he promptly had a full-blown panic attack in my arms. He proceeded to bite and scratch me, then climb to the top of my head. It seemed prudent to put him back in his cage. This poor animal, a survivor of a horrific car crash, after all, was so obviously stressed out. *Surely a relapse of his post-traumatic stress disorder, no doubt,* I concluded. Besides, I couldn't tell which leg, or legs, had sustained the damage from the car anyway.

That could wait. We had a whole lifetime together in front of us, he and I.

It happened, then, when the cat was back in his cage.

He staggered.

Staggering would not be unexpected in a cat who has survived a car crash, after all. Besides, they had told me very forthrightly that he staggered.

But this cat's staggering caught my attention and held me spellbound, then horrorstricken. I no longer heard the meows from the other shelter cats, as I fixated on this one brown tabby, adorned with mongoose-looking stripes.

The cat was easily bearing weight on all four straight and normal legs, which each moved easily. His ambulation, however, was similar to a post-surgical animal first coming out of anesthesia. There were no dilated pupils, but try as he might, this cat could not stay on his feet. Had he been doing an impression of the stumbling seen in a newly born wildebeest calf, he could not have done a better job. With Herculean efforts, he would try to stand up, try to take a step, and crash back down to the ground each time. The stumbling and tumbling was utterly heart-wrenching.

I was agape. *This is* neurological!

After my horror-struck reaction, I quickly assumed a poker face. All the shelter workers had fallen silent. They cast worried glances at one another as the silence from me continued. The story of this cat having been hit by an Indian car didn't seem quite so certain to me. *Does he have brain damage? If he has brain damage, was it from birth or from being hit by a car?* When the TAWESO staff took in the cat, did the person bringing in the animal lie to them?

I had no doubt that I could have easily dealt with musculoskeletal issues in a cat, but this new prospect of a brain-damaged cat was daunting.

Dr. Thomas arrived then, and having caught sight of my face—did I still look so shocked?—he greeted me warmly but, thankfully, briefly. He went on to tell me more about the cat. I only absorbed stray fragments, but no, the cat was not in pain. The senior vet to whom he had taken the cat diagnosed some sort of brain damage. From disease? From birth? From the car accident? Was there any proof of any car accident? No one knew. Perhaps an American would have dubbed him "one big hot mess." He went on as if I had gotten the email he had sent me about this brain damage.

"And do you want to continue with the adoption?"

"What email?" I looked at him blankly.

"*Mamma,* would you like a chair?" A white plastic chair. Of course it was.

Africa seems to have thousands of white plastic chairs, I found myself thinking dully, while nonetheless sinking gratefully into it. My legs felt none too steady just then.

What email? Did it go to my spam folder? I most certainly

never received any such email.

Had I gotten that email, would it really have changed anything?

"*Mamma*, would you like bandages?"

"Bandages?" I looked up at Dr. Thomas uncomprehendingly.

"Allow me, *Mamma*." He quietly busied himself bandaging up the various bites and scratches I had just sustained.

I looked, dazed, over his shoulder, at the cat—*my* cat—simmering down, over in his cage.

Dear God, what am I going to do? *How do I cope with brain damage?*

The animal cast baleful looks at all and sundry. And staggered.

Before all the bandaging (accompanied by much sympathetic tongue-clicking) was completed, I had reached several conclusions:

My previous love for this cat, sight unseen, had expanded to a bottomless well of sympathy, tenderness, and compassion.

Missed email or not, this cat was coming with me back to America. And if an American vet assessed this cat as being too severely impaired, then perhaps I would have to consider euthanasia.

But this scrawny animal was certainly going to have several good meals on American soil first.

Chapter 11
Mongooses Make Dreadful Pets

Dear Bob,
The Cath dearly loves the mongooses, and her dog Alice is jealous and gets spat upon every time she goes near them.
—Mother

Dar es Salaam, early 1970s

The reason that a wild animal should not be kept as a pet is because it is a wild animal.

This irrefutable logic can be temporarily eclipsed, however, when one is face-to-face with a very cute, very little, baby wild animal.

A very young wild animal, somewhat similar to a ferret, perhaps six inches long, lay at the bottom of the sisal *kikapu*,[24] blinking up at us with the utmost of innocence.

Craig was dubious.

I was charmed.

Pravin, who had brought us this gift, was one of Craig's Indian friends. He dodged all questions about his age, which could have been twenty-two, perhaps thirty, or anywhere in

---
[24] basket

between. He constantly wore rather flamboyant shirts, and had a little stall in the Arab quarter of downtown Dar, where he worked as a cobbler. Unnervingly, presenting us with unexpected gifts was a habit of his. Craig and I had been reading in the living room when Pravin dropped in one day for a visit, bearing an animal-laden sisal basket.

He looked slightly tired from the day's humidity, and Craig promptly offered a chair. "Hey, just rest a moment, eh, *rafiki?*"

An impish smile as he remained standing and handed my brother his present.

"A meerkat!" Craig hurriedly closed the basket and tried to hand it back to Pravin. "Ah, my *rafiki*,[25] I am allergic to cats, *pole*, I'm sorry."

"No, this is a mongoose I'm giving you! This is not a meerkat. Meerkats are *wild* animals." Pravin took a step back, clearly not willing to take back the basket and leaving the implication hanging in the air that he would most certainly never dare to presume that a wild animal could become a household pet. Although related to meerkats, the mongoose is a small, carnivorous mammal with a greater variety of coloring and sizes. Like many children, I had first learned about Indian mongooses in the Rudyard Kipling story "Rikki-Tikki-Tavi." I had been delighted to see mongooses here in local game parks too. These African ones were prettier to me, some with handsome stripes, none of which I'd seen in pictures of Indian mongooses.

"Uh, right. Mongoose then. Uh, so, do these—" Craig cast another doubtful glance at the basket he was holding at arm's length. "Do *mongooses* make good pets?"

"Oh, plenty of *wazungu* keep mongooses!" his friend

---

25   friend

assured him, neatly sidestepping the question. Pravin also did not disclose where he had gotten the mongoose.

"But this is a wild animal, isn't it?" Craig pressed, still holding the closed basket away.

It wiggled.

I glanced sharply at my brother's face and was thankful to see no allergic reaction starting. Perhaps Craig's allergies only pertained to cats and not African mongooses. Not willing to chance it, I gently took the basket from him.

While the two fellows continued to debate the virtues of mongooses, I opened the basket a safe distance away from Craig and examined the tiny animal more closely.

"And," Pravin continued from the other end of the living room, "you will never again have to worry about a single snake, ever! Mongooses are *experts* at killing snakes. Nothing better!" This was his trump card. Snakes were undeniably a frequent sight in Tanzania. A few of them were even venomous.

The baby mongoose uncurled himself at the bottom of his basket and allowed me to pick him up. I could see dark bands of brown fur crossing the gray-brown fur of his back, rather like tabby-cat stripes, and I paused, scrutinizing the small animal I held aloft. This was an East African banded mongoose. He had the same little pink nose, thin horizontal eye pupils, and tiny rounded ears, just like all the banded mongooses we had seen in the game parks. He was irrefutably cute. He was also irrefutably wild.

Pravin had shrewdly noticed our family's tendency to rescue animals. He didn't fail to mention that over half of mongoose pups die in the first three months. "This one is an orphan with nowhere to go."

As if fully aware that he needed to ingratiate himself, the small wild animal cuddled into my lap and unfurled a tiny pink tongue with a yawn.

"Do they need any special sort of food or vaccinations?" These additional questions from Craig were sidestepped as readily as his first had been.

"What vaccinations?" Mother asked, intrigued by the conversation fragment she had just caught as she entered the living room. "Oh, hello, Pravin!" She smiled at the young man in earnest conversation with her son. Then, turning to me, she said, "Cathy, have you put away your bicyc—" She caught sight of the small creature on my lap, who was looking as winsome and guileless as possible. "Oh! Is that a meerkat?"

"It's not a meerkat!" came the chorus from Pravin, Craig, and me.

"Isn't he *darling*!" exclaimed Mother over the animal that was not a meerkat. "A mongoose?" she asked, after closer inspection. The three of us informed her that yes, this was a present from Pravin; yes, this creature was a mongoose and they were good with snakes; and no, I had not yet put away my bicycle.

"We have to have a good Swahili name for him!" said Mother.

Craig gaped at me.

I gaped at Craig.

Pravin beamed.

"We can call him Fupi." (*Foopie*) She lifted the mongoose off my lap and cradled him in her hands. "Because he's so little."

"Um, *Fupi* is not the Swahili word for *little*," Craig explained. "*Kidogo* would mean *little*. *Fupi* just means *short*."

"No matter. He looks like a Fupi," said Mother, snuggling her face into his fur.

Two days later, Pravin, never one to do things by halves,

gave us, again unbidden, a second mongoose. This animal was identical to Fupi in both size and weight, and our friend deftly avoided our questions as to whether this second one was a littermate of the first. Presumably this mongoose would be good with snakes too.

Dad, Craig, and I explained to Pravin that we would not agree to a second mongoose. The very idea.

"Wild animals should not be pets," Dad repeated for good measure.

"Steady on," said Pravin. "It's hardly a rhino calf I'm giving you!"

He laughed so heartily, and perhaps as a deflection mechanism, that we could get nothing further from him, and the matter was dropped. We implored him to not bring us any more pets. I could not shake the image from my mind of someone making pocket money by sneaking into game parks and stealing pups from mongoose colony burrows. We hoped no local zoos were missing an exhibit either. The adult mongooses we had seen in parks had fiery personalities. Pravin, in his jazzy shirts, remained stuck in my mind as a modern-day Prometheus bringing us these stolen, fiery gifts.

Mother took the *kikapu* from Pravin and peeked inside.

Pravin had calculated well.

By fair means or foul, we were now the owners of two Eastern banded mongooses.

The two mongoose pups soon made themselves at home, scampering and scuttling all over the house and garden—even my treehouse. They snapped up table scraps or *dudus* and were dubbed "Fupi" and "the other Fupi," since none of us could tell them apart.

Chapter 12
Did You Not Ask for a Snake?

Dear Bob,
Cathy has a tree house and she goes up there with the mongooses and with her friends.

—Mother

Dear Dad,
Mother is so worried about snakes, she doesn't even want me to climb a tree.

—Me

Dar es Salaam, early 1970s

Mother did not expect to find a snake eight inches from her face and, understandably, she screamed.

It had been a rather prosaic afternoon until that one startled scream. I had been coloring cross-legged on my bed upstairs, with my little dog, Alice, dozing beside me. I was thankful that it was only one scream and not a series of terror-stricken screams. Still, it was enough for me to jettison my coloring book. Alice bolted off the bed, with me scrambling to follow, descending the stairs three at a time as my happy scrawlings fluttered to the floor behind me, and crayons which

I had trodden on in my haste snapped in two.

Alice arrived on the scene first, all four paws skidding to a halt beside Mother as the dog caught sight of the scene and recoiled. I arrived to find Mother unharmed, standing by the open front door with one hand clapped over her mouth. In the doorway stood Yacob, our diligent *shamba* boy.

Mother remained agog.

"*Nyoka*, Madam!" he said, indicating—with a rather enthusiastic flourish—his offering, which was unceremoniously draped over the end of a long stick.

It had been less than a week since Yacob had assured us that our young banded mongooses were capable of vanquishing any serpent (and had recounted his own impressive record of killing countless *nyoka* himself). Mother had then requested that he bring to us the next snake to which he administered the coup de grâce. It was a request made rather begrudgingly, as she wasn't at all keen on snakes and pronounced every last one of them viscerally repulsive. But perhaps our mongooses would enjoy at least sniffing the dead body.

She hadn't expected Yacob to be *quite* so prompt. Mother's request for a snake had been made just days ago and yet here he stood, beaming with pride.

At least, he *had* been beaming while producing this fat, black, twelve-inch trophy.

But after the scream from Mother, he was overcome with profuse apologies instead.

"*Pole*, Madam! Ah, *pole*!" he said, mortified that he had startled her. He reassured her that the snake was dead: "Snake *kafa*! *Nyoka kafa*, Madam!"[26] This was rather an inescapable conclusion, considering the head was quite pulverized, no

---

26 The snake is dead, ma'am!

doubt from a flurry of well-aimed blows from Yacob's *rungu*.[27]

"Madam wanted snake, no?" Yacob asked, his face clouded with doubt and concern. "For mongoose, no?" He gave a slight wave of the stick for emphasis, the snake dangling gruesomely.

"Oh, y-yes!" Mother forced a smile as she remembered her earlier request. "Yes! *Ndio*," she continued, faltering both in English and Swahili while blinking rapidly. Then, in brighter tones as she regained her composure, she thanked him and gingerly accepted the unadorned end of the stick. "Why yes, I did ask for a . . . Um . . . Yes. *Asante, asante sana!*"[28]

"But, Yacob," I said, rather hoping he would take back the gift, "our mongooses are still babies. Perhaps too young to know what to do with a snake."

This particular potential contribution to our mongooses' education was rather pungent anyway, since it was encrusted in fecal matter no doubt emitted by the hapless reptile in its death throes. Both Mother and I felt rather reluctant to bring it into the house. A vigorous sneeze came from Alice, as she expressed her own disgust at the odor.

The gardener blinked, hesitating to find a polite answer to this little *mzungu* girl who doubted the unquestionable instincts of an African mongoose. He solemnly held my gaze. "A mongoose knows, Missy *Sahib*. They will know."

Seeing Mother barely suppress a grimace as she looked upon the cadaver, I took the stick, and the droopy "loathsome vermin" dangling from it. She flashed me a look of gratitude while bidding goodbye to our reassured gardener. The door closed, and the two of us stood there alone for several awkward seconds gawking at the grisly offering and not quite sure what to do next.

---

27 cudgel
28 Thank you very much!

Alice had lost interest and padded off with one more parting sneeze and a contemptuous shake of her head. I turned the stick this way and that, studying the dangling expired serpent from various angles. Minus any identifiable characteristics of the head, I had no way of knowing if it had been one of the few venomous African breeds.

Absent any green pigmentation, we decided we could rule out green mamba.

Had it once held the characteristic spade-shaped head of an adder? Was this a cobra, perhaps? How could one find the presence or absence of a hood on a snake whose head and neck were already flattened? The presence or absence of fangs and the position of any fangs, the shape of the pupil of the eye, were all lost clues due to the decimated head. I gazed at the piteous corpse of a creature who had once moved with a mysterious and sinuous grace as he patrolled our gardens, providing the inestimable benefit of keeping rats at bay less than an hour ago.

Catching the sorrowful expression on my face, Mother gave me a stern look. "Now, before you start with 'oh, poor little *nyoka*,' perhaps you had better go find the mongooses so we can give them this . . . this . . ."—another grimace—"*thing*."

Ri-ki-ki-ki-ki-ki-ki-ki! came the delighted chattering as one of our mongooses arrived on the scene. Fupi, barely larger than a kitten, waddled up to us. His dull orange nose quivered as he caught the scent of the reptile.

"Oh, do take this outside, Cathy. *Do!*" Mother pulled another face.

But then Fupi leapt.

Stunned, we watched as the mongoose launched, soaring about three feet off the ground, an astounding distance I would have thought impossibly high for such a small animal.

He cleanly snatched the snake off the stick at the peak of his leap, then landed on the floor and scuttled off toward the downstairs bedroom with his prize.

I was no longer in any doubt that the mongoose knew what to do with a snake.

Mother and I remained agape.

The mongoose disappeared under the bed with his trophy.

"Wait, Mother, the venom sac!" I vaguely remembered a zookeeper once telling me that a venom sac (was this even a venomous snake anyway?) could be found toward the back of the head. "Are mongooses immune to snake venom?"

"I'm most certainly not fishing that snake back out." Mother left the room. In her mind, this matter was all sorted.

In the minutes that followed (interspersed with crunching sounds from under the bed) I gathered my own courage to get the snake away from the wee beastie myself. I was loath to be bitten by Fupi, who could be irritable at the best of times but would be more so if anyone tried to separate him from this most delectable morsel. My agonized dithering came to an unexpected end as Fupi emerged from under the bed and toddled out of the room. Relieved that I would be able to avoid a bite from a fiercely protective mongoose, I scrambled to the spot where he had been feasting, to grab whatever was left of the snake. Especially that venom sac.

Nothing remained.

The mongoose had eaten the entire thing.

Chapter 13
All We Ever See Are Wildebeest

Dear Bob,
Cathy is only interested in the fauna so far.

—Mother

Wildebeest were the most numerous.

—Craig

Tanzania, early 1970s

It was the wildebeest who made the strongest impression on me during our first journey into a game park in Africa. The Kiswahili word for journey, *safari*, was the widely used term throughout East Africa for these trips. One could go on safari in any number of ways, we found. It could be a day trip, or an overnight trip, with or without a professional guide, depending on the park and the distances involved. As we approached the main gate of the park, my excitement level rose, seeing the welcome sign written in multiple different languages and accompanied by artwork of various animals. I couldn't even decide which animal I most wanted to see. It would be a thrill to see any of them outside of a zoo, after all. My young Canadian brain, while thrilled, was still trying to absorb the fact that there were no bears in Africa.

At the gate, they gave us a game park pamphlet. Clutching it in my hand, I attempted to identify each creature we encountered. We drove past ostrich, the largest bird on the planet. We saw a secretary bird—a raptor with bizarrely long legs. Perhaps the ugliest creature we saw was the marabou stork. This really *is* a stork, the pamphlet declared, even though it flies like a heron, with his neck retracted. The most beautiful animal, in my opinion, was the greater kudu, pictured on the pamphlet, but we didn't see any that day, to my regret.

I giggled to see banded mongooses skittering across the potholed road. It seemed as though every road in the area was riddled with bone-jarring potholes. Paved roads only existed in cities.

At our first zebra sighting, I announced, *"Pundamilia,"* very proud that I had memorized the Kiswahili name of these walking barcodes. Mother said their stripes had something to do with repelling insects. Dad countered that it was a confusion tactic to thwart predators from picking out one individual animal in a milling herd. Craig turned to me in surprise when I called them donkeys with stripes.

"Donkeys with stripes? Kiddo, these are not donkeys with stripes."

I was certain this was the meaning of the name of these animals that somewhat resembled donkeys. The Kiswahili name for donkey was *punda*, and zebras, plural, were *pundamilia*, I pointed out triumphantly.

"I still don't think that means donkeys with stripes," Craig replied, thinking hard.

Fast-forward forty years ahead, I was an adult sitting at my computer one cool afternoon in America, exchanging emails with a friend who happened to be a native Kiswahili speaker. On impulse, I broke away from the conversation she and I had been having about the weather. A zebra had just crossed my mind.

"Please, can you tell me?" I emailed to her. "I remember that *punda* was *donkey*. Is that right?"

"Why yes," she wrote back. "The Kiswahili word for donkey is *punda*." She followed this with a smiling emoji.

"So then," I typed as confidently as I had verbally answered my brother all those years ago, "zebra, *pundamilia*, means a donkey with stripes. Is that right?"

I hit *Send*.

No answer for several minutes.

Then my computer screen filled with her reply of multiple emoji all laughing with tears wildly spurting from closed eyes, clearly overcome with mirth.

"It does *not* mean a donkey with stripes?" I wrote.

"No, my *rafiki*," and another laughing face symbol was inserted here, "*pundamilia* does not mean a donkey with stripes." Her reply gave me the impression she was still doubled over with laughter, complete with tears streaming down her face. Pulling herself together, she wrote again, saying very kindly, "No, it does not mean a donkey with stripes. *Pundamilia* roughly translates to 'a donkey with something different.'"

Well, at least I got the donkey part correct.

However, on that sunny day in Tanzania back in 1971, I was still confident, at age eight, that my animal knowledge surpassed that of my brother. and I did not stint on sharing all that I had learned with Craig. These wild equines would remain as donkeys with stripes in my young mind for years to come.

A Billion Blue Wildebeest

I had been somewhat amused by the zebras, but I loved the elephants on first sight. Their sheer mass stunned me and their trunks intrigued me. They moved grandly through the parks, with no predators daring to bother them.

But for sheer numbers, nothing could surpass the wildebeest. These are a very bizarre-looking, large antelope standing maybe four and a half feet high at the shoulder. Their coloring varies between gray and brown, but "white bearded blue wildebeest" was the name of the ones that we saw throughout Tanzania. Both males and females have horns, and they existed in vast migrating herds here, whereas the breeds of wildebeest in southern Africa, which do not migrate, are black, with horns that curve in a more forward angle. Neither looks graceful. Both have blocky heads, short necks, and thin legs. Nor do they have the gift of silence, but instead emit a near-constant stream of grunts varying in tone and pitch.

Wildebeest are not one of the Big Five specimens of African wildlife that tourists long to see. In almost every souvenir gift shop I've ever seen in Africa, they will (begrudgingly, perhaps?) feature wildebeest in postcards or sculpture, along with the more spectacular African wildlife. However, most of the time the animal is featured either in its mating dance (which is charming) or at a river crossing (which is dramatic). Souvenir gift shops will seldom sell sculptures of wildebeest dozing in the middle of the road, or in the grass, as the ones in front of me were that afternoon. Two hours of nothing but sleepy wildebeest eked by. A billion blue wildebeest. None of whom were dancing or engaged in a river crossing.

"Wow! Look! A wildebeest!"

The initial novelty soon wore off. "Ah. More wildebeest."

"Well. There certainly are a lot of them, aren't there?"

Everyone was good-natured, if slightly tepid, and lapsed into an amiable silence.

Except me. "Wildebeest, wildebeest. All we ever see are wildebeest. I'm fed up with wildebeest. Can't we see something else?"

Over the following years, this one quote from me, at age eight, became legendary in the family. I never did quite live it down. In contrast, however, I soon developed a deep affection for wildebeest (or "Wil-duh-beastie," as one friend nicknamed them). They became comforting symbols of stability for me, perhaps because they were so very ordinary and plentiful besides their comical and endearing qualities. Somehow the word *perseverance* came to mind for me when seeing wildebeest, and I used them as a reminder to myself not to give up during difficulties. Their perseverance was especially obvious to me in their annual great migration, as they continued plodding along, mile after mile after mile, over four hundred miles, against all odds.

Besides, could a wild beast be given a more unimaginative name? I couldn't shake the image that one day, long ago, a Dutch man and an Afrikaans man might have come together and admitted they had run out of attractive names to bestow upon animals, and so this wild beast became simply a wildebeest.

Or, to some, a Wil-Duh-Beastie.

CHAPTER 14
He Eats Funny Too

Dear Dr. Thomas,
May I please confirm that exporting a cat to the US involves the following. I will need:
1. Current vaccination certificate.
2. Veterinary export certificate issued by the Director of Veterinary Services. It is valid for ten days after issue.
3. Booking of airline. KLM, SWISSAIR are the preferred airlines.
4. Cost of freight will depend on weight and volume of cat and box.
5. Customs and zoosanitary clearance.
Is there any other information I might be missing . . . ?
Sincerely,
Catherine

Dar es Salaam, February 2017

I was a grown adult, sitting in a white plastic chair at the TAWESO animal shelter, trying to rally my thoughts together as I gazed upon the tabby cat I had agreed to adopt. Some unnamed brain damage seemed to be present in the animal, leaving me daunted but determined to carry through with the adoption regardless. "He's not in pain," the staff reassured me again.

With my *alea iacta est*[29] plan firm in my mind, I turned my attention to the fish.

"Oh, the fish! Yes, the fish!" The Tanzanians, who had also temporarily forgotten, all burst into smiles . . . of relief? Had they been worried I would decline to proceed with this adoption? "Yes, we shall get the fish ready!" they said, and hastily assembled feeding bowls for the cats.

Is it possible to be horror-struck twice in one day, minutes apart? Yes, it was, and that day I learned why. Amongst the shelter cats there were two who had only arrived the day before, and they were still shockingly thin. These two had been mewing up until now, as shelter cats do in every shelter that I have ever visited.

Until they caught the scent of the fish.

Then those two screamed.

I had never heard screams from cats before. Caterwauling, yes. Yowling, yes. But this was screaming. Shrill, strident, screeching, screams. It was surreal. These frenzied animals scrabbled at the wire of their cages. Sweet little plaintive mews were no longer in their vocabulary. I froze in place.

Fights broke out as the bowls of fish were brought into their cages. I had never seen anything like it, and my mouth fell agape once more. Unbelievable cacophony. It was almost as though a wave of electricity had zapped through the cages. The staff had considerable difficulty portioning out the food to the cats. The shelter staff, accustomed to the soundtrack (of starvation?) beckoned me to come watch my own cat being fed. Once again, I forced myself to compose my face. Whatever his impairment was (neurological?), it caused not

---

29   the die is cast

just staggering but head tremors too. This was my first time seeing head tremors, and it was heart-wrenching to see this cat try, again and again, to aim his wildly flailing head into the food bowl.

I now saw Saul's mimicry, in the car ride over here, of this cat's head movements while attempting to eat, had been spot on. My heart sank.

Perhaps to hold his head steady, I began to reach in, only to be met with a hiss as he lunged at me in fury at having disrupted his meal.

Right. I'll leave you to it.

Clank, click, clank! The sound of his teeth striking the rim of the metal bowl startled me as he kept trying to get his mouth down to the fish. Several agonizing attempts later, the wobbling, careening, and swaying head finally reached the fish. Frantic gobbling ensued.

Now that's the second thing I will change, after his name, I thought. No *more eating out of metal bowls. Otherwise he might chip a tooth. My God, look at those violent head tremors.*

The cat, almost choking and convulsing, continued its rapid-fire eating while I stared, fingers clutching a fold of my *kanga* and eyebrows raised almost to my hairline.

I just couldn't take my eyes off him. I was racking my brain as to what his disabilities might be, what particular form of brain damage, but could only come up with the dazed assessment of *This . . . This . . . This is a brain-damaged cat.*

"Now, here are all his papers."

I tore my eyes away from the animals to see a large, fat manila envelope in Dr. Thomas's hands. He had drawn up his chair next to me and was pulling each document out of the envelope, one at a time.

He showed me one printed on green paper. "This is his

export certificate. And here"—he pointed to another—"is his rabies certificate. You will be asked for these at the airport."

I nodded dully, my oversaturated brain unable to grasp much of what he was saying.

This . . . is . . . a . . . brain-damaged cat.

The recitation of the meticulous recordkeeping of every single dollar I had ever wired to him from America continued. I barely absorbed it.

This is a severely brain-damaged cat. I thought it would be a bone problem.

Dr. Thomas laid more papers in my lap. "Here's his distemper vaccine, his rhinotracheitis vaccine, his microchip, oh, and his feline panleucopenia vaccine." One after another. My wobble-head cat had also received treatments for ticks and fleas. A promise was made to trim his claws for me tomorrow. And did I have an airline-approved carrier for him?

This was then gently repeated. Perhaps they could see I was still in some degree of shock.

"Do you mind if . . ." I raised my head and faced Dr. Thomas. "If I give a different name to the cat?"

He considered this and agreed that naming the cat after the car that may or may not have hit him was perhaps not ideal. "I can see how it might be a bad reflection," he conceded. "What name would you like to give him instead?"

I mentioned the name "Stanley," which Dr. Thomas thought was fine. He added that the cat had been neutered and one ear tipped as proof of the neuter.

Unsurprisingly, he never asked me which particular Stanley had been chosen to be the cat's namesake. In Central or East Africa, the name "Stanley" only ever refers, it seems to me, to Sir Henry Morton Stanley. This famed nineteenth-century explorer, a Welsh-born American journalist who had been tasked with finding Dr. David Livingstone, was indelibly linked to our memories of Tanzania. So, over many years, the name "Stanley" had been given to various pets my family had, including two dogs.

Sir Henry Morton Stanley was tasked with this particular mission because there had been no word from missionary and explorer Dr. Livingstone, deep in the African Interior, in over four years. Was he still alive? Livingstone had been searching for the source of the Nile. Stanley went searching for Livingstone, who he found, and eventually neither man would be credited with finding the source of the Nile.

The ancient Romans even had a saying describing their view of any extremely difficult task: "Facilius sit Nili caput invenire," meaning it would be easier to find the source of the Nile. Stanley, however, would receive some acclaim when he was, in fact, able to confirm the findings of another explorer as to the location of the source.

Sir Henry Stanley had crossed Tanzania in several of the exact spots our family had visited, in his search for Livingstone. We had arrived in Tanzania about ninety-nine years after his "Doctor Livingstone, I presume?" meeting near Ujiji/Kigoma, Western Tanzania, on November 10, 1871. I was surprised to learn, years later, that about an hour from Kigoma was the Gombe National Park, where Dr. Jane Goodall had conducted her ground-breaking studies on chimpanzees.

On this September day of my TAWESO visit, I took assorted photographs and videos of this cat who was—or perhaps was not—a survivor of a car collision, Indian or otherwise.

Not long afterward, I was being driven back to my hotel in silence, head still reeling.

I was alone, without the cat, since the arrangement was

made that they would bring Stanley to me in my hotel a few hours before I would leave for the airport.

Back in my hotel room, I soaked my *kanga* in cold water, having found more blood from being bitten, and sent off emails to family, with descriptions of the cat who didn't seem to have any bone problems after all. And then:

What about that email he talked about . . . ?

And sure enough, sitting there in my spam folder was the email from Dr. Thomas, laying out the discovery of the brain damage in his typically forthright manner.

"I would understand if you do not wish to go forward with the adoption."

Perhaps five whole minutes went by of me staring at that screen in utter silence and just shaking my head.

A deep sigh, and I squared my shoulders and shut down the computer for the night.

Stan was mine, until death do us part.

I turned and studied the papers once again, reading and rereading this cat's various documents. *Animal Health Export Certificate* was printed across the green document, which was further specified as *Permit number 0000004788* and issued by the director of veterinary services in Dar es Salaam, Dr. Sekidio. He had affixed his seal, certifying *one cat being exported to USA through Julius Nyerere International Airport by Air*.

Poring over the veterinarian records, I could find no documentation of brain damage, whether from trauma or congenital. When Stanley's little tabula rasa of a brain had been forming in utero, did some neurons and cells go awry?

Tucking all the legal documents back into the manila envelope, my brain was staggering just as much as the wretched cat.

A cat who I was not convinced had once been hit by a car of any make or model.

I had no idea what sort of future to expect for Stanley and me. *I will be the owner of a brain-damaged cat. How will I ever cope?*

Wildebeest came to my mind just then. Their resilience. *I must have the resilience and the perseverance of the wildebeest*, I concluded. They just kept putting one foot in front of the other, mile after mile. And I could too. Exhaling then, I sat up straighter.

I knew with complete and utter certainty that I would see to it that my *paka wangu kipenzi* would be given ample meals, and never again from metal bowls, and he would have every possible chance available to a cat in America. The idea of euthanasia was too unbearable for me to consider just then. The word was Greek, meaning "a death that goes well." My brain wasn't willing to think of any form of death just then. No. Instead, this cat would get all my love, every day, for however many days he had left.

Chapter 15
The Word for Ten

Being a teenage boy, I was the first to learn that word.
—Craig

Dar es Salaam, circa 1971

I resolved, very early on, that I would just avoid the Swahili word for *ten*. Life was just simpler if I didn't try to say it.

Craig and Mother lingered at the dining room table long after dinner, absorbed in writing letters to family back in Canada. I strolled in and plopped down to join them, my rescued pet tortoise in my right hand and a banana in my left.

"Isn't it funny," I mused, gazing at the banana from various angles, "how they don't turn yellow when they're ripe?

"Yes," murmured Craig, still immersed in composing his letter, "yellow when they're ripe."

"But they *don't* turn yellow when they're ripe," I corrected Craig, but he and Mother's attention had already turned back to their aerograms.

It was in Africa when I first encountered these long blue sheets of ultra-light, tissue-thin paper (which our relatives back in Canada had to be careful not to tear). They were

A Billion Blue Wildebeest

folded and sealed to form a letter, without need of a separate envelope. Aerograms had been introduced in the early thirties and gained more popularity during World War II as an inexpensive method of international correspondence. Each aerogram was distinctive to its country of origin, and the ones we bought from our local post office always featured illustrations of African wildlife.

I perched on my chair, swinging my legs back and forth, and tried to catch my tortoise's attention with her banana treat. Delilah, however, had stretched her crepe-lined neck to its fullest extent, having noticed the elephant hair bracelet I was wearing and wanting to see if that, instead, was edible. The street vendor we had bought it from had told us that Tanzanian children in the country villages made money by gathering the stray tail hairs caught on bushes. These were then woven into bracelets with two knots. They were not designed to be eaten by African leopard tortoises, but Delilah was unconvinced.

"That shopkeeper from last week." Mother turned to Craig, her pen paused above her aerogram. "He was going to sell me ten small fish, right? So if I write it in Swahili, then it's *samaki nane wadogo*, right?"

My tortoise chomped down on the banana.

"Almost," Craig answered, not lifting his head, "but *nane* is *nine*, not *ten*."

Mother's brow furrowed. "Oh, right. *samaki kuma wadogo*, then." She shrugged and resumed writing.

A slight gasp from Craig.

Mother and I stared at him. Craig doesn't gasp.

My brother's shoulders were shaking. His mouth was clamped shut.

"What's so funny?" Mother said, slightly indignant. "I

corrected my sentence. It doesn't say *nine* any longer."

"It doesn't say *ten* either!" By now Craig was laughing openly. Mother stared at the sentence she had written, then back at Craig in bewilderment. Craig sobered down and gently but very firmly explained that the Swahili word for *ten* is *kumi*. "Don't ever say that other word. Better cross that out of your letter. That's not the word for *ten*."

Mother and I stared at him. I put Delilah on the floor and came to see what Mother had written. "That isn't the word for *ten*?"

"No." Craig looked a little uncomfortable. "That is not the word for *ten*. Don't ever say that word." Here, he shot a sideways glance at me, then a significant look at Mother.

She turned to me. "Darling," she suggested sweetly, "perhaps Delilah would like to go out of the room and into the garden?"

I wasn't going anywhere.

"So that other word?" I prodded, sitting back down, but now on the edge of my chair. The forgotten tortoise roamed free on the floor. "That other word means something really, really bad, then, eh?"

Mother looked apprehensively at Craig. Craig looked unhappily at Mother. I could almost hear the two of them groan.

Craig, realizing the futility of any further delay of the revelation, took a steeling breath, laid down his pen, and faced his little eight-year-old sister. "Kiddo, that word means, as you would say, *little bottom*," my brother said, using the baby talk term I had come up with years ago to describe female genitalia.

Mother pulled a face.

"So don't ever, ever use that word," he said. "It's not even the proper word." And here Mother looked at him sharply.

"It's not even the medical word, the clinical word that a doctor would use. It's instead a really, really vulgar, really dirty word."

A gasp from Mother and me.

My face burning, I dropped my eyes, hastily searching for my tortoise.

Mother vigorously crossed out the word that wasn't *kumi* from her aerogram. It tore from her vigor.

As I fled the room, Craig had already handed her a fresh aerogram and was shredding her old one.

Perhaps unsurprisingly, I developed an almost veritable phobia, for the rest of my life, about mixing up the two fraught and perilous words. It became such a Sisyphean task for me to try to avoid the error that I resorted to carrying *kumi* on an index card in my purse when I visited Tanzania in later years as an adult.

"How many would you like to buy?" a Dar es Salaam street vendor asked me one day, pointing to the candies I wanted to purchase.

Keeping a poker face, I pretended to reach into my purse for money, intending to carefully sneak a peek at my trusty index card first.

Thousands of people say the correct word for ten. I can too. No big deal.

I couldn't find the card.

What was the last syllable? All I need to remember is that last syllable. And where is that card?

"How many, *Mamma*?" the smiling vendor persisted.

With shoulders slumping, I stood before him and silently held up ten fingers.

The Swahili word for *ten* surfaced again and again in my life.

I was in a departure lounge—of which airport, I've

forgotten—where I had changed seats to position myself next to a couple who I thought might be Tanzanian. After greeting them and confessing that I had overheard them speaking Kiswahili, I asked if they were from Tanzania.

"Ah! We are from Kenya!" they replied in surprise, beaming at me. Then they both plied me with their own questions of where I was from, and how it was that I knew Kiswahili.

"Oh, but I *don't!*" I replied, switching back to English with a sheepish laugh. I went on to explain my upbringing in Tanzania and ended with my lament about how much Swahili I had forgotten. My new African friends were turning out to be as delightful as I'd expected. Contrasts and comparisons between Kenya and Tanzania were discussed at length, since we still had quite a while before our flight, and I basked in the joy of being back amongst East Africans. I barely noticed two other travelers, who seemed American to me, seated on the other side of Mr. and Mrs. Kenya. Were the Americans eavesdropping? This seating area we were in was, come to think of it, rather quiet.

My new friends earnestly suggested that I study Kiswahili once again, promising how quickly it would all come back to me. This then led to me describing, to their great mirth, all the mistakes I had made in their language.

"Trying to remember the numbers in Swahili is where I really used to stumble," I confessed. "And of course, I no longer dare to say the Swahili word for the number *ten*. That second syllable, you know."

"Oh! Oh, yes!" Mrs. Kenya responded, giggling. "We hear *mzungo* make that mistake with *kumi* all the time!" She spent the next minute or so clicking her tongue in sympathy, but then laughing once again.

By now Mr. Kenya was guffawing along with the two of

us. "Oh, that syllable!"

And we missed the Americans, who had lowered their magazines—*Southern Living, The Delights of Dixie, July issue*—and were asking us a question. "What syllable?"

They repeated their question, in undeniable American accents, but apparently not whatsoever inclined to drop the issue until they had an answer. Our giggles and guffaws trailed off awkwardly. My African friends shot me a look. I realized that it would be up to me alone to explain to these Americans the perils of the Kiswahili word for *ten*.

I turned to the American couple, slightly embarrassed. "If you mispronounce that word, it comes off as a rude word," I replied weakly.

"It does?" asked Mrs. Dixie.

"What rude word?" Mr. Dixie wanted to know.

I looked at the wife, and then at the husband, and they looked back at me, clearly still in dog-with-a-bone mode. Mr. and Mrs. Kenya, meanwhile, had retreated behind their own magazines.

"What rude word?" Mr. Dixie persisted.

I scoured my mind to think how best to phrase the explanation about this Swahili word but finally mumbled that, when pronounced incorrectly, it referred to a woman's private parts.

"Oh. It just means *lady bits* if you say the word wrong?" said Mrs. Dixie. "That's all? Well, that's not so bad."

I caught a side glance from Mrs. Kenya, who seemed to be wondering if I was going to allow the American to persist in her thoughts that the word was "not so bad."

"Well, let me put it this way." I turned to Mrs. Dixie, my voice stronger. "You know how when there's a litter of puppies, and one puppy is the smallest and weakest of the lot?"

"Sure." She shrugged, unsure as to why I was talking about dogs.

"So that smallest, weakest puppy in the litter," I continued. "What is that one called?"

"The runt."

"Well." I spoke slowly and clearly for emphasis and gave her a long steady look. "It rhymes with that."

Now three pairs of eyes were staring at the Americans in silence.

The penny dropped.

"Oh . . ." A weak gasp from Mrs. Dixie, who flushed crimson.

"Oh. Y-yeah," stammered Mr. Dixie, equally crimson.

Our flight was called just then, a diversion gratefully seized upon. Dozens of passengers got to their feet in the departure lounge and began gathering up their assorted carry-on bags. Mr. and Mrs. Kenya and I had our heads down like everyone else as we sorted our own bags.

When next we looked around, the Americans had vanished.

Chapter 16
Only A Mock Charge

Dear Bob,
The Cath is a scream. She is not timid, and this worries me, as there are snakes here, and I always worry that she does not pay attention to where she puts her feet while chasing lizards, which she brings into her room. You should see her FEET. They are so long. I hope they stop growing.

—Mother

Dar es Salaam, early 1970s

Nonna pointed out the car window, drawing my attention to how the African soil was becoming redder as we left the Dar coast and headed inland to a game park. Craig had recently gotten his driver's license and had happily agreed to drive Nonna anywhere she wished. When she requested a game park, Mother and I came along as well.

Nonna was delighted we had been posted to Tanzania and visited often. She was no stranger to Africa. All four of us were looking forward to the wildlife, but Nonna in particular had fond memories of baobab trees from Eritrea and was looking forward to seeing them once again. I had been intrigued by how she had described them as "upside-down." She drifted into French or Italian to describe the other aspects of these trees (which can have a lifespan of over one thousand years) since English was not her first language. Many years later, as an adult, I returned to Tanzania and gazed at baobab trees, and wondered, *If they do have such long lifespans, am I seeing the exact individual trees that Nonna and I saw here in my childhood?*

On this sunny day in the early 1970s, however, my grandmother sat beside her little granddaughter earnestly attempting to decide which language to use to convey her thoughts about baobabs. It was not the English word for *upside-down* that she stumbled on, because these particular trees were upside-down in any language. By the end of the day, however, one particular elephant had succeeded in making me forget about any baobabs.

We had already visited multiple parks so far in Tanzania, but Mikumi National Park was a particular favorite. Mikumi was fairly small, only about one thousand square miles, and still very new, having been designated as a national park three years after Independence. We were visiting it about six years into its new chapter as an official national park.

After two hours' worth of blue wildebeest, everybody in the car had fallen into a polite, tepid silence. We scanned the sky but saw no telltale circling vultures, signifying any nearby predators with a kill. Craig kept listening for any alarm cries of any animal reacting to some other animal, with no luck.

Nonna, I noticed, was being very good-natured about not seeing one baobab yet. Upside-down or not. I still held to my belief that *billions* was the correct term for the number of wildebeest we were seeing. The polite silence continued.

Until Craig saw something.

"Wait . . . Is that . . . ?" Craig slowed down the car and peered deep into the bush. "There! Do you see it?" We all stared in the direction in which he was pointing.

I saw bush.

"Oh!" said Mother and Nonna. "Yes! Over there!"

I saw bush.

"Wait, I'm going to position us over there." Craig drove down a different little side path. "That way we are downwind."

Downwind of what?

The largest ear on any animal on the planet is around two feet across and four feet from top to bottom. These are found on the African elephant, and finally, with binoculars, I saw the tiny edge of one part of one elephant's ear that my brother had seen, deep, deep in the bush. I lowered the binoculars and gazed at Craig agape. My brother's sharp vision never failed to astound me, and this *tembo*[30] had been almost obscured in the bush.

Elephants! I was seeing elephants again. Wild African elephants, not in some zoo. Back home in Canadian zoos, I had only seen Asian elephants, with their one-finger trunks. The Asian ones had ears that seemed absurdly small, whereas the ears on African elephants were magnificent. The rounded backs on the Asian ones were another contrast from the sway backs I was seeing here in Tanzania. Nonna and I sighed, captivated. Mother, however, fell silent and swallowed hard. Nonna's complete lack of fear around elephants must have skipped a generation.

We could just make out several individuals in a herd. Soon these individuals were filling the viewfinder in the binoculars. They were walking toward us. Craig, Nonna, and I spoke to one another in reverent whispers, loath to disturb the magic.

---

30   elephant

Mother held a stiff smile and watched. Craig was sharply watching one young bull off to the side. I was distracted by the half-dozen spellbinding cows and two charming calves milling around, quietly grazing.

"Tools," whispered Nonna. "Do you see? They use tools!" She pointed to a young cow who had broken off a small branch and was holding it in her trunk.

Just before I could whisper back, "What tools?" I realized that the elephant was methodically scratching one shoulder with the branch instead of rubbing her shoulder up against some scratchy surface.

"Notice how you don't hear their feet?" Craig said, sotto voce. We could hear the calm slow flapping of the ears. We could hear the rumblings of elephantine tummies and throats. We could hear bits of foliage being broken here and there. But each footfall of each elephant was utterly silent. These great galoots with the gossamer feet had more spongy padding than cat paws.

One calf, the smaller of the two, was enchanting.

"Just a little titch!" Nonna smiled. The little chap was still so young that he was having considerable struggles with his how-do-I-control-this-thing trunk. Try as he might, Titch did not yet have mastery over his rogue appendage and frequently thwacked his mother in the ankles or tangled it around his own forelegs. His flailing and flopping reminded me of a previous Christmas morning when I'd plopped a sticky Christmas bow on the top of our dog's head. The annoyed dog shook and shook his head, but the bow wouldn't come off until he scraped a paw repeatedly over his head and at last removed the sticky nuisance. Here was Titch in front of me, with his own puppyish charm, doing that same frustrated headshake, bumbling and blundering and even tripping over his most versatile but noncompliant extremity.

"Ah, he is saying, 'Mama, what *is* this? What do I *do* with this?'" Nonna whispered to me as we both giggled over the baby's struggles.

"He's not sure if it's his upper lip, or is it a hand, or is it his nose!" I whispered back. Then, seeing Titch pause, still puzzled about his unruly limb, I added, "He's thinking to himself, 'If I step on this thing and pull backward, can I get it off my face?'" which got a chuckle from everyone in the car.

"*Bene*,[31] is no broken tusks down near the root on anyone here," murmured Nonna, surveying the herd. Tusks are modified upper incisors, and the largest teeth of any animal in the world. Each of these modified upper incisors, all solid dentin and denser than bone, weighed as much or more than my entire body. I wasn't even seeing the entire length of each tusk because about a quarter of it, the hollow part that does contain nerves, was embedded inside the elephant's skull. Nonna explained that a broken tusk down near the root might mean an exposed nerve, hence a terrible toothache for the elephant. Any wild animal suffering a toothache can become a danger, or the pain might diminish its ability to eat.

Yes, I, too, was glad that I saw no broken tusks in this group today.

One cow, adorned with tusks that crisscrossed, stood at a slight distance, staring at us and flapping her ears with increasing briskness. We could see no obvious reason why CrissCross was annoyed with us. She had no calf, and both tusks were whole, precluding any toothache. Mother watched this particular cow with keen attention.

"Well, somebody's out of sorts," I observed, leaning forward from my seat in the back to talk to Craig. Mother

---

31 good

had her head leaning out the window for a better look and missed most of our whispering.

"I'm not worried about her," Craig said very quietly, his eyes on a different elephant, farther away. "I'm keeping my eye on the grumpy old sod over there." He nodded toward an older bull whose body language was more languid than CrissCross, though Grumpy Old Sod did have a broken off tusk that I hadn't noticed earlier.

"Toothache?" I kept my voice equally low. No need to worry Mother, who was never entirely at ease around elephants anyway.

"Actually, I didn't think about that," Craig said, "but I'm wondering . . . *musth*?" The mention of *musth*, a periodic condition that male elephants go through of heightened aggression, made me take a sharper look. Ever observant, it had not escaped my brother's notice that this bull was flapping his ears at the elephant next to him, lashing his trunk, and dribbling urine. Secretions were seeping down the side of his face from his temporal glands. All possible *musth* symptoms.

I caught Craig's eye and raised my eyebrows.

"I didn't think of toothache," my brother whispered to me.

"I didn't think of *musth*."

"Let's hope Mother doesn't think of either one."

Both of us knew full well that Mother would request that we leave, right there and then, if she caught wind of what we had seen. Nonna, however, had the same hawklike vision Craig had, and sure enough, she soon raised a finger toward Grumpy Old Sod.

"Uh, Craig . . ."

Craig and I quickly caught Nonna's eye, then gave a tiny nod toward Mother. Our grandmother understood immediately.

"Oh, Anna," said Nonna brightly, turning to Mother,

who had brought her head back into the car. Nonna quickly moved her pointing finger toward CrissCross instead. "That elephant is nothing to worry about."

"Yeah, Mother," I said, bringing my voice back to normal volume again. "No problem there." I could see that neither of us had managed to convince her, as her eyes remained riveted on the bothered cow. Little did any of us know, but Grumpy Old Sod would soon become the least of our problems.

The herd who had been grazing and drifting in our direction began to cross the road a few yards behind our vehicle. Several trunks facing us rose up as the elephants assessed the wind and our scent, then lowered with an occasional snort. Those large ears slowly flapped, tails flopping casually as the largest land mammals on the entire planet crossed the road, still with incongruous silence. The mothers with calves passed behind us. One young cow, ambling across the road just behind our car, extended her trunk and gently touched our back bumper.

"Yes, we smell funny, don't we?" I murmured to the young snoop, who soon lost interest and plodded on to join the others. Mother still had her eyes on CrissCross, who hadn't yet even come close to us. I shot up a silent prayer of thanks that she had somehow missed this encounter with Little Miss I-Touched-Your-Car, skillfully distracted by Craig pointing out other elephants and their bizarrely silent feet.

Nonna had noticed her, and the two of us beamed at each other, silently delighted in our close encounter.

Let's not tell Mother about that one until we leave the park was our mutual resolve.

Grumpy Old Sod, I was thankful to see, was a considerable distance away from the front of our vehicle, placidly munching grass on the roadside.

Whenever I saw elephants up close, my brain could not

even grasp the sheer height of these creatures. Elephants can be ten feet high at the shoulder, taller than a polar bear back home in Canada standing up on his hind legs. One adult can weigh as much as four cars. And all of that is balanced on feet that make less noise than the average house cat. This close to the car, though, all I could really see were legs. I did get a good look at the tip of the trunk of Little Miss I-Touched-Your-Car during those three or four seconds when she was only about a yard away, noting the two fingers on the end.

Mother had other things on her mind right then and would not have been receptive had I shared with her my musings about elephant trunks. She remained fixated on that one fraught female.

"She's going to charge at us, Craig-O," Mother told my brother apprehensively. "I think we should split." I noted she carefully chose the slang *split* instead of *leave* in her appeal to her teenage son.

Craig smiled at Mother. "Relaxez-vous," he said, responding her use of slang with made-up slang of his own.

The cow was pacing back and forth perhaps two hundred feet away, with her tail stiffly held up and trunk swinging. She flapped her ears more briskly, then faced us.

A profile view of an elephant, with those nice shoulders, has always seemed less confrontational. But now she was facing us squarely, and her massive ears were fanned out, unnervingly hiding those comforting shoulders. She could be planning anything.

All four of us had our eyes fixed on CrissCross.

I don't like it when I can't see shoulders.

"It would not be *groovy* . . . " wheedled Mother, her widened eyes fixed on the elephant cow. "It would not be *far out* if she charged at us." Her voice cracked. "I would not *dig it.*"

Craig was unruffled. "We'll be fine."

The five-ton beast came toward us. She began picking up speed.

"*Craaiig!*" One of the very few times we ever heard a scream from Mother.

"Mother, this is a mock charge," said Craig, never taking his eyes off the elephant, but remaining enviably calm. "Don't worry, this is only a mock charge."

This mock charge looked absolutely identical to a real charge to me, but I noted that Nonna had remained as calm as Craig, so I silently clenched my jaw and prayed fervently that this really was only a bluff.

Mother's panic was fully florid. "*OhCraigOhCraigOhCraigOhCraigOhCraig!*"

The elephant gave out a deafening trumpet as she bore down on us, ears fully spread forward.

"Mother, this is a mock charge," Craig repeated, hands resting in his lap, not even reaching for the keys.

Mesmerized, I tore my gaze away from the charging elephant barely seven car lengths away to check yet again for my grandmother's reaction. And still saw no fear on my Nonna's face. She must have heard the sobbing whimpers that I thought I had successfully stifled, because she reached out and clasped my hand warmly.

Mother, however, was putting into words the same feelings that were going through me. "Oh! Oh! B-bloody hell! Craig, start the car. Quickly, quickly." For good measure she repeated, "quickly, quickly" in multiple languages, since slang hadn't worked. "*Haraka, haraka! Vite! Vite! Veloce!*"

"This is a mock charge," Craig replied in English, still supernaturally calm. He then added a Swahili phrase, since language-hopping was where Mother's mind was. "We'll go *pole pole.*"

The elephant, who was not going *pole pole*, was still thundering down on us and by now only about five car lengths away, ears unfurled, trunk loose, head and tusks held high, and still trumpeting.

"This is a mock charge," Craig repeated.

And he was right.

The furious elephant came to a stop two car lengths away from us. She blew another infuriated trumpeting blast, then wheeled around in a swirl of red dust, and with one final haughty toss of her head, she stomped off to join her herd.

Mother and I exhaled.

"Do you know people can *die* from *heart failure* during a mock charge?" Mother wanted Craig to know, smacking his arm with her *Welcome to Mikumi* brochure instead of praising him for his sangfroid. "*Now* can we go?"

"All right, I guess we can split now," said Craig agreeably. The sound of that engine starting up was the most blessed relief.

My quavering voice piped up. "Craig, how did you *know*? How did you know the difference between a real charge and a mock charge?" I was vastly impressed, though not completely surprised, that my brother had shown the same calmness today as he had when we had all received our injections-for-Africa in that Montreal clinic.

"Kiddo, you watch the ears. When elephants are serious about charging, they pin their ears back, tuck in their trunk and just go for it. But if they're not serious, they flap out their ears to make themselves look bigger, wave their trunk around, make lots of noise, and—"

"And they do mock charge. Is almost always only a mock charge," said Nonna. "Buffalo instead never do a mock charge."

"And watch the trunk too," Craig continued. "The trunk is sensitive and vulnerable, so they will curl it up carefully against the chest, protectively, if it's a real charge. And you must never try to run. Just stay put."

"Quite right. You cannot outrun an elephant," Nonna agreed. Then, after a slight pause, she added, "I still think she had toothache. She had no good reason to be so irritable with us."

Mother decided she had had quite enough of a game drive for one day. As we headed straight back to the lodge, I tried not to think what might have happened had this been a real charge.

At the dinner table that night in the Mikumi Lodge, Mother was back in her element. A hearty cup of tea had settled her frayed nerves, and she was once again relaxed and gregarious with the other tourists we encountered that night. She made mention of the mock charge at least three times, with the "rampaging" elephant portrayed as more murderous or more enraged or more crazed with each successive telling. Some of our dinner companions might well have been confused as to whether this was the same elephant that Nonna and Craig had referred to as merely "a spot of bother."

Nonna and I had decided to not share the news with Mother about Little Miss I-Touched-Your-Car, and how that youngster had come far, far closer to us than CrissCross ever had. Craig had similarly decided that Grumpy Old Sod did not bear mentioning either. The adorable antics of Titch remained a safe subject, and because of our somewhat aborted game drive today, there remained upside-down baobabs still to be seen.

Mother agreed to come back out on another game drive with us tomorrow.

Catherine MacLaine

"But only if you don't turn off the car."

Chapter 17
Eponymous Animals

"The Serengeti plains are webbed with the paths of eland and wildebeest and Thomson gazelle and their hills and valleys are trampled by thousands of zebra."

—Beryl Markham, *West with the Night*

Tanzania, February 2017

I didn't notice the names of certain wild animals during my childhood in Africa, but decades later, I found myself somewhat unsettled by a pattern.

Thomson's gazelles, for instance, are beautiful animals. Dainty little gazelles with straight, ringed horns, a white rump patch, and a broad, dark, horizontal band on their flanks, they stand a little over two feet high at the shoulders. Having returned to Tanzania as an adult, I was enjoying the sights of hundreds of "Tommies" during a visit to a game park. My guide, Alex, was recounting various facts to me about the wildlife and happened to mention that the namesake for these Tommies had been a Scottish explorer from the late 1800s. Joseph Thomson had the Thomson waterfalls of Kenya and five different African flowers named after him as well. Mr.

Thomson had been a contemporary of Dr. David Livingstone and Sir Henry Morton Stanley, two other European names that I seemed to find everywhere in East Africa.

My instruction continued on eponymous animals. Grazing next to the Tommies was another example.

"That one is a Grant's gazelle." Alex pointed out a bigger gazelle missing the broad black flank stripe found on Tommies. He explained that this gazelle, too, was named after a contemporary of Stanley and Livingstone, also a Scot, as Thomson and Livingstone had been. James Augustus Grant had been on one of the many expeditions during the 1860s, attempting to locate the source of the Nile River. And he didn't only have a gazelle carrying his name.

"Zebras too?" I asked, somewhat surprised. "There are zebras named after people?"

"Oh, so many zebras," Alex said with a dismissive wave. He followed this with a recitation of the Grévy's zebra, Boehm's zebra, the Wahlberg's zebra, the Hartmann's mountain zebra, the Chapman's zebra, and the Burchell's zebra.

As if on cue, a zebra herd materialized up ahead of us. The striped and snorting steeds were soon everywhere around us, swishing their tails, nonchalantly grazing, or raising their chevron faces to stare at us before resuming their grazing once again. Their ages varied from one rather ancient-looking mare down to a tiny foal so young that he still had his brown baby stripes.

"And besides that zebra," Alex added, "William John Burchell also had, I think, a lizard and an insect of some sort or another."

"Really?"

"Yes," he said. "And a couple of birds too. Ah, but *Mamma*, did you not grow up here? How did you not learn the different zebras?"

Not certain if he was teasing me, I responded somewhat huffily that I had ample knowledge of zebras.

"Some zebras," I stammered, "do not have belly stripes, for instance. And some do not have stripes that extend all the way down their legs to their hooves. Some of them do not have shadow stripes and . . . and . . ." I tried to go on, but then meekly admitted that I had exhausted my sum total knowledge of zebras. Furthermore, in terms of species, I had been aware of three species of zebra (Grévy's, mountain, and plains), but not the half dozen or so that he had so blithely rattled off.

"Ah, *Mamma*, I was joking with you," he admitted, with a laugh. "Yes, those three are the three species of zebra." He went on to reveal that five of the names he had just mentioned were just subspecies of the plains zebra.

Somewhat mollified, I mentioned how I hoped we would see a Grévy's zebra today, because I could tell at least the Grévy's apart from the others.

The zebras had decided to continue cooperating, and one stallion (a plains zebra with wider stripes than the Grévy's) lowered himself to the ground and rolled.

"See?" he seemed to be saying, as he flashed his fish-skeleton patterned tummy up at me. "I'm one of the ones who does have belly stripes!" His big, round tummy brought me a smile, while I also caught myself wondering why they were all so plump. I had never seen a skinny zebra. Not even once.

Determined to cement my newfound knowledge of zebra monikers, I attempted to repeat his prior recitation. "So, it's Grévy's, and Burchell's," I said, ticking them off on my fingers, "and Grant's and Boehm's?"

"Ah, *Mamma, pole*, I should have clarified, Boehm's is

another name for the Grant's zebra."

"Oh."

"And you forgot Chapman's."

Seizing on this one zebra, because the others perplexed me, I asked, "Who was Chapman?"

"Well," Alex said, becoming less animated, "he was another contemporary of Dr. David Livingstone." Perhaps this subject was beginning to grate on him.

In any case, I failed to read the room and continued my ruminations on wild African animals with European names.

"What about the Grévy's zebra, then?" I pressed on. "Who was Grévy, and when did he come here?"

Alex took a deep breath and took an extra second or so to compose his face into a polite expression. "He never came here."

I stayed quiet after hearing such a short and blunt reply. Still, I hoped that he would go on, and continued fixing a steady, expectant gaze on him.

"Grévy never came here," Alex repeated. Seeing my expression, he continued, "He was a French president in the 1800s who was given a zebra from here. And so we have the Grévy's zebra. That's it."

Even I knew that it was now time to drop the subject of European men, some of whom had never even set foot on the continent, who slapped their names onto animals in a country that was not theirs.

As ubiquitous as the zebra had been, we were also seeing vast quantities of wildebeest during this game drive, and my Wil-Duh-Beastie buddies afforded me a graceful transition to other subjects.

"Um, so tell me, Alex, these wildebeest, are these the blue wildebeest or the black wildebeest?"

"Oh, blue, *Mamma*!" he replied, cheerful again, but with perhaps too much obvious relief in his voice. "These are the blue wildebeest," he repeated, sounding happy to be on the subject of animal coloration or markings.

All tension dissipated, the two of us chattered on throughout the rest of our drive about other non-eponymous animals. We chattered about jackals (who are either side-striped or black-backed). We chatted about hyenas (who are either spotted or striped). And wouldn't it be nice if we saw a rhino today? (Those are either white or black.) Alas, the rest of the day passed without the sighting of a rhino, nor of any Grévy's zebras, who had decided not to cross the border from Kenya into Tanzania on this particular day.

Weeks after that game drive in Africa, I booted up my laptop in my home in America and began to research more on the subject of dead European men whose names were attached to various African animals. The Grévy's zebra, I learned, had indeed been a gift to a French president, and most of the men that Alex had named had lifespans that overlapped with most or all of Dr. David Livingstone's. The Scottish doctor/explorer had become one of my frames of reference for East African history, the other being the scramble for Africa, the seismic event that came after him. Few of these men were still alive when the scramble began, with perhaps the exception of Baron Lionel Walter Rothschild, who had been the namesake for African birds, insects, reptiles, and perhaps most famously, the Rothschild's giraffe of Uganda. ("Ro-cheeeld gee-raff, if you're German," said Alex.)

The morning after that game drive where I had first begun to learn about eponymous animals, Alex and I were once again in the Land Rover, rattling along the rutted dirt roads crisscrossing the game park with our eyes peeled for wildlife.

Zebras were once again everywhere, but at least we could avoid the topic of their nomenclature and discuss instead how amusing their barking vocalizations were. Hearing a member of the equine family who doesn't whinny or neigh but can only bark has always struck me as funny. As the day progressed, we had no sightings of any particularly remarkable animals, although it must be stated that all African animals are remarkable.

Eventually I reached the uncomfortable realization that I was in need of a bathroom, and there were none to be had far, far out here in the bush.

"No problem," Alex assured me. "You can do bush toilet."

Which is precisely what I had been hoping to avoid.

Alex reassured me he would find me a spot with no trees featuring low-hanging branches (I wanted to avoid snakes). I scanned the ground carefully (I also wanted to avoid *siafu*[32]). Bathroom breaks such as this were the only times that I was ever on foot, out of the truck, in an African game park, and I always sought to keep these vulnerable and unnerving moments to a bare minimum.

A suitable spot was soon found, so there was nothing left to do but grab my large cloth *kanga* wrap and head on out. Alex kept a sharp eye out, and I was soon able to rejoin him in the truck having had no interruptions from any wildlife at all.

Minutes after my bush toilet stop, Alex spotted something in the bush.

"Oooo! *Mamma!* Do you see!" He was pointing at—what was he pointing at? "Wait, wait, we will get closer." He turned our Land Rover toward whatever this was, this mysterious prize in the small nearby cluster of tall trees. The something was coming in our direction, and Alex was well capable of

---

[32] army ants

anticipating its path.

Then it happened.

Alex had positioned us perfectly, and soon a splendid animal sauntered across the road in front of us.

"You see, *Mamma*! I have found you an African animal with an *African* name! You see? You see?"

I saw.

The two of us beamed with delight as a resplendent Masai giraffe languidly crossed the road.

Chapter 18
African Cat on A Dutch Airline

Try to book with KLM airlines; they're great with animals.
—Dr. Thomas.

Dar es Salaam, February 2017

I was just praying this cat would not bite me. Again.

Stanley and I had arrived at Julius Nyerere airport in Dar es Salaam, and the two of us were facing a very long journey ahead of us.

This was my first day with him, a cat I barely knew.

This was the day that a scrawny little African street cat was brought onboard a Dutch airline by his middle-aged Canadian owner (whom he had bitten when we first met) and flown from East Africa to go live the rest of his life in America. Actually, it was two KLM Dutch flights, and the poor little wretch did end up having quite a withering journey.

Over that whole traveling day, I found myself murmuring, "*Salaam, salaam, tulia*" to this frightened African cat who seemed to only know Kiswahili. It was not clear to me how much English he had ever heard in his short life so far.

Thankfully I had made arrangements for him to be with

me in the aircraft cabin instead of in the cargo hold of the plane, stacked alongside the luggage. I settled into my seat, with Stanley in his black Sherpa cat carrier in my footwell.

Stanley still appeared calm and perhaps dully resigned to his fate. Cautious optimism began to creep over me while our plane roared down the runway.

Wheels up.

My optimism was premature.

For the first time that day, Stanley launched into a panic attack, thrashing about as our plane climbed.

His body careened back and forth against the sides of his carrier at my feet, thumping against each of my ankles in turn.

It was possible that the altitude was hurting his ears, and yet there wasn't anything I could do to ease his discomfort. Several more minutes ensued of a frightened cat flailing in his confinement, unaware that he was being taken away from the only home he had ever known.

"I couldn't just leave you there, *paka wangu kipenzi*," I murmured to Stanley, adding some *salaams*, but my words were drowned out by the roaring jet engine anyway. "I'm sorry to take you from your homeland, but you would have just eked out the entire rest of your life in that cage. In America, at least, I can get your brain damage assessed. In America, at least, I will . . ." My voice trailed off as I remembered that the sword of Damocles still teetered above this cat's head. There was still a chance that this cat's case would be assessed as doomed, and he would be slated for euthanasia after all.

A wave of utter misery threatened to sweep over me then, at the thought of this long-planned-for, deeply loved cat being put to death by an American vet. *Will they say his brain damage is hopeless?* With a deep breath, I pushed the thought away.

"In America," I continued, "I promise, darling, that I will

feed you amply every day for the rest of your life." *For however many days you have left.*

A potential bite notwithstanding, I unzipped a tiny corner of Stanley's carrier lid, inserted one hand, and gently stroked the brown tabby fur.

My *taka taka paka* settled down, and I was soon able to withdraw an unbitten hand and close the carrier securely once again.

I was desperately tired but still willed myself to stay awake for those last few minutes that I was in Tanzanian airspace. I fought back tears, wondering if this would be my last trip back to Africa. Slumber overcame me shortly afterward, and I barely awoke in time to catch the moment we flew over the coast of Libya.

"Hey, Stan." Again, my murmurs were perhaps for my own benefit rather than my moggy's. "This is it. We are actually leaving African airspace." My mongrel-moggie cat slept on, blissfully unaware of the milestone.

Not long afterward, we were wheels down in Amsterdam, where I could turn my attention to finding a quiet corner to feed Stanley. We soon settled in a large bathroom stall. I eased Stanley out of his carrier and unpacked the needleless syringes with which I could dribble water down his throat. He drank gratefully and was surprisingly meek, perhaps traumatized from his first-ever flight.

To my dismay, he declined to eat anything. I was very anxious for him to eat at least enough to keep body and soul together until our next stop, but Stanley turned away from any morsel I brought to his mouth. Any tidbit, even diced chicken pieces from my salad that I gently placed inside his mouth, was pushed out by his tongue. The tables had turned, with Stanley being the calm one and me instead fighting off panic. How long was he going to continue to refuse food?

I squashed down the feeling of the little girl deep inside me who just wanted to sob and scrub her bawling eyes with both little fists. Just a few short days ago I had imagined such a very different scenario. I had been expecting to be blithely striding through this airport with a cat who had a mere bone problem, an easy fix. This would be remedied by a veterinary surgeon, waiting at the ready, back in America, who would soon have him right as rain. Nothing more complicated than that.

But instead—brain damage.

I slumped on that airport bathroom floor, gulping hard and wiping away any tears before they had a chance to fall. It slowly dawned on me that I had been absentmindedly stroking Stanley all this time without being bitten. I gazed down at the tabby fur that still reminded me so much of the stripes on my childhood mongooses. What quality of life was he facing? At least I had photographs of Stan to always remember him by, in case an American vet assessed the brain damage and told me that—

No, it doesn't bear thinking about.

"Hey, Stan!" My voice had a note of forced cheer, "Come on, here's some more chicken!" This was refused yet again, so I gave him one more syringe of water before I packed up again, and we trudged on through the airport to catch our next flight.

By the time our second flight was descending toward Washington DC, Stanley once again began to ricochet in his carrier between my ankles. Any meowing was drowned by the roar of the engines, but his misery tore my heart.

My animal's distress was clearly not unique. A few rows away, a baby began to wail as the altitude change wreaked its

Catherine MacLaine

havoc on the ears of man and beast alike.
    And then—wheels down.
    Karibu, welcome to America, Stanley. This is your new home.

Chapter 19
Tingatinga

Mother bought quite a few. They were always very happy to see her and show her their latest offerings. She would bargain with them and didn't pay much. Today the style has spread across East Africa and every tourist store and stand in Nairobi, Mombasa or Dar has them.

—Craig

Dar es Salaam, 1972

Seeing great artwork can often inspire some people to pick up a paintbrush themselves. I, on the other hand, was inspired to get on a plane and travel to the other side of the world.

The inspiring painting had been an old artwork done over forty years ago by an artist from the Tanzanian Tingatinga school, and after seeing it again, I booked my ticket back to Tanzania. Over four decades ago, when our family had been posted here in Dar es Salaam, Tingatinga paintings had graced almost every wall of our home.

A few years before that, before our family was posted to Dar, most Tanzanian artists did not paint but rather created wood carvings. The wood carvers would shake their heads as Edward Saidi Tingatinga, a Tanzanian man in his late thirties, gathered panels of Masonite ceiling board and bicycle paint and, *pole pole*, created his artistic vision. African birds and wildlife flowed from his paintbrush in bright colors and simple compositions. He displayed his paintings at the Morogoro stores, a little strip mall in Oyster Bay, just south of the peninsula where we lived—then again, everything was south of the peninsula. The Morogoro stores consisted of a couple of food stores, a general goods store, and a post office where we had our postal box. An assortment of vegetable vendors had stalls there as well.

Just behind the stores, to the west, was the large African village of Msasani, where several of the artists and the wood carvers lived. The carvers spread out their wares toward the first part of the Morogoro strip mall, but in a master stroke, Edward positioned himself down at the end where the *wazungu* expats would have to pass right by him to get to their post office boxes to collect their mail. Mail was something we *wazungu* deeply coveted while out in Africa in the early 1970s. To receive a letter was usually the high point of one's day, and these were read and reread and savored at length.

The carvers soon dropped their initial dismissive attitude as Edward's paintings began selling well. So well, in fact, that he soon gathered about half a dozen students to join him, and a painting school was born there, next to the post office. The little group of men did a brisk business, since the expat community (who had to collect their mail, after all) grew to love their artwork.

One particular Canadian woman was an especially happy repeat customer.

"Another painting?" said Dad as Mother proudly showed

him her latest purchase. He stood back, studying the artwork. "That really is nice. I like it. Shall we hang it in the dining room with the other one?"

Not long after that, Mother came home from collecting our mail with another one from the painting school.

"Um, how many Edward paintings do you plan on purchasing?" Dad asked, while still admitting that he did really like them.

"I'm not sure," Mother answered casually. "But I like these. And these are not Edward paintings. These were done by his students of his school."

And so it was Mother who introduced us to Tingatinga paintings. Edward had several relatives working with him, and most of the paintings Mother bought were done by his stepbrother, Simon Mpata. Amongst the Mpata ones was a large fishing scene done in tones of gray and dark blue, as well as one featuring a bright pink bird with green plumage, pecking at an insect.

Mother came home one day with a Tingatinga painting that depicted a zebra on a red background.

"Golly, this artist ran out of space for the head of this zebra!" I laughed, noticing the head was straight down, inches from the border of the frame.

"He's grazing," Mother replied, slightly defensively. "Just a whimsical view of a grazing zebra."

"I like it!" I replied, to her relief. And I kept that painting for decades, amongst my most beloved possessions.

Some were not quite so whimsical. By now, I had begun to wait by the door to see what new Tingatinga painting Mother had acquired, which seemed to be a couple each month. My Tingatinga enthusiasm did wane somewhat, however, when she brought home a scene depicting one bird attempting to drink from a black gourd with diagonal striping while a second bird clamped his beak on his neck, attempting to strangle him.

"No," said Mother, explaining this was a rescue scene instead. It was one bird helping another bird dislodge his head where it had gotten stuck in a gourd. I was not convinced. The birds were of similar size, each golden with dark green wings, against a reddish background. Rather cheery colors for such an incongruously grim scene.

"Oh!" I said, crestfallen.

"Oh, no," Craig agreed, equally crestfallen.

"No more sad bird paintings!" Craig and I declared. Mother then did her penance by presenting Craig soon afterward with a lovely blue Tingatinga painting featuring guinea fowl.

Mine turned out to be birds on a blue background too, done by one of Edward's students, who signed his work *Hizza*. He had also painted the bird strangulation/possible rescue scene. This particular Tingatinga was smaller and showed a charming pair of birds with their necks crossed. One of them was seated on a clutch of four eggs. I had secretly hoped for a wildebeest painting but was enchanted with these beautiful birds. Decades later, I quietly gifted two of my Mpata paintings to a family member, who was delighted to receive the gray-toned fishing picture and was not whatsoever bothered by the strangulation scene. Perhaps it *was* a rescue? Indeed, the golden plumage of the birds enchanted her to the extent that she meticulously painted the wall on which she hung the painting the exact same hue.

None of us ever expected that a case of mistaken identity would shatter the Tingatinga school.

Mother went to the Morogoro stores as usual one morning

in 1972, once again promising herself that she would walk past the Tingatinga artists without succumbing to the urge to buy yet another painting. The artists never failed to call out to her, as was their wont, greeting her and exhorting her to see their latest creations.

But that day, there was only silence from the artists.

Emerging from the post office, mail in hand, she could see that every Tingatinga artist was uncharacteristically subdued. Some faces bore shock; others were etched in grief. Two nearby women were sadly ululating. And Edward's face was nowhere to be seen.

Mother chose not to pry and returned to the car. But Jacob, our driver, didn't start the car right away. He nodded toward the artists and asked Mother if she wanted to buy a painting, to which she replied, "Not today. They seem sad about something."

"Yes, they are sad," he told her. "Edward has died, Madam. They don't know if they can continue the school."

Stunned silence from Mother.

Her hands shook as she fumbled through her purse for some shillings, exited the car and marched straight back to the artists.

"May I buy a painting, please?"

She came back to the car, having spoken at length with the artists, with her face as sad as theirs had been. The loss of this artist had struck her to the core. Horrific shocks can sometimes cause forgetfulness, and Mother only realized once she got halfway home that she had left behind the painting for which she had just paid.

Over the following days, when she went back to collect her paid-for Tingatinga painting, and the mail, conflicting accounts emerged as to what had happened. But the final outcome was that Edward had been shot to death by the police.

"But it was a case of mistaken identity," one Tingatinga artist explained.

"It happened during a car chase," said another.

Then a third artist stated that, no, the tragedy happened in front of the local museum.

Yet another mentioned that Tedo, one of Edward's cousins, had also been wounded in the shoot-out.

Over the coming days, after Edward was buried in a local Dar cemetery, the remaining artists struggled to keep the school going.

Less than a week had passed since Edward was shot when Dad found Mother discussing the death amongst her other expat friends. He had not failed to notice her (and their) acceleration in buying more paintings from the rudderless students left behind.

"Darling, you can't save the Tingatinga school just by you lot buying heaps of paintings."

"I'm not," Mother huffed. "I'm just spreading the word about, um, how nice the paintings are."

"Right." Dad wasn't convinced.

"They *are* very nice paintings. You . . . you said so yourself."

"Right." His tone was softer now. He had not failed to notice the crack in her voice. He knew perfectly well that she had built many friendships in the Tingatinga community. This particular death was an irreversible tragedy, regardless of whether or not sympathetic and grief-stricken friends of Edward began "buying heaps of paintings."

Ultimately, what saved the Tingatinga school was the indomitable vision of Edward himself. His students had caught the vision and had faithfully carried on the particular style he had pioneered during his four years of painting, honoring his original vision. The paintings sold themselves, and in great numbers, and the students, no longer rudderless, could barely keep pace with demand. Within a few years, the art movement bearing his name grew in popularity throughout East Africa.

When I returned to Africa in 2017, I didn't dare hope to find any of the original artists still there at their original location at the Morogoro stores, partly because the life expectancy in many parts of Africa was tragically short, but also because several of the original artists had moved to other countries or into other professions.

When my driver and I arrived at the Morogoro stores, even the Tingatinga paintings themselves were different. They barely resembled the Tingatinga artworks with which I had grown up. Now I was seeing artworks created on canvas instead of Masonite board. The compositions no longer featured one solitary animal or bird depicted in linear fashion against a plain background. Crowded scenes of people and groups of animals were being painted instead. I didn't even find any wildebeest. And it was not clear to me if the bicycle enamel paints of the early days were still being used.

I wandered through various market stalls, all featuring paintings done with foreshadowing and shading, and asked vendor after vendor if they recognized my photos of our original Tingatinga paintings. Several people could only point to the paintings done by Simon Mpata and tell me that he no longer lives in Tanzania. Everyone seemed to draw a blank about any of the other artists, or whether any of them was even alive any longer.

Until one young man pointed to my zebra-on-a-red-background picture, featuring a signature of "Mr. Kainne."

"Kuh-ee-nee," he said, tapping the zebra photo with his finger. Up until now I had not been aware of the pronunciation of Mr. Kainne's name.

"Kuh-ee-nee," the lad repeated, continuing to study the solitary stylized zebra. Then he raised his head, met my gaze, and said, "And this artist is still alive."

"Truth-truth?" I was so stunned with delight that I found myself tongue-tied. I barely noticed that I had lapsed back into the tendency I sometimes found overseas that if a word is repeated, it is accorded yet greater emphasis, weight and credibility. *Ndio, ukweli*[33] was another expression in Tanzania, but I tended to use *truth-truth*.

The young man smiled at my incredulity. "Yes. Truth-truth, he's still alive. Want to meet him?"

---

33   Yes, truly

Chapter 20
Her Mother Bought Your Painting

TingaTinga started the style but he was shot dead by police in 1972. Mpata and a few others, all of them related to Tingatinga or at least came from his same village, worked with him and continued to paint and sell their work after he died.

—Craig

Dar es Salaam, February 2017

I can't imagine what Mr. Kainne must have felt, answering his cell phone that afternoon and hearing that he needed to come home right away because some *mzungu* wanted to meet him.

"Her mother bought your paintings forty years ago, and the daughter wants to meet you."

The casual young man I had just met and my driver had gone into rapid conversation as they hyperextended themselves to arrange this meeting for me at such short notice. I felt deeply touched by their kindness. It's possible they were amused at my surprise that an original founding member of the Tingatinga school was still alive. They were determined to assuage my concerns that I was disrupting his day.

In any case, the artist—now a taxi driver—turned his taxi around, missing who knows how many other fares that he might have picked up.

I had been waiting on the front terrace of his home, making small talk with his family. My presence caused a bit of a stir amongst his neighbors. This neighborhood didn't get many *mzungu* visitors, I gathered, and sure enough one middle-aged man approached me with undisguised curiosity.

"*Karibu*! You are an American? I remember the day your embassy here was bombed." He might have been hoping to impress me.

He did.

I didn't even bother to mention I was born Canadian, but gaped at him instead.

"Truth-truth? You actually remember?" I said, abandoning any customary preliminary greetings.

"Yes, truth-truth!"

Seeing he had my attention, this neighbor launched into his recollection of the day. Was this true? I'll never know. According to him, nineteen years ago, his father had witnessed the bombing firsthand. His father still remembered the days when the building had been the Israeli Embassy, and he had been a *dala dala*[34] driver at the time. His day consisted of seeking out would-be passengers for his *dala dala* with his cheery greeting of "*beba, beba!*"[35] The explosion on that August day had changed everything. Large numbers of wounded needed to be taken to Mumbili hospital, and multiple private cars as well as *dala dalas* began to serve as

---

34   public minibus
35   Come aboard! I'm carrying passengers!

makeshift ambulances. Indeed, anything that could move was being used as an ambulance that day. He immediately brought his *dala dala* on the scene too.

"My father was screaming *beba, beba!*" this neighbor went on to say. His father had come home that day grateful that he had been able to help transport some of the wounded, but stunned by the horror he had witnessed.

Just then, we were able to pivot from the subject of death and destruction—a taxi had pulled up. I held my breath as the driver emerged. And there in front of me was an original Tingatinga artist, as spry as a man half his age, sound in wind and limb. The *beba beba* neighbor retreated to his own house. All eyes were on the taxi driver.

"I am Mr. Kuh-ee-nee. Or you can call me Mr. Kainne," he said with a smile, kindly brushing aside my "*Shikamoo*" and shaking my hand warmly.

He wore a cross, was neatly dressed, and spoke perfect English, to my relief. After the initial lengthy greetings (in English today), I drew out the photographs from my purse, handed them to him, and waited for his feedback.

He peered at the bird pictures. "Simon Mpata did these. I'm sorry I can't take you to meet him. He left Tanzania, you know." He murmured about how long ago it had been. Whether Mpata was even alive any longer was a question that I did not ask, and an answer that he did not offer. And Edward's death was only touched upon.

"And Tingatinga . . . you know."

I nodded sadly.

A respectful silence from Mr. Kaine. Then, slowly, we turned our attention back to the pictures.

When Mr. Kainne came to the zebra picture, I held my breath.

"Yes, I painted this." He nodded matter-of-factly. He had just spoken a sentence so seismic that my legs almost buckled, yet he was as calm as though he had informed me that the sky was blue. My brain still was reeling just from being in the presence of one of the original artists. This exact individual gentleman could have easily been sitting next to Edward, outside the post office, greeting my mother as she went to fetch our mail.

In my mind I found myself addressing my departed mother and stealing a quick glance skyward. *Are you seeing this, Mother? Look who I met! Did you help arrange this meeting? Wait until I tell Craig!*

My reverie was broken then as Mr. Kainne turned to me hopefully.

"I can paint you another, if you like?"

With keen regret, I declined, since my flight home was in two days' time and I hadn't space in my luggage. With the typical Tanzanian gracious spirit, he changed the subject, and we discussed our families and his taxi business.

Later, after we said our goodbyes, I turned and lingered, watching Mr. Kainne's taxi drive away down the road.

I had just shaken the hand of one of the original Tingatinga artists. This was the hand that had painted the zebra that had so pleased my mother four decades ago. I had told him how much my family had loved his painting. I had told him how it had hung in pride of place on our main dining room wall for years. I had told him about how I had grown up here and how much I loved zebras. I had told this Tingatinga artist how I had loved his choice of color and the composition of his painting.

The taxi turned a corner and went out of my sight.

But I had forgotten to tell him one thing.

A Billion Blue Wildebeest

I had forgotten to tell him that it had been specifically *his* painting that inspired me to jump back on a plane and travel here, to the other side of the world.

Chapter 21
A Brown Dog

Dear Bob,
Life is still quite confused here. Shopping for food is a time-consuming effort, but it is quite interesting. Lately my main concern is food. All my mornings are spent hunting for it. We have been without butter now for two months. Before, it was milk and sugar and meat. It is really difficult.
—Mother

Dar es Salaam, early 1970s

During our earliest days in our new house, a single vendor had ventured up our driveway on his bicycle to visit us bearing his fresh catch of the day, hoping this was a *mzungu* house occupied by people inclined to eat fish. My parents purchased his offering, delighted that it was fresh and being sold for less than the local store prices. The bicycle vendor was, predictably, also delighted and from that point on, visited us regularly. The word must have spread through bush telegraph, and soon we were being visited by any number of bicycle vendors offering as much fresh fruit, veg, and fish as could be found during that time. This would vary, depending on drought conditions or the season.

There were various food shortages in our area, and these could range from annoying to critical. It didn't take long before Mother and Craig put their heads together and came up with an arrangement to bypass the shops that were so often *hakuna hapa*.[36]

Enter the bicycle vendors, who were only too happy to oblige.

Our household had the good fortune to even have a fisherman who would come to the house two times a week with fresh fish, which previously we could not find. Now barracuda, rock fish, lobsters and prawns were being brought to our door, all still alive.

We soon had no shortage of bicycle vendors to help us weather the food shortages.

"*Hodi!*" would be the greeting we would hear as a new vendor cycled up our driveway, accompanied by the *gling! gling! gling!* of his bicycle bell.

He would be answered by our servants' "*Karibu, karibu!*" They would then summon us. Craig always came promptly, since he, the only vegetarian in the family, had a keen interest in seeing what vegetables were being offered. For some Africans, to learn that my brother was vegetarian *by choice* dumbfounded them.

"Why eat only vegetables when you can afford meat?"

When a vendor arrived, one or both of my parents would come, along with our cook, and from time to time I, too, would join the assembly. That is, if I could be sure it wasn't someone selling chickens. The necessity of the death of livestock for food consumption still distressed me somewhat, so I would avoid it when possible.

---

36   There is none here; out of food.

Along with the honest fishermen and food vendors who would visit us, we would also get the occasional minor extortionist. On one particular day, punctuated by the *gling-gling-Hodi* routine, a lone cyclist arrived with a bundle of cloth. I was carrying one of our mongooses down from my treehouse. Fupi had made it abundantly clear he would much rather be on *terra firma*.

As the cyclist reached our front entrance, I peeped around the door tentatively and was relieved to see no live chickens hanging off his handlebars. I couldn't bear the sight of poultry tied by the legs and hanging upside-down, occasionally uttering faint and plaintive clucks. I ventured out to find out why he was carrying a bundle of cloth instead.

My parents were already engaged in the lengthy preliminary greetings.

At long last, this gentleman approached the reason for his visit.

"Your dog has bitten me." This was followed by claims that he had been chased *by our dog* and been mauled *by our dog* and that his trousers had been shredded *by our dog*.

None of our dogs happened to be present right then, probably having chased Craig as he had left on his *piki piki*[37] an hour ago for errands.

Dad took advantage of our pets' absence and queried the vendor further. "How can you be so sure that it was one of our dogs?" He flatly requested further proof.

The vendor untied his bundle with a slight flourish, and out fell the remains of a pair of trousers.

"Shredded!" the man exclaimed, waving his hands indignantly over the wreckage of his garment. "Torn and shredded! And this was all done *by your dog*." What followed,

---

37 motorcycle

to nobody's surprise, was a claim that he was owed damages.

Squatting down, I retrieved some of the remnants of "shredded, torn and shredded" trousers and turned them over and over in my hands, failing to find one tooth or claw mark. What I found instead was only trouser portions torn quite carefully and methodically along existing seams.

"These are hardly shredded by *anyone's* dog," Mother remarked, examining the one of the eight or so pieces of trouser material.

Our visitor protested more vociferously that his trousers had indeed been torn by a dog (torn *and* shredded!) and that the offending animal in question was irrefutably one of ours.

"Is that so?" Dad said. "Perhaps you can describe what the dog looked like?" Dad knew perfectly well that the gentleman's claim was preposterous. In mere seconds, this self-proclaimed, victimized, paragon of virtue was going to be sent back down our driveway without one shilling.

"Yes, I can describe the dog who tore my trousers, for which you owe me," the vendor persisted. "It was, um . . . It was a brown dog."

Dad replied that we had no brown dogs, which was technically correct, since the closest candidate we had was my little tricolor mongrel, Alice.

I, however, was also thinking of Alice, and the undeniable fact that brown was a prominent color in her coat.

Little girls who have a dismaying tendency to blurt before thinking should never, *never* be present during financial negotiations.

"Oh!" I piped up. "Yes, we *do* have a brown dog! Alice is a brown dog!" Three pairs of eyes turned to me.

The vendor failed to hide a triumphant smirk, knowing full well that a wheels-screeching turn of events had just taken place. My parents both glared at me, and I was then bidden very firmly to go play in the backyard.

The scam artist departed that day with quite a few shillings in his pocket after all, but not before carefully repackaging his destroyed-by-a-dog trousers and retying the bundle to his bike.

Chapter 22
A Present for Mother

To be aroused in the dark by five feet of cold, green snake gliding over one's face is unpleasant.
—Dr. David Livingstone, 1865, *Expedition to the Zambesi*

The rainy season is coming. I guess Mother or Cath told you that that's when the cobras come.
—Craig

Africa, circa early 1970s

In all the years we lived in Africa, no cobra ever made it into the house, but this trifling fact never assuaged Mother's lifelong abject terror of any snake whatsoever.

It was Mother's birthday, and the family had been relaxing on the outdoor patio after dinner as Mother thanked us for the various presents she had received from us. The nearby mosquito coil's scent wafted through the air, punctuated by the crinkling of the birthday wrapping papers that Mother was neatly folding back up again. Our teacups were almost empty. Craig had drifted off somewhere, and only my parents and I remained as the evening was drawing to a close.

Mother noticed, almost with a start, that Craig was back

on the terrace, approaching her with an enormous black plastic bag. She eyed the bag with increasing suspicion.

"I brought you something back from the game park," he said.

Earlier that day, I had reproached my brother for having chosen to take a trip to the nearby game park rather than going into town to get a present for Mother. He had reassured me that he had indeed not forgotten. He then showed me—briefly—a large, closed plastic bag in the trunk, but refused to reveal what it held. I had poked the bag as my curiosity metastasized, but my inquisitive fingers only discerned a squishy *something* before Craig closed the trunk once more.

"You'll see it after dinner," he said cryptically.

Now, Mother's original trepidation morphed into real horror. "*Craig*! Is that a *snake*?" Her blue eyes were now white-ringed. She edged toward the front of her seat.

Craig stopped in front of her and began to open the bag.

"*Is it a snake?*" she cried.

Craig opened the bag.

Mother jumped up from the outdoor sofa. A teacup crashed to the floor.

Peak hysteria.

Craig was, however, between her and the house, blocking her panicked flight.

And as he recounted later, "I dumped out the dump, so to speak."

Out of the bag rolled several large balls of elephant dung.

Mother collapsed with relief into the nearest chair. Dad burst out laughing. And I was aghast, recoiling at the memory that earlier I had poked that bag with my bare hand.

Alerted by Mother's scream, several of our servants, including our gardener, arrived on the scene just then. Finding no snake and that no harm had befallen us, they soon left us once again.

Only the gardener remained, his eyes were riveted to the excrement.

"Madam . . ." He tentatively approached Mother, who had been rendered inarticulate and was still gulping and panting, trying feebly to regather her shattered composure. "Madam, did you know that this elephant dung would be excellent fertilizer for your flower beds?"

Mother, wan and wordless, raised her eyes weakly to him from the chair where she had shudderingly sat down, inches from the reeking droppings, and looking for all the world like one who had just cheated death by inches.

"F-fertilizer?" she quavered, her nerves still utterly frayed. Finally it dawned on her that the fecal matter was something he was actually requesting. She readily surrendered her entire pungent birthday present to him with the utmost relief, and he promptly gathered it up in his bare hands.

Mother, who still had not removed her splayed fingers from her collarbone, and Dad retreated into the house. This left only me and Craig out on the veranda, gazing at the retreating back of the gardener who was triumphantly marching away toward the flower beds with the last of the elephantine excreta.

I turned to my brother with a million questions writ large upon my face.

During his trip to the game park, he then told me, he'd come across a big, fresh, steaming elephant dump in the middle of the road, and he had the bright idea to bring the dung back to town and leave it somewhere to give the impression that there was a rogue elephant roaming our local streets at night. An impish grin stole across his face at this point.

"But"—the grin faded—"by the time I got back, I had come around to the thinking that no one would realize what it was."

Contrite now, his gaze fell to the floor. "But I hadn't meant to frighten Mother."

"But it will be terrific fertilizer for her flower beds," I said hopefully.

He gave a rueful smile at his little sister's attempt to comfort him.

"Why would she think," my brother's miserable mutterings over his clumsy joke continued, "that I actually had a snake in there?"

I had no answer. We fell into silence, punctuated only by a slight clattering of intact teacups and the gentle clinking of teacup shards as we gathered them up.

"It was really hot," he went on. "I was amazed."

I turned to him, puzzled.

"When I went to get it out of the trunk," he continued, "to my surprise, the bag was very hot—the chemical reaction of the dung, I guess. I wonder if the whole car would have gone up in flames if I had left it there any longer."

***

I never fully understood why any snake—any snake at all—never failed to send Mother into a fully florid panic attack. Although snakes were plentiful throughout Tanzania, there were thankfully only a very few that were actually venomous, and these greatly outnumbered the poisonous ones. But I understood even less the time when Mother very calmly informed Dad that a snake had fallen on her head.

She and Dad had been enjoying a light breakfast one

morning, in their guest cottage at the Tanzania Leopard Lodge, when something fell from the thatched ceiling and landed on her head. The unexpected visitor then rolled off her head, slid down her face, and landed quietly on the floor.

"John," Mother said with uncharacteristic calm, as the snake—for it *was* a snake—took cover underneath the bed. "John, a snake has fallen on my head."

Dad, seeing no snake on Mother's head, and hearing no hysterics from her, chuckled and continued buttering his toast.

"He's under the bed," Mother went on, still deathly calm.

"Whooof unduh da bed?" asked Dad, his mouth full of toast.

"John, the snake is under the bed."

He stopped chewing and looked at her sharply. Following her gaze, he put down his toast. Still no hysterics from Mother, who had quietly gotten to her feet and was pointing silently at the bed, eyes huge, face pale but still freakishly calm. After checking under the bed himself, Dad blanched, scrambled back up to his feet, and straight away reached for the phone. The Leopard Lodge front desk staff came immediately. The unfortunate snake was quickly dispatched, and when the reptile's nondescript black body was stretched out on the floor, he measured about a foot and a half. Mother had hoped for enough time to call me to come see it, but the staff hurriedly left, taking the corpse with them.

"I begged them to tell me what kind it had been," she said, filling me in later, "and they assured me they would get the snake identified and tell me later on in the day."

Six hours passed with no word. My parents went to the manager of the Leopard Lodge, begging to know the identification of the snake that had fallen on Mother's head.

"There was no snake, Madam," the manager said.

Mother protested that this was about the snake that had fallen on her head this morning, and then the staff had come and killed it just a few hours ago.

"There was no snake, Madam."

Mother protested again. This was the snake that had fallen on her head this morning, then was killed by the staff. And that she and Dad and two staff members had all seen this snake.

"There was no snake, Madam."

My mother was never, *never* that calm for any snake again.

Chapter 23
Hello Mr. Africa

Hello, Dr. Thomas,
I am very relieved to say that now ALL his blood lab work has come back and ALL his results are normal! No diabetes, nothing contagious, no vitamin or electrolyte imbalances, all is normal. So basically all we're dealing with is the severe brain damage.
Kind regards,
Catherine

Virginia, February 2017

The morning dawned of Stanley's first full day on American soil. We had awoken a while ago, and I had gone to the hotel breakfast area to have my "back from Africa" ritual glass of milk. During my childhood in Tanzania, each time we took our annual summer return trip to Canada, after months in Africa, one of the first things I reached for was a glass of milk. I never did develop a liking for the milk we had in Africa. Craig had no such silly little ritual, but my glass of milk always made me smile. It was also a pleasure to be back in the land of carpets again. It always puzzled me how Africa has so few carpets, on any floor, anywhere.

Turning my attention to our departure, I eased my newly adopted cat back into his carrier. Gratefully I loaded Stanley into my own car, which I had parked here in this hotel parking lot weeks prior, and we drove the remaining three hours home. *That* vet appointment was hours away, an appointment I had eagerly made over a month ago when I began making the arrangements for *some* African cat to be coming home with me.

I felt only half caught up on my sleep at this point, and uppermost in my mind was to get this cat all the way home safely, and to that long-awaited vet appointment.

Stanley's brain damage, I decided, I would not mention until the vet herself gave her official professional assessment on the matter. I didn't trust myself to speak objectively about it, since I knew next to nothing about brain damage. I already loved this poor cat deeply and had no idea what the life prognosis for such a cat would be.

When the time came, I lifted Stanley's carrier onto the vet's examining table and the happily chattering technician unzipped the lid. At this point Stan lifted his head up.

"What now? Are we at another airport?" he seemed to say, and peered around at these new surroundings.

As I had expected, his head swayed drastically in various directions, not unlike some drunken submarine periscope, as he attempted to gaze around with bright green eyes slightly crossed from the sheer effort to concentrate.

The happy chatter from the vet tech vanished as she stared very sharply at this swaying, wobbling, unbalanced cat.

"Um . . ." She kept wide eyes riveted on the severely uncoordinated animal. "Do you mind if I take him to the back office so the vet can examine him there?"

I obediently zipped Stan back in again, and she gingerly

took the carrier from me, carefully held it out at arm's length, and hastily left the room.

This can't be good, I thought. Why the haste? What had she seen? *Are they going to euthanize him before I can say goodbye?*

Not long after, she and the veterinarian, both with wide smiles, strolled back in together with my cat cuddled in her arms.

My vet greeted me with "Well, I'm amazed!" which was followed by "Welcome back! Did you have a nice trip? Was Africa the same as you remembered it?"

I replied that it had been a lovely trip, Africa was quite different from how I had remembered it, and what was it, exactly, that she found to be so amazing? It had not escaped my notice that I was the only tense one now in the room, surrounded by relaxed and smiling vet staff and a content cat.

"Well, you are not going to believe this, but your cat is only the third CH cat that I have ever seen in my entire thirty-year career! It's amazing!" She lowered Stan to the ground, and we all gazed at him as he explored the examining room floor.

"I'm so glad it was only CH!" the vet tech chimed in. "I was so scared that he had rabies! That's why I took him back so hastily! You see, in the later stages of rabies, cats can have seizures where they can't control their head, and the head sways all over the place and—"

"But this is not rabies," the vet interjected, placing a gentle hand on the arm of the exuberant tech.

"What is CH?" I said.

The somewhat sheepish vet tech glanced at my non-rabid cat, respectfully held her tongue, and looked at her boss.

"Have you heard of wobbly cat syndrome?" the vet asked me. I shook my head. "Wobbly cat syndrome is a congenital neurological condition, found in cats the world over." She went on to explain that it was officially called cerebellar hypoplasia, and that drunken head swaying is known as "intention tremors."

"So his cerebrum is—"

"His cerebellum," the vet gently corrected me.

I made a mental note to later make an index card for my purse with the words *cerebrum* and *cerebellum*. If I could just remember that second portion of the word, I dared to hope, then perhaps I wouldn't make the same mistake as with the Swahili word for the number ten.

The cerebellum was the portion of his brain that was supposed to control fine movement. But his was underdeveloped.

"A brain scan," she said, "might show the brain as internally disorganized, or even show us a large portion missing from his brain, which might have been due to his mother having a disease while he was in utero." While effortlessly rattling off these facts, the vet also managed to scrutinize all of Stanley's Tanzanian documents.

"These cats are defenseless, you see, so they can never be an outdoor cat." She proceeded with a meticulous physical examination and found no atrophied legs or fracture malunion that might have possibly pointed to a history of being, perhaps, just hypothetically, struck by an Indian car careening through the streets of Tanzania.

That was that sorted then. There had been no car accident.

The TAWESO shelter staff had innocently named him after a car only after being erroneously told by the person who brought the cat to them that his condition had been a result of a vehicular collision.

I momentarily stared at the floor. So the entire chain of events had begun with an actual lie. Someone had lied to the

TAWESO staff. Did that person hide the truth to increase their chances that the staff would agree to take in the animal? I'll never know. A slight wave of anger, maybe even betrayal, was rising in me. I swatted it out of my mind.

It is what it is. My beloved cat would get definitive care, at least.

The vet kept crooning to Stanley as she conducted her exam. Her crooning was interspersed with remarks to me as well, until I wasn't always sure which one of us she was addressing. "Oh, yes, you are such a *big* boy—The word *cerebellum*, you see, is the Latin word for *little brain*, and his little brain is yet littler because of his cerebellar hypoplasia—No, sweetie, you can't chew on my stethoscope—He is really only missing some parts of his brain, or some parts in internal disarray. The parts that deal with coordination of movement. His intelligence and decision-making abilities, though, are intact. With a few reasonable accommodations, these—Yes, you are *such* a big boy, huh, sweetie? Thank you for behaving so well for your blood draw!—these CH cats can live a long and happy life." At which point she placed him on the floor, and my cat commenced exploring.

"And that"—she pointed to Stanley's goose-stepping attempts to walk—"is what we call hypermetria."

My cat paused, swaying slightly with his legs all splayed out in a very wide stance ("Truncal sway," the vet explained), before trying to look up at us, losing his balance, and crashing down on his side.

"Oh!"

It was very shocking to see a cat fall down. Cats are silent and graceful.

Stanley was neither.

He had fallen with an almighty crash, legs flailing and a

flash of his pale belly, just as he had done back in Tanzania on the day we met.

Before I even realized what I was doing, I had gathered him back into my arms, wondering if he had perhaps dislocated a hip or a shoulder from the fall. The vet reassured me that CH cats do this all the time, but kindly reexamined him just for my peace of mind.

"You're fine, Mr. Africa!" she crooned, and gave another quick affectionate scruffle of his fur. "Do you mind if I call you Mr. Africa, sweetie?"

The tech too stroked Stanley, joking how a "neuro cat" has a chronic condition in contrast to an acute short-term bone problem. "If you had a broken bone, that would be a piece of cake!"

"But instead you're a piece of work." The vet chuckled, smiling at my cat.

She also scanned for his microchip, which was found to be present and accounted for. I mentioned that I had gotten rubber food bowls for him due to the uncontrollable head tremors, and she agreed that these accommodations were necessary.

Turning her attention back to my pet, she said, "You don't want to chip any more teeth, do you, Mr. Africa?"

"Chipped teeth? He has chipped teeth?" I was taken aback. How had I missed that?

My vet gently lifted the lips of my perfectly compliant and meek, nonbiting cat and showed me how both upper canines were indeed chipped with broken-off points. An appointment for Stanley's dental care was then planned for the near future. She also mused about how very, very short his fur was. I joked that every single animal in Africa seemed to only have very short fur.

"Unless," I said, now that I was thinking about it, "you count the beards on the wildebeest."

She countered that the only long-haired African animal that had immediately sprung to her mind was the lion. "Now *there's* an African animal with long hair."

Of course. I had missed this too, along with the chipped teeth of my own cat who was still on the floor, wobbling around.

"So, about CH cats," I said quickly, trying to regain face. "There are very few CH cats born, then? He is only the third one you've seen? Why are so few born?" I did not lift my eyes from gazing at Stanley lolling and lurching about, again doing his best impression of a clumsy newborn wildebeest calf as he tried to cross the examining room floor.

"Oh, quite a few are born," she replied, "but then many don't survive kittenhood. Or they are euthanized."

Which brought me to the question that had been burning on my mind since I had met Stanley.

I gulped, trying to think how to phrase my question.

"His prognosis is fine." She turned to me, accurately guessing what was on my mind. "This will never get any worse. A neuro cat, a CH cat, can live a long happy life. You don't need to euthanize him."

Crash!

Once more, Stanley had fallen over.

Chapter 24
School

Dear Bob,
The Cath is very tall and thin. She is good in school but lousy in math. She loves her school, which is a very good one.
—Mother

Dar es Salaam, early 1970s

The school I attended from age eight to eleven was known as the International School of Tanganyika, established less than a decade before. It was accessed by smooth paved roads, in stark contrast to the potholed roads found in some other parts of Dar. The classes there were only taught in English, and the students were mostly multinational. Many easily switched between multiple languages when conversing with one another. We would all switch straight back to English once class was in session, however. This was the first school where I was surrounded by so many different races, nationalities, ages, cultures, and tribes.

New Year's Day, I soon learned, was only celebrated on January 1st by some cultures. Instead, my Chinese and Korean classmates had theirs in February, then came the Iranians in

March. In April it would be the Hindu students' turn, and for the Arab students, New Year's landed in October. One thing most of us had in common was the tendency to shorten the names of some of our large cities. My Ethiopian classmates simply said, "Addis," and my Egyptian classmates said, "Alex."

The African students didn't seem to see all these stark demographic differences. They referred to everyone else as "my sister" or "my brother." They took especial delight in teaching me various games, and we spent many hours together playing various versions of tag, or Rock Paper Scissors and any number of games featuring pebbles moved from various little depressions in the ground as one would move chess pieces on a board.

School bullies were sometimes dealt with in a rather unique manner by the African students. A bullied child would calmly state that a witch doctor had placed a curse, at their request, upon their tormentors. Nobody bothered them after that. An Indian friend of mine stoutly swore she would come to my aid if I was ever mocked for having a crossed eye.

"Don't ever fix that eye," she said. "It's good luck." Thankfully the occasion never presented itself.

When established *mzungu* students met newly arrived *mzungu* students, we loved to compare our first impressions of Tanzania.

"Sisal is a big deal here, isn't it?"

Invariably the humidity was mentioned, but I especially waited for them to describe what they thought of the game parks. When they mentioned wildebeest—and they always mentioned wildebeest—I listened in silence, with a gleeful grin.

"Oh, we saw heaps and heaps of those!" groaned one student.

"For hours and hours," another student replied.

The school had western-style toilets, which made many parents happy. Many parents were unhappy, however, that the school stopped at grade nine, leaving older students to search for other avenues of education. Many turned to overseas correspondence courses, as my brother did.

Our biological father back in Canada had been as sad as any of our relatives when we moved to Africa, but he had been considerably anxious over whether our education would be neglected. He had purchased the *Encyclopedia Britannica* for us while my brother and I were still little, to leave no stone unturned, and was relieved when we brought the volumes with us on every move.

He, my mother, and my stepfather had always remained friends, and the three of them, to their everlasting credit, had always remained focused on the best interest of "the Craig-O and the Cath."

So Craig and I wrote him frequently about our schooling, carefully hiding any fact that would betray that we were not, just as he had predicted, keeping pace with our Canadian peers back home. It brought a smile to my face seeing my mother adding her own notes in these letters, continuing the same deception, as she, too, wrote how well we two were doing.

"Craig is taught by tutors here, all Canadians!" one of her particularly cheery letters stated. She went on to describe his lessons taking place out on our terrace "in the fresh air." All of which was bluntly refuted by Craig in an email to me in later years.

"There were no tutors."

My brother had educated himself without any tutors, Canadian or otherwise. He did correspondence courses from the University of British Columbia in Canada, sitting on his bed with the door closed, and not in the fresh air, either. Later in life, when I began to realize that Mother occasionally told white lies, it bothered me. I took small comfort in that her fibs usually didn't concern any serious issues. Once Craig and I left Africa, we caught up to our grade level in short order, so really, our father was never any the wiser.

During my adult years, I found the old "Dear Dad" Tanzanian aerograms that I had written to my father during my childhood, all of which he had meticulously saved. In one, my mother, still seeking to reassure him about our access to knowledge while in the depths of Africa, had added a sentence of her own: "The encyclopedia is a great help to the Craig-O and the Cath here."

My father might have raised his eyebrows to see the outdated curriculum I had in my history classes, however.

My history teacher felt a keen responsibility to her little flock of African, Arab, Asian, and white expat students and strove mightily to keep us apprised of current events. She regularly brought in news clippings to supplement our lessons. There was never a time when her desk was not strewn with papers: our daily Tanzanian newspaper, *The Standard*, or from *Time* magazine or *Newsweek*.

The alternative, but for her Herculean efforts, would have been that we would have gained only outdated information from the archaic materials she had been issued for her classroom. She carefully put the old globe on a high bookshelf, and she would only bring it down when she could supervise our perusal of it.

We did especially enjoy poring over the globe, happily ignoring our instructor wincing over the outdated names of African countries.

"Ignore where it says Dahomey. That's Benin now," she

would typically instruct. And Italian Somaliland was now Somalia, and Basutoland was now Lesotho. Sometimes I would hear the teacher's sotto voce mutterings: "I can't keep up with these name changes," and "I quite feel as though I were drinking from a blasted fire hose . . ."

"Ooh, look!" one student would point out, with a finger on the pale green splotch. "*Our* country, right here! It still says Tanganyika!"

I never did remember where the prefix of *Tanga-* had come from, or its meaning, but the suffix of *-nyika* simply meant *wilderness* or *bush*.

The teacher quizzed us. "And before we were Tanzania, and before we were Tanganyika, what were we?"

"German East Africa and Deutsch Ostafrika," we recited.

Discreetly omitted was that before this country was known as *German East Africa*, it had been free and independent, run by Africans for Africans. Less than ten minutes' drive from our classroom was the Indian Ocean, which had been known as the Great Lake before the colonists came. And before the colonists were the missionaries, and before them were the slave traders, and in the earliest days, foreigners had simply divided Africa into "the coast" and "the interior."

Many maps of Africa in the early 1800s still left blank mostly everything below the equator (the interior that foreigners had not yet explored), except for a few small coastal features.

Our science teacher never missed a chance to impress upon us the significant paleontology discoveries that had been made, right here in Tanzania. One resident of Tanzania was Dr. Louis Leakey, a paleontologist famed for demonstrating that humans evolved in Africa, and author of multiple books pertaining to his discoveries in the Olduvai

A Billion Blue Wildebeest

Gorge. Mary Leakey, matriarch of, arguably, the First Family of paleontology, also made discoveries in Olduvai Gorge. Her most important, about eleven years before we arrived in Tanzania, was known as "Olduvai Hominid 5"—better known as Nutcracker Man, a rather undignified nickname inspired by the fossil's unusually large jaw and huge molars, perfect for cracking large nuts. The sheer size of these teeth astounded the scientists and caused an upheaval in their understanding of the hominid diet.

Unbeknownst to anyone at the time, still buried in the Ethiopian soil, about fifteen hundred miles north of us, were portions of an ancient skeleton: Lucy. She was not found until the end of our time in Tanzania. Back then, Donald Johanson, the paleoanthropologist who would discover her bones in 1974, was still just another college student in America, studying for his master's degree. Maybe he was humming "Lucy in the Sky with Diamonds," never dreaming that he would one day choose it as the namesake for his stunning African hominid discovery.

Did we students go to the National Museum of Tanzania in Dar to see the reconstructed replica of the Nutcracker Man? I don't remember. In fact, I have no memory of having gone on any school field trips. That museum did have a bust of the German man who introduced sisal to East Africa (very important, you see), but the original Nutcracker Man fossil was tucked away (for safekeeping, you see) in the Smithsonian in Washington, DC.

Indeed, many African artifacts are housed in museums overseas instead of in Africa. Had we wanted to see the earliest known documentation of the Swahili language, written in Arabic, those were in a museum in India. The taxidermied lions who had been globally known as the Man-Eaters of Tsavo were no longer in Africa either but in the United States. Lucy was still in an Ethiopian museum, but the Rosetta Stone had been moved from the Egyptian Nile town where it had been found to the British museum, over two thousand miles away.

In later years, it struck me as slightly bizarre to think that I had moved from one former British colony, Canada, to another former British protectorate, Tanzania—which previously had been a German colony. I had lived on land where a plantation had once been, and in places where humans had been exploited by fellow humans. Slavery had taken place and resources plundered. Perhaps an argument could be made that such atrocities are global. But perhaps Mwalimu[38] said it best when he captured the thoughts of millions during a speech he made about two years before we arrived in Dar:

"No nation has the right to make decisions for another nation; no people for another people."[39]

---

38   Teacher, Tanzanian President Julius Nyerere
39   From "A Peaceful New Year" speech, Tanzania, January 1968

Chapter 25
Just Keep Going, Mr. Nyoka

Dear Bob,
Last month, some friends that live near us killed a seventeen-foot python with their car. He had raised up in the middle of the road like a huge column. They were scared. They ran him over two or three times and brought him back in the trunk of their car in a plastic bag. It was enormous. However, we were told not to do that ever, that they were stupid.

—Mother

Dar es Salaam, early 1970s

Each time I see a snake, I am reminded of a river.

So when I encountered an enormous snake a few scant inches from my feet one morning, the words *river* and *fluid* occurred to me. A multitude of other, different words and feelings also occurred to me that morning, though, given this particular snake's impressive size and proximity.

My friend Heidi and I had been riding our bicycles on a dirt road in our Msasani neighborhood one morning, not too far from my house, and I was taking particular delight in how the bright pink tassels on my handlebars fluttered in the breeze as we pedaled along. She was teasing me that I had been making some mistakes in my school work the day before. Until—

"*Nyoka!*" she hollered.

"You can just *say* 'snake,' you know!" I hollered back, pedaling and giggling. "After all, we both speak Engl—"

She screamed.

The scream was guttural. She screeched and skidded her bike to an abrupt halt, slightly ahead of me. Her back wheel generated a swirl of dust.

Then I saw it.

She had just barely gotten her bike past a stunningly large snake that was unhurriedly materializing from the swirl of dust mere inches behind her. The snake had just emerged from the bush on the right-hand side of the road we were on and had begun to cross over to the left side. There would not be enough time to get ahead of him, so I skidded to a halt too.

The snake was heading toward the front wheel of my bicycle.

He was very large.

Phenomenally large.

His head alone looked the size of my bicycle seat. His body was as thick as my leg. No mongoose in all of existence would have agreed to take on that snake.

Time stopped. Heidi didn't move. I didn't breathe.

Frozen in place, we stared at the enormous snake, mouths agape, eyes wide, and faces blanched. My knuckles turned white as I clenched my pink tasseled handlebars.

The gleaming snake came, *pole pole*, within inches of my sandaled feet, before he thankfully changed direction and decided to inspect my front wheel instead. The scent and the feel of my bicycle wheel was casually examined by a tongue,

A Billion Blue Wildebeest

which had always thrilled me when seen in the safe confines of a zoo. Today, too, I felt more thrilled than actual fear, but still—he was *this* close?

Had he heard the thunderous pounding of my heart in my chest?

I remained rooted to the spot, not even daring to roll my bicycle backward out of his way. A slight bulge in his middle led me to hope fervently that he had supped recently and would therefore be disinclined to bother trying to devour two little girls. His flicking, bifurcated tongue finished its leisurely assessment of my front bicycle wheel.

He decided he was further disinclined to bother trying to squeeze through the spokes, and languidly slid in front of my bicycle wheel instead. Had he scented the sweat that was soaking my shirt?

This *was* an ordinary, nonvenomous rock python, wasn't it?

Unbothered, the colossal, lustrous reptile wound his way across the dirt road. During the several long seconds that it took for a squillion jillion miles' worth of sleek snake to meander past my bicycle, my disassociated brain was flooded with what felt like a hundred hours of thoughts.

"Keep going, *Bwana Nyoka*,[40] just keep going . . . Just keep going . . . Keep going," I whispered to the mesmerizing snake, except that my whisper came out in a tiny, high-pitched, and raspy squeak, as my gaping mouth had dried out. I hoped he would not change his mind and turn his attention back to my almost bare feet.

Keep going . . . Keep going . . .

Never taking my eyes off the formidable creature seeping past, bizarre thoughts continued to whirl through my brain.

Gee, snakes really are like a river . . . They just really are . . .

---

40   Mister Snake

They move exactly like a river... There's no better word for it...

He was taking his glacial time to ooze across the road. There was just so *much* of him.

Keep going... Don't coil up, Bwana Nyoka... Stay nice and stretched out... Keep going...

The very last inches of his meandering tail slid past my bicycle and finally the whole, entire snake, every gleaming last inch of him, slipped into the scrub.

I exhaled.

Raising my head for the first time, I saw Heidi slowly making her way back to me, face still ashen as she rolled her bike backward to where I was still rooted to the spot, wordlessly pointing to the spot where that last inch of scaly tail had disappeared into the bush.

"W-w-wow," she said as she came over to me, slowly shaking her head, eyes still large as saucers. "Wow."

"Wow," I agreed, unable to think of any adequate reply. I was only just starting to breathe again, in long, deep shuddering breaths.

We clutched our faces and gasped to one another how huge, huge, *huge* he had been, how he was the biggest we'd seen, and what a massive relief it had been that he had just kept going.

Finally, we wiped our sweaty palms on our shorts. The shakiness in my legs was wearing off, and I was breathing through my nose once again.

It wasn't every day that I was visited by a snake *that* size.

"I want to figure out how big he was!" I said, now that my heart rate was returning to normal. "My brother is never going to believe this!"

With the utmost reluctance, and several nervous glances at the surrounding bush, Heidi helped me decipher the tracks the serpent had left behind in the dirt road.

Eventually we were able to pinpoint a spot on the road where his head had started and another spot on the road where his tail had ended. But little girls don't habitually carry around a tape measure.

I positioned my bicycle along his path, and we both concluded that the snake had stretched two and a half lengths of this impromptu unit of measurement.

"Yes, yes. Two and a half lengths. Now can we go?" Heidi cast another tense glance at the bush surrounding us.

"But I haven't measured its circumference!" I replied, to her dismay.

Again, absent any sort of measuring aid, all I could think of was to measure the width of his tracks against the palm of my hand laid down in the dirt and then measure my palm once we got home.

Heidi hastily agreed with my assessment that the snake's girth, most certainly, quite definitely, oh, absolutely, had equaled the width of my palm, and now could we go? Chafing at the delay, and nerves frayed, she prodded me back onto my bike. She had long ago remounted hers, and was clomping down on her pedals before I could linger to contemplate any further aspect of the snake, entreating me once again to vacate the area.

So we pedaled back to my house with the utmost haste, our hair flying, elbows high and heads down, legs piston-pumping, each shouting to one another our sharply differing motivations for our haste.

"I want to get out of here!"

"I want a tape measure!"

We peeled into my driveway, and there was a clang and a clatter as I flung my bike down and galloped into the house.

Heidi lingered outside on hers and, as she expected, I soon reemerged with a tape measure hastily pinched from my long-suffering brother. We measured my bicycle and my palm, and concluded that the snake had been about eight feet long and three inches thick.

"Wow," said Heidi, as we stared at the tape measure and then back at each other. Our gardener had come to join us by then and listened to the story with interest.

It was his conclusion that I had been singled out for this visitation by the *nyoka*. "Is good magic, this. Is an ordinary python, but you were given a blessing."

The unblessed Heidi was only too relieved not to have had such a close encounter. Getting back on her bike to head home, she shouted over her shoulder how her family would be amazed at our story as I waved goodbye.

Craig had come out of the house by then to retrieve his tape measure from me and inquire why I had pinched it. "Wow," he said, after I'd told him about the snake, and how long and how wide he had been. "Good thing that snake just kept on going, eh?" And then, "What color was the snake?"

Color?

My shoulders sagged. I bit my bottom lip. I stared down at my feet.

"Kiddo, you don't remember what the snake *looked* like?" My brother strode back into the house chuckling.

I do remember that it most definitely looked like a river! I wanted to shout at my brother, but by then he was out of sight.

While Craig was no great snake enthusiast, he always kept my secrets from Mother about how I would throw dirt clumps or twigs at any big snakes blocking my path until they moseyed along and I could safely pass.

"Just never tell Mother about any cobras or mambas you come across," he said. "Or vipers."

My brother was, predictably, more reliable about remembering what not to say than I was. There was more danger that I would inadvertently tell Mother myself. At the dinner table that night, it was me, of course, who started it.

"I was given a blessing today!" I announced proudly.

"Were you then, Beloved?" Mother smiled. "That's nice."

"Uh-huh." I nodded happily.

Craig, instantly realizing where this was going and knowing full well that his little sister would periodically get The Blurts, gave me a warning look.

I launched straight into a description of today's python anyway, which was not, after all, a cobra, mamba, or viper.

Mother's eyes were widening by the second.

Craig cleared his throat very loudly, a stern look on his face.

"What?" I turned to my brother blankly. "That wasn't one of the snakes that I'm not supposed to ever tell Mother about."

Mother's fork clattered onto the plate.

And Craig shot me a withering look.

Chapter 26
Halcyon Days at the Zebra Park

Dear Diana,
I last visited Mount Meru Game Lodge and Sanctuary as a child, when my family visited forty years ago during the years between 1971 and 1975, at the invitation of your father. I was between ages nine and twelve at the time.
I've never forgotten my happy memories at your lodge
I was so impressed with your sanctuary, with the enclosed paddock containing other herbivore wildlife. I was horse-mad and therefore spent most of my time at your stables.
Amongst my fondest memories were mornings when your father took me riding (he was on Canasta and I was on little Simba) through the enclosed paddock with the various gazelles, giraffes and ostriches. He was so kind to me and very patient, to take me riding.
My most vivid memories were your sanctuary animals though.
Kind regards,
Catherine

A Billion Blue Wildebeest

Tanzania, early 1970s

"He won't bite?" I asked in a stage whisper, nodding toward a zebra stallion meandering unnervingly close to my horse. I had been reluctant to voice this concern, lest I appear impolite, but really that barcode-emblazoned face with its inscrutable eyes was rather too close for my liking. Zebra may look sweet, but I was well aware of their mercurial temperaments, which is precisely why so few have ever been successfully domesticated. And it did feel bizarre, there on horseback, to be looking down onto the spine of this zebra as he rambled past me, perhaps my first good close look at the dorsal stripe on a living specimen instead of a zebra rug.

"You needn't worry," the count said with a smile. "They're all quite accustomed to us riding here."

The Hungarian count Dr. Andreas Von Nagy, owner of Mount Meru Game Lodge, had created a small animal sanctuary. The site, on the Usa river, had its beginnings as a safari lodge and family business about two years before Independence. By the time we arrived in Africa in the early 1970s, it had expanded to include multiple guest cottages and five-star service.

There was a large courtyard area lined with cages, one with adorable porcupines, and walkways, as well as grassy areas on which various antelopes and small deer would wander. Mother had met the count through mutual friends, and our visits to his lodge were always a joy—especially for me, since Dr. Von Nagy invited me to ride with him from time to time. Nonna also accompanied our family on these lodge visits, whenever possible.

The enormous park (which I nicknamed the "zebra park") was encircled by impenetrable hedges and fences and contained, besides zebra, an enchanting assortment of a great many African birds and wildlife. All the animals were either orphans or in varying stages of recovering from injuries. Each one was on its journey to be eventually rehabilitated back into the wild, or when that was impossible, they would live out their days in the safety of this park. There was nary a carnivore to be seen, notwithstanding one caged Nile crocodile and a large population of omnivorous Colobus monkeys who rarely emerged from the tree canopy overhead. This woodland area was teeming with wild animals, all of whom, it was emphasized to us, were *wild* animals.

These were also rescued animals. Each animal on his property was rescued due to their disability, injury, or other acute need. Dr. Von Nagy's rescue efforts made a profound and lifelong impression on me.

On the front lawn was a break in the park's encircling hedges and fencing, giving one an optimal view of the wildlife. A low stone wall stood above a moat to safely separate human from beast. I would spend hours at that stone wall, just gazing in rapt delight at this stunning vista.

My delight turned to stunned amazement one day when the count took me on yet another ride, but this time . . .

My brain could barely absorb it.

Today we were actually *inside* the zebra park.

The park I had gazed at, mesmerized, from a safe distance only that morning.

The park nobody was allowed in, except veterinarians and the Von Nagy family. I had no idea why the count made an exception for me, but I was overjoyed.

The beautiful park was a veritable microcosm of any of the national game parks, albeit it with, thankfully, an absence of carnivores.

A Billion Blue Wildebeest

I am inside the zebra park! Inside! With the pressing issue laid to rest that I would not be bitten by the zebra stallion, I gazed around in wonder.

Here I was, inside, riding amongst the familiar wild herbivores and in close quarters. I was almost weakened from the emotions coursing through me. Were I not already seated, my legs might well have given way. Here were the familiar ears and tails, always flickering, since flies are more plentiful around game. The animals were none too bothered that we were there, and we were regarded impassively, if at all.

An ostrich wafted by in this waking dream, and then a Masai giraffe. I was taken aback by the realization that being on horseback placed me almost at eye level with the ostrich. Close enough to look down at his feet, I was fascinated to see only two toes on each foot. Close enough to watch his huge, long-lashed eyes blink, the lower lid traveling quite a distance up to meet the upper. And the feathers! The only other time I'd ever seen ostrich feathers close-up had been in millinery, and here were those long quills and soft feathery strands not on a hat but on their original source.

A dik-dik skittered across my path, barely avoiding the legs of my horse. This tiny spaniel-sized antelope with its dinky little toothpick legs was perhaps the only animal there slightly unnerved by our horses, although it must be said that dik-dik are not renowned for their boldness to begin with. This one had been mincing his way along the field, giving me a close look at his bizarrely shortened nose before scampering off into the bush.

Yet no creature present here gave out their familiar alarm calls. Antelopes didn't whistle, wildebeest didn't snort, and the zebras didn't bark. Nor did the oxpeckers perched atop their backs take flight. Every single oxpecker remained in place on the backs of their various host animals, as tranquil and passive as their companions. None of them cared one jot that we were there.

In stark contrast to the tiny dik-dik, an eland, the largest antelope in Tanzania, came walking alongside me, each hoof making its distinctive click as it was raised off the ground. An oxpecker was astride his smooth sepia coat, and the eland's impressive spiral-grooved horns were tantalizingly close to me. I had only ever seen horned heads this close as stuffed displays. Then, as now, I could see the distinctive grooves in the spiral horns. Spirals that reminded me of the paper curling as I peeled it off my crayons.

This close, I could see between the eyes framed by absurdly long eyelashes, how the fur patterns on the foreheads whorled in graduations of brown. It was utter agony to refrain from touching the creature, but, stealing a glance at the count, I could see his hands never strayed from the reins. I followed his example, keeping my hands to myself even when I was close enough to clearly see a brownish tick in the eland's flicking ear.

Might I pluck that tick off your ear, perhaps, Mr. Eland?

In later years, I read how a Kenyan wildlife warden, Richard Leakey, had also ridden his horse amongst the African wildlife in the game parks during his childhood. Instead of keeping his hands to himself during those rides, he instead took great glee in smacking rhinoceros with his open palm as he rode past them. I can easily picture myself succumbing to the same temptation had I ridden alongside him.

Trekking through this dreamlike domain, the count and I spoke very little and then only very quietly. Birdsong competed with monkey chattering, and the soft clomp of our horses' hooves through the rustling grass was yet more pronounced to my ears. The hoofbeats came from both horses, but the distinctive squeaks of saddle leather came only from me, as I alone kept shifting around in my saddle, my head spinning, trying to take it all in.

Soon we approached the low stone wall where I had previously stood watching the animals. Now I was approaching from the interior of this herbivore heaven.

Too soon, my time in the dream landscape came to a close. Horse hooves clopped sharply once again on the stable yard cobblestones, the magic was fading, and the *syces*[41] came to take our horses. They chuckled as I dismounted with unsteady legs, and I watched wistfully as they led the horses back to the stalls. As I tried to verbalize my thanks to my host, my voice emerged as a hopelessly breathless stammer.

The count beamed, already guessing what I was incapable of articulating about this halcyon day. "I'm so glad you enjoyed your ride today."

---

41   Stablehands

Chapter 27
An Original Animal, & the Empty Water Bucket

The Park [Serengeti National Park] is huge and beautiful.
—Craig

Stealthy forms of carnivora stole through the dark woods outside our camp.
—Sir Henry Morton Stanley, How I Found Livingstone

Tanzania, February 2017

When I booked a return trip back to Tanzania during my adulthood, among the very first sites I revisited was the Mount Meru Game reserve, where Count Von Nagy had taken me riding in his animal sanctuary, full of the orphaned or injured animals he had rescued, which I had nicknamed "the Zebra Park." Fast-forward four decades later, and here I was back at the lodge, still as beautiful as ever, for a visit with Diana, his daughter and grandson.

We had exchanged emails prior to my visit, reminiscing about our families and shared memories. Diana also braced me for the fact that, with her father now departed, far fewer animals were now kept on the property. I mentioned how her father had impressed me to no end with his efforts to rescue injured animals, and I had been inspired to come back to Africa to rescue a disabled cat.

Upon my arrival at the Mount Meru Lodge, I was warmly welcomed by Diana and her family, and soon she and I were once again walking around the estate. Logically, I had known not to expect a completely unchanged, trapped-in-amber site. And yet I felt—was it sadness? The quote "You can never go home again" stabbed my brain just then. My heart, too, was pierced with pangs of missing my mother, Nonna, and the count, all now passed, all of whom had been at this exact spot with me decades ago. The sanctuary was still there, but I found only one zebra there sharing the space with a solitary ostrich and some assorted waterfowl.

That was it.

Over forty years had now passed, so this particular zebra was surely not any of the original ones I had seen, nor was the ostrich.

She and I lingered at the familiar stone wall for a few moments.

"Your father took me riding in there." I continued to gaze into the sanctuary with its solitary zebra. "So many rescued animals in those days."

"I know." Her tone was warm and supportive, and she kindly changed the topic to my "Von Nagy-inspired rescue cat."

The two of us continued our rapt contemplation of the beautiful sanctuary a few minutes longer, before resuming our tour of the grounds. It was a pleasure to see a cage of porcupines was still here. Like the zebra and the ostrich, these, too, were not the original ones I had seen so many years ago.

"Alas, we no longer keep horses," Diana said, as she showed me around the old stable yard, now simply used for storage.

I made another wistful remark about missing her father's original animals as we walked past the gap in the trees through which one could see an impressive view of Mount Kilimanjaro.

Diana did not fail to notice my sigh, and she glanced at me sympathetically. "Yes, sadly, none of my father's original animals are—Oh!"

She turned on her heels just then, warmly clasped my hand, and marched me off in a completely different direction, a huge smile on her face. "Come! Come!"

I found myself being trotted past the sanctuary, where the ostrich and the zebra were not the original ostrich and zebra I had known. We passed the porcupine enclosure once again, where the porcupines were no longer the original porcupines that I had known, and we passed the stables that were not even stables any longer.

"This!" Diana now pointed triumphantly into a very strong, very sturdy enclosure that I had not noticed previously.

"He is the *original* animal!"

Inside this enclosure there *did* reside an animal with a typical lifespan of fifty or more years. This animal had indeed been here during my childhood visits. This *was* one of the original animals from the original menagerie assembled by Count Von Nagy himself.

"Ah!" I said to the creature. "Do you remember me? I'm back!" Although it was nonsensical to address the animal, still I was barely able to contain my excitement. "Do you remember me? I knew you over forty years ago!"

Inside the enclosure, that enormous Nile crocodile gazed back at me impassively.

A Billion Blue Wildebeest

***

On the day I found myself back in the Serengeti, I almost sobbed with joy.

My ubiquitous wil-duh-beestie buddies were still there and resolutely marching through the park as they progressed through the great migration. At one point, our vehicle was surrounded to the point that I felt as though I were a small foreign object, blissfully embedded in a carpet of wildebeest. The sights and scents and sounds of the game I saw during that day's drive had been a complete and utter joy. I hoped that at least the sounds would continue to some degree throughout the night as well. One of my highest priorities, when planning this trip, was to feel close to African wildlife once again. I yearned for it.

I'd planned two nights inside the Serengeti park, in a small, tented bush camp as opposed to one of the more comfortable lodges nearby. The bush camps had an excellent reputation for safety, with neither guests nor staff ever coming to any harm—that I'd heard of.

My private tent was tall enough to stand up in and had space for one narrow cot, a table and, to my delight, a small western-style camp toilet. Having expected to use an outdoor squat hole, this was a very welcome surprise.

The water for the indoor toilet was in a bucket outside my tent, and clean and plentiful enough to be used for a bush shower or sponge bath also. This *maji*[42] was trucked in to the camp, the staff explained to me, since there were no lakes in our particular vicinity. It had not been merely an act of kindness that toilets were included inside each of the five tourist tents at this camp. I was soon to learn that it had been,

---

42   water

instead, an act of safety.

"Because many wild animals, you see," the camp staff explained to me and the other four tourists that night. Yes, I was a tourist this time, I had to remind myself, with a slight shake of my head.

Somewhere out in the bush, not too far away, we could hear lions coughing. Occasional roars wafted over the bush to us. Closer to camp were the yipping cries of hyena. Certainly I would not have heard any of it this clearly had I been in a lodge.

During the cleanup after dinner, I plied the staff with questions and learned that these sorts of tourist camps in the Serengeti were mobile, being repositioned several times a year according to the migration paths of the local wildlife. Setting up the camp each time was an endeavor, taking more than a week of work by perhaps a dozen men—and men alone—who would stay out here in the bush for around three months before being replaced by the next shift. These camps were too mobile for planting or harvesting crops. Absolutely everything was trucked in. With the constant proximity of dangerous wildlife, these camps had *hakuna toto* and *hakuna kuku*.[43] Women, children, and poultry were always such a mainstay of any African village I had ever seen that their absence here was remarkable to me.

The *hakuna kuku* aspect also really surprised me, and I asked again whether wildlife was really *that* close as to threaten poultry.

The cook gazed back at me with ill-disguised incredulity. "You come, *Mamma*." He picked up a flashlight—somewhat indignantly—and beckoned me to follow him. The peril to poultry was obviously a point he was determined to prove.

---

43   No women or children, and no poultry.

Shrugging, I followed him perhaps several dozen paces into the surrounding bush behind the kitchen tent. There in the darkness, he shone his flashlight around and soon found what he had been so determined to show me.

"You see, *Mamma*?" His tone was triumphant.

I scrutinized the bush: Nothing.

No ravenous carnivores poised and waiting to pounce. No salivating lion, leopard or slobbering crazed cheetah. Hardly any great threat out here to hapless poultry.

"*Fisi*,[44] *Mamma*," the cook clarified.

And there, in the beam of his light, one pair of *fisi* eyes gleamed back at us. The hyena's eyes blinked, lingered a few more seconds, then disappeared back into the bush.

"You see, *Mamma*?" He could not hide the triumph in his voice.

I saw.

I most hastily and heartily agreed with him that without doubt, no chicken could be guaranteed safety from the jaws of any number of Serengeti predators out here. It seemed safe to assume that the chicken dinner that had just been served to us had been, like the avocado, trucked in. The vindicated cook spun on his heels and started his victory march back to camp. I followed very close behind, thrilled to have had an encounter that close but still not in the mood for any *fisi* to start nipping at my heels. Hyenas are well capable of killing a human adult and are notorious for their extremely strong jaws that can crush bones.

Exhausted from that day's game drive, I joined the other tourists, all *wazungo* like me, seated around the campfire.

The others were as weary as I was, and our leisurely conversation proceeded with frequent periods of contented

---

[44] Hyena

and companionable silence as we all gazed languidly into the mesmerizing flames. The warmth melted our bodies as the light flickered across drowsy faces. Several people were deep in thought, perhaps reviewing in their minds the sights they had seen that day. In the sky above us, somebody spotted the Southern Cross, but peer as I might, I could not find it. Smoky tendrils from the crackling fire slowly curled around our murmured and sparse sentences.

"This is bush television, this." The camp boss broke into our reverie as he came to join us.

"I much prefer it to ordinary television," I mused. Murmurs of hearty agreement from my companions.

We bade him join us, but the camp boss remained standing. He had come to explain to us the camp rules, which involved that none of us could go anywhere without an armed escort, now that night had fallen.

"Because many wild animals, you see."

We were each to be escorted from the bush television the whole distance through the scrub grass (well illuminated by the escorts' flashlight) over to our tents, tents spaced about twenty feet apart. Once safely ensconced inside, our escort would zip up our tents from the outside, and we were under strict instruction not to emerge until he came back at daybreak to escort us back to the main gathering area.

The "because wild animals, you see" point was reiterated twice more to me as my own escort walked me to my tent for the night. He took pains to point out the whistle hanging on a hook inside.

"To call us," he explained, as I looked blankly at the whistle. "Because . . . because wild animals."

I nodded wearily, and the young man answered with a nod of his own.

He added, "Sleep now," pointing to my cot with a smile. It crossed my mind that this was perhaps how a Labrador retriever feels when he is bidden to "Sit. Lie down. Stay."

Do wild animals breach these tents that often that a whistle is even necessary? Before I could ask anything further, the escort zipped the tent closed and I was alone. I entertained the notion of calling him back to ask more about the whistle, but gave in to fatigue instead and settled into bed.

So great was my exhaustion that I had fallen asleep fully clothed, and hours passed before I heard the first noise.

I had not been expecting to hear any noise *this* close to my tent.

But there was, undeniably, a noise.

It punctuated the complete silence.

My eyes opened in the pitch darkness. Where was it? *What* was it?

Sitting upright, I strained my ears.

It was an animal of some sort, but *where*?

Slowly freezing horror crept over my brain. Perhaps a monkey had breached my tent.

Please, dear God, no. Not a monkey.

My shaking hands closed over the whistle, and I shot up a silent fervent prayer that I would never have to use it. It could well be that I would become a laughingstock amongst the other tourists were my terror of primates to be known, but on the other hand, yes, I was petrified of all things simian and in no mood to be bitten. By now my other hand—equally shaky—had reached my flashlight. Holding my breath, I turned it on and shone the wobbling beam around my little tent.

Nothing.

Nothing but me inside the tent.

Outside the tent, however, the strange sounds continued.

Almost sobbing with relief at the absence of any monkeys, I hugged my knees and exhaled. But the original question remained as to the author of the rumbling, shuffling sounds I could still hear. A herbivore, perhaps? My gut instinct wasn't picking up any sense of lion or hyena . . .

I crawled across my tent to where the sounds seemed closest, on my knees and the heels of my hands—still gripping my flashlight and the "wild-animals-you-know" whistle. Even amongst the Serengeti's grass-eating fauna, there remained some dangerous species. Buffalo, for instance, were never to be trifled with, and the idea of nothing but a sheet of canvas separating me from one of them was not particularly pleasant.

The rumbles and the shuffles were accompanied by soft, muffled tummy gurgles, such as I've heard from horses or cattle. Then:

Slurp, slurp, splash, slurp.

My outside bucket of water was evidently being emptied. I sat back, stunned with awe and delight as I realized who my visitor was.

Those rumbles were elephant tummy rumbles!

The unneeded whistle dropped from my hands as I hugged my knees again, this time giddy with joy.

A quote from Beryl Markham's *West with the Night* came to mind: "The bowels of peacefully occupied elephant rumble continually, like oncoming thunder," and for a few more seconds, I just savored the comforting sounds as my visitor drank.

Of course she'd found my outside water bucket—the sense of smell in an elephant is nothing short of phenomenal—but I wondered if she (a female, I'd decided, though I couldn't be sure) would trip over the guy wires of my tent and send the whole contraption crashing down. She would then be startled and depart, and I would lose my chance to really see her. Even in my childhood here in Tanzania, I had had very few encounters this close to a *tembo*, and I was not about to lose this opportunity to see her (and perhaps touch a foot?).

It must be said that sensible tourists do not unzip their tent flaps, especially after having been strictly forbidden to do so. Sensible tourists do not attempt to touch the foot of an elephant. That would be incalculably foolhardy. Nonetheless, lacking any such sense, I resolved to attempt to touch her foot.

Mamma Tembo, however, had intelligence yet greater than her thirst, and though I tried to unzip the flap as silently as possible, she heard me. I peered out earnestly and directed the beam of my flashlight in her direction, but all I saw was a massive retreating elephantine silhouette that blocked out the stars. I marveled once again at how silent her colossal feet had been. No guy wires had been tripped. This two-ton thistledown simply drifted away, impossibly and noiselessly, leaving only my overturned bucket in her wake. She left me also with the greatest burst of joy in my heart at the sheer privilege of her presence.

The following morning, my armed escort arrived as promised and caught sight of my overturned bucket. I watched with a grin as he studied the tracks around my tent with growing dismay on his face.

"Daaaah! Tembo!" He apologized profusely and hastened to refill my bucket.

Upon querying the other tourists, I learned that nobody else had had such a visit, whether their own water buckets had been full or empty. None of the staff had seen hide nor hair of any large wildlife either. The only pachyderm tracks found had been those around my tent.

The elephant's visit remained the pinnacle of my time in

this camp. It left me with a feeling of having received almost an angelic visitation. Why did she choose me? Did she somehow know that I love the African elephant above all others? Was she giving me a blessing? If a cloud were a living entity, that was my *Mamma Tembo*, almost otherworldly, gently wafting over, gathering water, and silently drifting away.

I have always known Africans to be generous in sharing their food and drink with others. Indeed, it strikes me as a gesture of community, of camaraderie and inclusiveness. Perhaps as the elephant partook of my water, the message she was conveying was "You're amongst friends."

Chapter 28
A Graceless Cat

Dear Catherine,
Stanley is a good boy and was a friend to everyone here at TAWESO, and he is remembered with fondness.

—Dr. Thomas

Virginia, circa 2017

My little African cat with half a brain (as I joked), and no longer under any threat of euthanasia, was still settling into his new life in America. He was delighted to no longer be in the carrier, was using disposable pee pads, and was back to doing his *choo*[45] properly in a litter box again. The litter box was, alas, one more place where he would fall down, and this he did frequently, soiling his fur. Almost daily bathing quickly became a routine. Soon I bought some washable pee pads, since Stan was not always successful in reaching his litter box. One of my neighbors stared, in those early days, as I hung my daily laundry out on the clothesline, now featuring multiple pee pads. Perhaps she concluded that an extremely incontinent senior citizen had moved in with me, tripling my

---
45   toileting

laundry load. I never did bother to persuade her otherwise.

The incontinence also caused me to purchase a dog crate in which Stanley could spend each night. Some precious square footage of my small kitchen floor was ceded to his enclosure, but bodily waste was at least more reasonably contained and cleaned.

Stan would also soil his fur if he lost his balance near his food dish or water bowl. As his entire body weight slammed full-force into the dish or bowl, the contents were sent flying. Result: another bath for sticky, soiled tabby fur. This happened only a few times before I resolutely marched back into my local pet store and brought home kennel cups that were bolted to the wire sides of the crate. His rubber dishes and bowls were inserted in those, and it seemed to me that Stanley preferred this new arrangement too.

He loved all the cat toys I had given him but ignored the cat scratching post.

"No matter, darling," I murmured, kissing the top of his tabby cat head. "I think the sisal on that scratching post didn't even come from Tanzania anyway."

He was catching on to English better than I had dared hope, for which I was deeply thankful, given how little Swahili I could still remember. Indeed, he didn't seem to mind what language was used as I cooed over him. If I tried to sing "Malaika" to him—badly, apparently—he would give me an "Aw, Moth-*urrr*" look. Can a cat roll their eyes? Nor was he particularly impressed each time I held him in my arms and danced around the kitchen to "Pata Pata."

He certainly gave me the impression that he was delighted to find so many carpets on the floors here in the USA.

Now that we were here in America, when people learned my cat's name, the explorer Sir Henry Morton Stanley never sprang to mind as it tended to do in Africa. Instead, my pet was the cat "with that Canadian hockey trophy name."

For decades I had been among the thousands of pet owners with a disabled pet, but now I could count myself among the legions of owners with a neurologically impaired animal.

Besides scouring my veterinarian's knowledge, I was able to glean considerable CH cat information from various online sources. Online, I also did find some more severely incontinent CH cats than Stanley. Diapers, even. Sometimes next to their photos would be pictures of the seizure-impaired cats, with their little heads cushioned in small foam rubber protective helmets. Occasionally there were matching colored diapers, along with the safety helmets.

I studied everything I could find on cerebellar hypoplasia in cats and realized there was a considerable spectrum. Stanley, alas, seemed to be at the more extremely impaired end, because many CH cats could walk easily. Those enviable specimens could use a litter box effortlessly too. I found it curious that his CH didn't really show unless he was up on his feet. To watch him groom himself while lying down, not weight-bearing, he seemed as coordinated as any other cat. When walking, however, he would usually lose his balance after one or two steps. I soon found that if I supported his hindquarters with two hands, his forward progress was greatly improved. It made for a somewhat bizarre sight, like two children playing the "wheelbarrow" game, but it was certainly effective.

A graceless cat was still such an oddity to me that my brain could barely absorb it. I would flinch and cringe each time Stan did a white belly flash in the air, losing his footing and falling over in his random nosedive. It was still a horrific shock for me to see a cat fall down.

I would always wonder if he sustained bruises up and

down both shoulders and both hips from falling so often. The sight of an upended cat tore at my heart, and yet the two ends of this cat were never synched together.

"He has a loose caboose!" chuckled one vet tech.

He would invariably collapse, quite incapable of walking in a straight line. A cat who could not be graceful struck me as bizarre as a fish that could not swim, or a monkey who could not climb, or perhaps a flightless bird.

And the sounds from a CH cat surprised me too.

I would abruptly awaken in the middle of the night hearing a crash or bang that did not, after all, indicate an intruder but merely Stanley colliding with items in his crate. This new phase of my life, I realized, would involve things that go bump, blundering, and bungling in the night.

If I wasn't immediately on hand, it would take several long seconds for the poor wretch to right himself. His limbs would thump and thrash, not unlike a capsized turtle, complete with madly oscillating head. After a series of ever stronger lurches, like a fish on dry land, he would regain his feet and proceed on his merry way, teetering and tottering along until the next toppling tumble.

A cat cannot really continue on his merry way *hakuna ubongo*,[46] I joked with my pet as I stroked his head, before correcting myself. "*Pole*, Stan, *nusu ya ubongo*."[47]

He had one ear where the very tip had been removed as proof of his neuter, many months ago. During our cuddle sessions, Stanley soon became accustomed to me playfully waggling his tipped ear, sometimes resulting in another "Oh, Moth-*uurr*" glance from him. When he came back home from having some dental extractions done, he was too tired

---

46   without a brain
47   Sorry, half a brain.

to give me any sort of glance and mostly slept straight through the following day.

In Stan's first week on American soil, I zapped off an email to Dr. Thomas with a photo of the cat in front of our local post office, the only obvious American landmark I came across in my local area. Instead of Stanley's face showing a triumphant "Look! I arrived in America!" expression, his "Oh, Moth-*urrr*" look is in place.

Stan was the latest addition to my household of other cats, most with varying disabilities. The exception was Saba,[48] who I had found years ago at our local kill shelter. Saba had had no disabilities, but he had stretched out one paw from his cage and tapped my ankle with such urgency that my rescue gland predictably flared up. He came home with me that day. My fingers would always trail down the length of his tail as he walked past. He would gaze back at me serenely, and I felt deeply grateful he was here. Poor Saba soon developed a chronic digestive tract condition and so joined the ranks of my disabled cats after all.

Thankfully, my multi-cat household soon adjusted to the African newcomer, and we settled into our new routines.

Each morning I opened the door of Stanley's crate and coaxed the sleepy tabby out. With some reluctance, he would eventually stumble and stagger out to greet the day. Seizing the day, however, was the furthest thought from his mind. Instead of carpe diem, Stanley would make it known in no uncertain terms that he really only wanted to go straight back to bed. This he would do with astonishing rapidity unless I closed the door in time. I was determined for him to spend the next hour or so getting exercise. Stan was determined to do no such thing.

---

[48] Seven

The thwarted cat would stand there for a moment, swaying on four unsteady legs as he gazed longingly into the closed crate at his own enticing bed, complete with heating pad, now so cruelly out of reach. His vet had recommended daily exercise, so I hardened my heart against Stanley's beseeching look.

"Come on, cubbie," I said gently. "Time to get some exercise."

Stan knew full well that I was clearly intent on putting him through his paces. And he was fully intent on not being put through them.

"No matter," his eyes seemed to say, and he would turn and march off. I would soon find him nestled cozily in some other cat bed, having rudely rousted the previous occupant—and still not exercising. So adamant had been his desire for a bed that he had ignored all manner of appealing cat toys strewn about and various inviting scratching pads in his quest to go back to sleep.

"No, no, no, darling," I said, lifting him gently out of the bed and back onto his feet. "You should be walking around and exploring now. The vet said so." And I removed the bed out of his reach, for good measure. Predictably, as soon as my back was turned, Stan made a beeline for the very next cat bed. I evicted him from that one too.

"Nuh-uh. Vet said."

By the time an hour had passed, a disgruntled Stanley had been dislodged out of every bed he could reach, and the other cats were none too amused about the resulting scarcity of beds either. The amount of exercise my tabby was getting simply going from bed to bed was not quite what I, nor the vet, had had in mind.

Despite some degree of brain damage, Stanley had enough

shrewdness to have one more card up his sleeve.

"*If I weave and weave and weave around her ankles constantly enough . . .*"

It never failed.

"Oh, for Pete's sake! Stan-leeee!" I cried, as I barely avoided tripping over him for the hundredth time. "Stan! No!" My attempts to carry on with my morning tasks were hampered by a tenacious tabby weaving as brilliantly as any skier on a slalom course. "Ugh, Cubbie! No!"

And then, "Fine. You win."

Conceding defeat, I begrudgingly opened wide his crate door.

And with that, Stanley marched triumphantly back to his own cozy bed, head held high and shooting me one last victorious look.

Chapter 29
Creeping Thieves

Dear Dad,
The mongooses are little thieves! They take our food and even Mother's cigarette. When you half open your mouth they try to open all the way! They both come if you call Fupi. They eat worms, thinking it's a snake. They eat bugs and snails.

—Me

Dar es Salaam, early 1970s

As our mongooses matured, they progressed from sweet, guileless, and hyperactive pups to shorter-tempered, unpredictable animals, still unfailingly hyperactive. Anything shiny caught their interest, as we learned one day when lunch was late and the houseboy came to Mother to report a shortage of spoons, that he said were readily to be had, but he was loath to put his hand into the mongoose nest.

"They bite, *Madam*" was his flat statement.

I was summoned.

"Beloved," said Mother, "he can't lay the table until we get those spoons back, and lunch is late, as it is. Would you?"

Girding myself for the near certainty of being bitten, I

went to search the nest myself. My findings indeed buttressed his claim that the mongoose pups (who have needle-sharp teeth and razor-like claws in their arsenal) had been stealing spoons. They had also stolen pens, a fork, various seashells, and several of my smaller toys. Mongooses, I had been told, were in the *Herpestidae* family, which means "creeping thief." Our pets were aptly named. I successfully removed all their ill-gotten gains and was bitten in the process.

Alas, the thievery only temporarily abated. It became my regular unpleasant duty to retrieve tableware from the mongoose nest. I was none too pleased with the bites. The mongooses were none too pleased with their nest being raided.

We also learned that the mongooses did not seem to be able to distinguish something that was shiny from something that was burning. More than once, a cigarette smoker innocently sitting in our living room would be startled by a flash of gray and brown fur sailing past his nose. One of the mongooses, at the peak of his leap, plucked the lit cigarette right from the mouth of the smoker, then landed neatly on the floor and ran off with his incendiary little trophy. The ensuing scramble of panicked humans chasing after a tiny four-legged potential arsonist usually only lasted a few minutes before, mercifully, the mongoose himself lost interest and dropped the potential tinder. Fire was no small threat in Africa, and these episodes would usually badly frighten us.

Inevitably it would prompt a muttered aside from Dad: "I *told* you wild animals don't make good pets."

The final result of these episodes was that smokers became very, very cautious about lighting up until they could be sure no mongooses were about, and our family members somehow squashed down any urge to turn on Pravin with annoyance each time they saw him with some sort of variation of "Those *wild* animals could have burned the house down!"

Lifting a forkful of food to one's mouth at the dinner table was similarly fraught with peril, since the mongooses would blithely snatch it right off the fork. During one particular dinner, one pup saw my mouth partway open and proceeded to shove his entire pointed head into it. After an unbidden mouthful of mongoose, followed by shrieks (which had followed my initial shocked gagging), the pups were decisively banned during mealtimes.

***

Pravin leaned over to whisper conspiratorially to me, "Do you want to see something funny?"

I nodded vigorously, and he continued, still in low tones, "Well then, see what happens"—and here he glanced furtively about, to be certain we were not being overheard, then turned back to me with a wink—"when you give an egg to a mongoose."

"An egg!?" I responded with surprise, and apparently too loudly, because Pravin hastily hushed me.

He glanced around again. "A whole, unbroken egg," he emphasized, one finger raised.

"Okay," I answered, now in matching sotto voce. "It might take a while to find an egg." I explained that the various burrows in our garden and in the surrounding area where I usually could find clutches of snake eggs might be already vacated with the babies hatched and gone.

"You needn't bother with snake eggs," he said. "Too leathery. Just an ordinary chicken egg from your kitchen will do."

I fell silent, considering this. Pinching anything from our kitchen would be no mean feat. Our cook had a gimlet eye. Besides, Mother had always made it clear, in no uncertain terms, that the kitchen was strictly off-limits.

"Do not go in the kitchen," she had always said. "Don't bother the servants." This constant admonition eventually resulted in me reaching adulthood having rarely set foot in a kitchen, and unable to relate to people who would tell me that the kitchen is "the heart of the home."

Back then, a kitchen was nothing more than a bustling, off-limits workstation occupied by busy workers, not to be bothered. Despite that, this egg idea was irresistibly intriguing, and soon enough our cook stepped away from his post. To my relief, his hawklike eyes did not notice the egg discrepancy. And now, clutching my little round plunder, I had only to find one of the mongooses.

I found the other Fupi—or perhaps this was the original Fupi—attempting to stalk a praying mantis on our garden patio. My arrival startled the insect, who promptly took wing. The thwarted mongoose turned to me, exasperation all over his pointy little face, then advanced upon me with obvious irritation.

"Hey, Fupi! Look!" I offered him the purloined egg, rather hoping to avoid being bitten again. The pup's eyes brightened as he caught sight of it. He came and took it gently from me, to my relief, and remained standing on his two hind legs, still holding the egg with the impressively long claws of his forepaws.

"Pravin told me," I whispered to Fupi, my new partner in crime, "to give you an egg because it would be interesting to see what you . . ." The mongoose had turned and was walking purposefully toward the nearest wall, carefully rolling the egg as he went along.

Fupi carefully positioned himself standing on his hind legs with his back to the wall and once again held the egg in his front paws. He crouched forward slightly. In the blink of an eye, the pup leapt straight up vertically and hurled the egg with full force between his hind legs and against the wall, before landing neatly back down on all four paws. As though this were a daily occurrence, Fupi then matter-of-factly turned and proceeded to lap up the splattered egg with the greatest satisfaction.

I was agog.

I began to pilfer eggs from our kitchen on a regular basis, each of which I surreptitiously passed on to the mongoose pups. Their antics had me convulsed in laughter. I mentally justified to myself this deception from my parents, just as I had previously with all the gecko eggs I had sneaked into my bedroom.

Occasionally I would give the mongooses a marble and watch as they tried to break it in the same way, to no avail. Their nonplussed expressions had me laughing until breathless.

Our cook grew suspicious, the pups grew glossy coats, and I grew yet more emboldened with each foray.

One day, as I was tiptoeing backward out of the kitchen with a stolen egg in each hand, Dad asked, "Can you keep it down to maybe only two or three eggs a week, please, darling?"

I spun around in shock, just barely managing not to drop the eggs.

After about two weeks of my larceny, I realized with hot shame that Dad, who was now casually leaning against the kitchen doorway, had been perfectly aware of my thievery from day one.

From that point onward, the mongooses received one

egg each per week, now handed to me by the cook himself, neither of us making eye contact with the other.

Chapter 30
Uncoated and Incomparable

Those bitter uncoated Nivaquine that we had in Dar . . .
—Craig

"Also, particularily if he is white, he is vulnerable as a peeled egg to all things that sting—anopheles mosquitoes, scorpions, snakes and tsetse flies."
—Beryl Marham, *West with the Night*

Dar es Salaam, early 1970s

Six days and twenty-three hours and fifty minutes out of each week in Africa was lovely. The other ten minutes involved me having to swallow the wretched antimalarial pill.

Uncoated quinine is harrowingly, harshly, horrifically bitter. It is not physically possible to suppress a facial grimace as it shoots through one's jaw, radiates through the skull and convulses the brain. My shoulders would hunch up to my ears, eyes tightly shut, as a violent shudder went through my entire head. Not only was the first taste of the quinine horrific, but its impossibly vile chalkiness would linger even after multiple gulps of water.

The very first time I had to take an uncoated antimalarial

pill had been back during our last two weeks in Montreal, before coming to Africa. That first tablet, an incomparable assault on my tastebuds, was unprecedented in my brain—or on my tongue, for that matter.

For several seconds, I alternated between various facial contortions.

"W-wow-wow!"

I gulped down tea, water being grossly inadequate.

Mother had come to my side now, murmuring sympathetically, "Only once a week, beloved," and stroking my hair.

"Every *week*, Mother? This *poison*?" I was aghast at this unthinkable prospect. "I have to take this *every week*? For years?"

"Quinine was utter misery for me in Africa too." She handed me tissues, having seen a tear or two course down my cheek.

In Dar, there was slight comfort in that the tea was delicious, but even though I took the pills every week, for years, it always took multiple attempts to wash down the aftertaste. If the tea failed, I would gulp down a Fanta Orange soft drink instead. I was still the only family member who complained. Everyone else was stoic and sensible about it.

To be precise, they didn't complain around me, but I did overhear a muttered aside that Dad directed at Mother one day: "You would have thought that pharmacies would have found some way to make a coated version of these pills by now."

Notwithstanding the preventive weekly pills, a female *Anopheles* mosquito, the vector of malaria, did somehow find our house. Craig came down with a case of the disease, which thankfully did not last long but was about three days of misery nonetheless. Cue the sympathetic tongue-clicking from our African friends. Not to be outdone, I too acquired malaria. More sympathetic tongue-clicking. The chills and shivering on the first day were soon replaced by sweats and fever, resulting in me flat on my back in bed, staring dully up at my geckos on my ceiling. Not for nothing did Sir Henry Morton Stanley dub malaria a "racking anguish of body."[49]

That evening, I had stoutly defended my splay-footed little protectors who had been impugned by Mother for not having intercepted that female Anopheles.

"Fat lot of good those horrid things did," said Mother, grimacing up at my beloved lizards as she brought me a drink of water.

With all the strength I could—just barely—muster, I sat up and retorted indignantly that the guilty mosquito most certainly had infected me when I was *not* in this room, where my little friends patrolled so diligently. I was about to say more but had to fall back on my pillow, shivering, and retreat in feeble haste and utter misery once more under three blankets.

Fat lot of good those horrid things did, I thought bitterly, grimacing instead at the bottle of antimalarial pills at my bedside.

Amongst the many thousands of people visiting or living in Africa who acquire malaria, I was felled with it twice, but thankfully each was a mild case that could be treated at home. Another saving grace was that in Dar we had ready access to doctors and a hospital. Malaria, one of the oldest diseases known to man, can advance quickly and in some cases can be fatal without timely intervention. In the previous century, certain parts of Africa had been known as "The White Man's Grave" because of it.

---

[49] H. M. Stanley, *How I Found Livingstone.*

"So," said the doctor on the phone with Mother, discussing proposed treatments, "you have been giving your daughter one quinine tablet per week as a malarial preventive, is that correct?"

Mother said that it was. "Really, doctor, you have no idea. It is utter torment each week when my daughter has to take that one little—"

"Madam, you must now give her the same pill again, once each eight hours, for seven days. My care plan for patients is this: quinine is the preventive for malaria, and *more* quinine is the treatment for malaria."

"Easy for you to say," she muttered after she'd hung up.

Moments later, Craig found her in the same chair, staring at the wall, at a loss as to how to possibly obtain my compliance for a fourteenfold increase in uncoated quinine pills.

"Oh, Craig-O . . ." She sadly explained the dilemma to him, and soon Craig found himself wheedled into being the pill-giver. "She *worships* you. She'll do it for *you*."

Noncompliance became a moot point, to my brother's great relief, because I was too miserably sick to resist anyway.

As Craig left my room, Nonna entered, dragging a chair with her.

"She doesn't feel well," Nonna stated flatly, cutting off any questions that Mother might have had. Nonna positioned her chair next to my bed and watched me all night.

And she smiled at my geckoes.

Those uncoated quinine pills resolved my symptoms so effectively that I emerged from bed too soon, prematurely assuming I was once again hale and hearty. I was forced to crawl right back into bed with a relapse. To my knowledge, a relapse is not common, but if the patient rushes too quickly through the recovery process, then they pay the price. Each of my two malarial bouts involved me losing just a few days of school. I lost a bit of weight since I lost my appetite. But the biggest change: I lost the will to fight taking malaria pills any longer. All histrionics were dropped forever afterward, and from then onward, Craig noted thankfully that I silently and glumly swallowed them. Grimace notwithstanding.

Chapter 31
Not a Mistake in My Chart

A man can be riddled with malaria for years on end, with its chills and its fevers and its nightmares, but if one day he sees that the water from his kidneys is black, he knows he will not leave that place again, wherever he is, or wherever he hoped to be.
—Beryl Markham, *West with the Night*

Virginia, circa 2017

Years later, living as an adult in the United States, I found the word *malaria* evoked varying reactions. It usually started when I'd arrive for the first time at a new medical provider's office, and the receptionist would hand me a clipboard with forms to fill out.

"Just take a seat over there, and we'll call you soon."

As I methodically filled out their forms, invariably there would be some section with the instructions: *Please add here any other pertinent past medical conditions not listed above.* I would sigh, and then I would print carefully in block letters: *Plasmodium (Malaria)*. With every new medical provider, I would carefully add it in, every time, for the rest of my life. I squashed the temptation to add in a quote from Beryl

Markham: "Africa has accorded me my full share of malaria and other illnesses."

Medical staff who saw my medical history for the first time often did a double take.

"It says here that you've had . . . malaria?"

"Yes, ma'am." I'd smile and usually offer nothing more, wondering if the nurse, rapidly blinking, would press the issue.

"Malaria." Now the nurse phrased it as a statement, holding her finger down on that spot on the page, doubt flickering across her face. Perhaps she was about to remind me that with that in my history, I could never be a blood donor (although in the last five years or so, I've heard some providers dispute this). Had she been African, she might well have clicked her tongue in sympathy with me then, accompanied by a "*Daaah! Pole sana!*"[50]

"Yes, ma'am. Malaria." I held my smile and held my tongue, squashing down the urge to say, "Well, overseas travel has its price."

Sometimes that price is a mild bout of malaria. Still, malaria is never something to take lightly. The fatality rate of the disease was never far from my mind, especially after the news hit our family that our cousin Alessandro DeRege had traveled overseas and caught malaria just like Craig and I had done. Both Craig and I had recovered, uneventfully. But to everyone's horror, Alessandro had not.

"What do you mean, died?" I asked, thunderstruck, when Mother telephoned me to break the news. I was twenty-eight, and my parents and I lived a few hours apart, in the USA. I sat quickly on the nearest chair as my brain reeled from this update. Alessandro and I had played together as children back home in Montreal, Canada. He had been disappointed, one

---

50   I'm sorry you had to go through that!

day, when he had failed to frighten me (perhaps around age five) with a spider. He then brought out a rather horrid frog, which did make me jump. His laugh was so infectious it was impossible to ever stay cross with him.

Mother's voice, raspy, uneven, repeated with a slight quaver the news my brain could not absorb.

"He *can't* be dead," I said, thinking of my own bouts with malaria.

"Nonna just told me. I need to call her back in a few minutes," she said.

"He *can't* be dead," I repeated. "Craig and I. We were fine."

"Meningital." Mother's voice cracked. His malaria had gone to the brain.

Alessandro had left Canada and gone to live in Ecuador, South America, where he was training people in biodynamic farming, so that they could grow their own food without chemical pesticides and fertilizers. He had contracted malaria while traveling to teach. Far from any hospital and unable to get immediate treatment, the disease had rapidly spread. By the time they identified it, it was too late.

"Beloved, I have to go," she said faintly. "I have to tell the others now."

"But . . . but he *can't* be dead," I said, clutching the phone receiver in my limp hands and not realizing she had already hung up. I felt somehow like a tiny figure seated in a cavernous hall.

Mother's telephone was very busy in the following days. Every DeRege relative was staggering with the shock and trying to absorb this seismic news.

"So young! Why? Why?"

Years later, I wondered if Craig felt any self-imposed survivor's guilt. I most certainly wrestled with it in the days following the loss of Alessandro. My cousin had been only a few months younger than me. Why were Craig and I spared?

But on the day of the news, I remained alone in that chair. At some point I'd dropped the receiver, and I picked it up with clumsy, shaking hands.

"He *can't* be dead," I said, into the wrong end of the phone.

CHAPTER 32
Not A Bad Nyoka

Last week there was a 16-foot pithon but the mongooses there killed it.

—Me, age eight

Dar es Salaam, early 1970s

It was deeply satisfying to be told that I clean rice very well. The compliment was not really warranted, truth to tell, but Tanzanians are inherently benevolent, and so when they laid eyes on a little *mzungu* girl making an earnest effort to clean rice well, they spoke kindly to me. Rice grains were always first poured into a wide, shallow pan to be examined minutely. Any errant substance, small stones perhaps, or *dudus* or grit can then be identified and picked out with ease, leaving one with clean, edible rice. The smile of approval I would be given as I handed over a cleaned pan of rice warmed my heart more than good marks at school. Perhaps I felt I had accomplished a feat more substantive than schoolwork. Perhaps my mother's philosophy that we are put on Earth to help others was running through my mind. Whatever the case, the immediate gratification was immense. If any of my

African friends suggested we clean rice together, I was only too happy to oblige.

Neema was perhaps my favorite of my neighborhood African friends. We were similar ages, and she had, at first, like all my African friends, made a considerable effort to pronounce the *th* in my name.

"What is your name? Cat-teee?"

Invariably, though, my name was dropped entirely. The two of us were simply "my *rafiki*" or "my sister" to one another. We cleaned rice together from time to time. She was sweet-natured and never failed to laud my efforts.

Her father had been a cook in a nearby house since before Independence, and she alternated her time living with her father here in my neighborhood and with her mother in their home village. Her own year of birth was described as "after Independence." When it came to the exact month of her birth, she described it to me in farming-related terms: "My mother was pregnant during the harvest, but I was born before she planted yams." None of which I completely understood.

I would often ride my *baiskeli*[51] over to see her when I had been given new candies. Sweets were a great bartering item, I found. In exchange for them, she happily found little gifts that thrilled me, like assorted leathery shell fragments from snake nests and brittle shell fragments from bird nests, some in lovely hues and speckled patterns.

"Ah, my sistah," she said one day, "I know you are liking *nyoka* so much, I will be showing you something." She took my hand and led me into a dense patch of bush.

Neither she nor I shared my mother's implacable distaste toward all things reptilian, yet there were gradations to our daring. I knew perfectly well that she was astoundingly

---

51 bicycle

brave—bold, even—around venomous snakes. Unlike the good five-foot-or-so distance I liked to keep between me and a venomous one, she would fearlessly walk past one at close quarters.

I hastily stammered, while following her somewhat reluctantly because my curiosity *had* admittedly metastasized by now, "I-I don't really like *every* snake, you know. Just certain snakes." And my stammering continued as I asked where we were going. And what exactly did she want to show me?

"You will see." She grinned. "I found something that you will be liking."

"Hey . . ." My timidity now rose to the fore. "Hey . . ." I tried to gently pull my hand from hers. "None of the *nyoka mbaya*.[52] Not up close now, eh?"

She giggled and reassured me that she would not bring me near any of the very few venomous snakes in this area. We soon came to a stop, and she pointed to an object next to a rough rock on the ground. "You see, my sistah, this is not one of the venomous ones." She gave my hand a warm squeeze.

She was absolutely correct.

It wasn't a venomous snake I was looking at. It was not, indeed, any snake at all, venomous or non-venomous. This was, instead, a beautiful snakeskin. It looked like it had been shed by its previous inhabitant fairly recently.

"Ooooooh . . ." I exhaled reverently. She grinned yet more widely, hearing my delighted awed whisper as I gathered up the tissue-thin cast skin gently. *"Intact! Almost completely intact!"*

We made our way back to the main garden. The British Crown Jewels were never carried as tenderly as I carried my incomparable treasure that day.

I had forgotten that a shed snakeskin might sometimes

---

52   bad snakes

be perceived as a sort of harbinger of doom. Neema had not.

"Soon baby *nyokas* come," she muttered.

I did remember that the eyes of snakes can sometimes cloud over right before shedding. But now it came back to me how pregnant mothers often shed right before laying their eggs. The impending arrival of baby *nyokas* was not always entirely welcome, considering the harm the venomous ones could do, upon reaching adulthood, to surrounding people and livestock. However, Tanzanians rarely complain about anything. True to form, Neema quickly recomposed her facial expression, graciously rejoicing with me about this exciting find and showing me how the skin had been shed starting at the head and was peeled neatly inside out.

"This is longer than the *nyoka* was!" I marveled.

My hooray about the snakeskin was not a sufficiently exuberant celebration to her, and she let loose a short burst of ululation, encouraging me to do the same. This high-pitched rhythmic trilling wail, "Vigelegele!" is often heard throughout Africa and Arab countries to express celebration or mourning. All my own attempts at ululation more closely resembled a donkey's bray interspersed with a sheep's bleating. Neema tried mightily not to laugh, but eventually she was doubled over in mirth and repeating a Swahili phrase that I later learned meant, "I'm laughing so hard that you will have to pick me up off the ground."

What did it matter if I could not ululate well? My rice-cleaning skills, instead, were irrefutable.

Chapter 33
African Jollification

Ngomas are big in Tanzania. They are basically huge parties focused on dancing.

—Craig

Dar es Salaam, early 1970s

My enthusiasm for *wanyama*[53] never failed to amuse Neema. When we were not cleaning rice together, she would take me exploring in the sisal or the nearby dense undergrowth to find various insects under rocks, eggs in snake nests, or a glimpse of assorted birds in the trees above us. For whatever reason, perhaps our shared love of nature, it was a happy and relaxed friendship. We would pass many long minutes in contented, companionable silence together. On some days, the two of us chattered nonstop.

On some days we danced together. Not that it was ever planned.

The first time this happened, the two of us were cleaning rice, deep in conversation while seated on the steps of the kitchen doorway. Her father's white plastic lawn chair

---

53 animals

remained untouched in the courtyard, which she respectfully left for him. Her father's little transistor *redio* was playing Tanzanian music while she chattered about how she hoped to have many children of her own one day (a barren African woman could be perceived as of lower rank, I came to learn) and how she hoped to be pretty one day.

"But I'll never be as beautiful as a Somali woman," she lamented. "They are the most beautiful, even more than Tanzanian women."

Since we were not on the subject of any animals, not even snakes, I felt somewhat at a loss and nodded, giving polite answers and weak smiles instead. With any luck, she might turn to the topic of farming, and then, I dared to hope, I could at least discuss livestock or small animal husbandry and feel on somewhat firmer ground.

"Come!" she exclaimed. She put her pan of rice to one side and leapt to her feet, extending one hand to me. "Come!"

I gaped at her, dumbstruck, one hand still poised over my own pan.

She whirled to raise the volume on her father's little radio, beaming hugely, then waggled her hand back at me again. "Come! We will have *ngoma yetu*!"[54]

I hurriedly set aside my own pan and stood to join her. Our own little *ngoma*? Here? Now? What if her father caught us slacking on our chores?

Neema, instead, did not seem to care two strings of beads if her father caught her or not.

Although tantalized with the diversion from our task, I realized with growing dread that my dancing skills were far below my rice-cleaning skills. I cast a furtive glance for her father. Perhaps he could abort this *ngoma*, sparing me the

---

54   our own dance

certain embarrassment.

Neema's father, alas, was nowhere in sight at the moment and the music *was* appealing. Soon the two of us little brown-eyed girls were swaying and swinging along to the last bars of the song that had initially caught Neema's attention. Perhaps it was not a proper "knees-up," but we smiled happily nonetheless. This African jollification was enjoyable enough, I found. It had amused me to learn the term *jollification* when I had first arrived here, which seemed to be the term for spending happy times together with one's friends. The song was pleasant, perhaps slightly ordinary, but certainly a welcome break from chores. As the song drew to a close I was about to sit back down again with my pan of rice. But then the next song came on, and that next song changed my life.

"*Khaa!* My sistah!" Neema squealed shrilly, electrified as she recognized it. "*This* is '*Pata Pata!*' Our *ngoma must* continuing!" Neema gave another shriek of delight and danced yet more gleefully than before, her own pan of rice obviously now completely forgotten.

A force began to move through me, an irresistible wave of such joy that I danced as though transported to another realm. What was it about this song that brought on such happiness?

I later learned it was a popular song from South Africa. On that sunny day, though, all I knew was that I was hearing euphoria set to music. My limbs took on a life of their own as I danced exuberantly along to arguably the most exhilarating song I had yet encountered.

A little while later, when the radio had moved on from music to the news of the day, and her father had come to check on us, he found two little girls seated together innocently cleaning rice. I for one was grateful that he didn't seem to notice our breathlessness or flushed faces. Neema had discreetly turned the volume dial back down to a sensible level, and I was asking her innocuous poultry-related questions while I picked through my rice. Nor did he notice that his white plastic lawn chair was slightly out of place from when I'd hurriedly set it upright after Neema and I knocked it over during our exuberant jollification.

From that day forward, after that *ngoma*, for the rest of my life, that one infectious song became my personal infusion of joy, a song I would play whenever I missed Africa or my spirits needed lifting. In later years in America, as an adult, I bought the album so that I could play it to my heart's content whenever I wished and spent many happy hours dancing alone in my American kitchen.

Although my rice-cleaning abilities still surpass my dancing skills, whenever I dance to "Pata Pata," nothing else in the whole world matters.

Chapter 34
Implacable Foes

Cry "Havoc!" and let slip the dogs of war
—William Shakespeare, *Julius Caesar*

Virginia, 2017

Cats will launch ferocious attacks on one another only when they have a very good reason.

But what if, just perhaps, that reason remains a mystery because it exists only in one very small, very impaired brain?

My beloved cerebellar hypoplasia cat was still stealing every cat bed he could, ignoring my entreaties to get some exercise. This caused mild annoyance among all the cats, but it didn't get any worse than that.

Until it did.

For whatever unfathomable reason, Stanley fell into a bizarre cycle of recurring fights with Saba.

Stan had barely passed six months on American soil at this point, and I was still not completely adjusted to the "my new cat has brain damage, not bone damage" thought. My neighbors still cast curious glances at me as I hung Stanley's freshly laundered pee pads out on the clothesline.

Aggression was another issue I had not foreseen, I thought grimly as I folded Stanley's towels from his frequent baths that prevented urine-scalded fur, baths that washed away the waste matter that stuck to him when he would lose his balance in his litter box. Ordinary life has sufficient tumult and turbulence. I wasn't in the mood for any more.

Stanley and Saba fought horrifically. The fights were always and only initiated by Stanley. And the sounds of them—ah, the sounds. The yowling would start before the screaming, with Stanley in a defensive posture, though no threat actually existed. Saba was just innocently going about his day.

Poor Saba, on the receiving end of Stanley's wrath, would initially be stunned by the unprovoked onslaught, as was I each time Stanley would inexplicably go berserk. Saba's formidable size, however, stood him in good stead, and he would spin around to face the crazed, capricious creature charging at him.

"Fine! You want a piece of me, you grumpy old sod? Bring it!" Saba would seem to say, and the two of them would go at it hammer and tongs.

Back in Tanzania, "*Ebooh!*" or "*Wewe!*" was a cry of exasperation, often from parents telling a misbehaving child that this was their very last warning before a punishment was meted out. Stanley did not always give a "*wewe!*" warning to Saba, however. Some of the attacks were launched in deadly silence.

I did not share Saba's grim resolve and instead was aghast when the two cats went at it hammer and tongs.

"Stan-leeee! What are you thinking! Stop that!" My own screams were matched decibel for decibel by the screaming, screeching and shrieking rolling ball of mingled fur spinning and writhing all over my living room floor.

This Stanley-Saba cyclone reminded me of the Stanley-

George cyclone of my childhood, when two of our dogs fought. In Tanzania, we had eventually ended up with three dogs in total, counting a white mongrel named George, my dog Alice, and one of her puppies, Stanley, not surprisingly named after Sir Henry Morton Stanley. The two male dogs, George and Stanley, got along well except for when Alice went into heat.

I had hoped they would not fight.

They fought.

Their fights always traumatized me and reduced me to tears.

Now, here in America, the fights between my two cats had no obvious trigger. Stan could be sniffing noses uneventfully with Saba one day and mere moments later attacking, always with full fury, always with deadly intent, and never with any clear cause.

If I attempted to snatch Saba and lift him up to safety, Stanley would not be in the least deterred. He kept his grip on Saba, the result being that both cats were lifted clear off the floor, still dangling in that one singular ball of fur. When Stan was finally bested by gravity and dropped back down to the floor with the utmost reluctance, he'd keep lunging at Saba, held safely aloft, still bent on destruction, until I forcibly separated both animals.

"Dude, this is *so* not over," his eyes seemed to say.

After each fight—and these became recurrent fights—I would check each cat for injuries, but to my vast relief, there was only one occasion where a vet was needed. Saba usually walked away, sometimes shaking his head as though he found this all rather tiresome. Saliva from each cat would be slathered on the neck and shoulders of both animals, but thankfully no broken skin, and nobody was limping. Saba kept his head high after he had trounced Stanley (and he always trounced Stanley), glancing at me undaunted as though he was saying, "Mother, I didn't start it, but I jolly well finished it." Meanwhile, Stanley would be heaving and gasping while I righted the various pieces of overturned furniture.

"Stanley, why do you *do* this!" I would wail at my mercurial moggie. He'd meow impassively back at me in a voice too raspy from all his previous screaming, while I miserably cleaned countless ripped-out tufts of tabby African fur and white American fur off the floor.

A visiting friend witnessed one of these outbreaks of fisticuffs. She joined me on the floor, helping to clean up the fur. She joked about a popular American television show she'd seen where the host of the show goes from house to house, helping people with their problem cats.

"It's a great show! Have you seen it? It's called *My Cat From Hell*." She then muttered how my cat was *just* like those cats.

"Well, my cat is a cat not from hell," I huffed. "Stanley is from Tanzania."

She laughed good-naturedly as she helped me load both cats into carriers to go to the vet, all the while still muttering, "*Just* like those cats."

Shortly afterward my two bloodied and beloved cats, neither of whom was from hell, were in the vet's examining room for this new problem.

Stanley's brain damage had been manageable—barely—up until today. This new ferocity stunned me. My pet had now crossed a line from being merely a high-maintenance cat to an actual danger.

We were first seen by a vet tech, who meticulously began taking notes regarding the various slings and arrows that poor Saba endured from my brat of a cat.

The vet tech, too, chirped up about how Stanley was *just like* those cats on *My Cat From Hell*." When she saw my wan smile, she tactfully took her leave, reappearing shortly afterward with the veterinarian.

That day, Saba and Stan both received wound care for the havoc each had wreaked upon the other, and I poured out my tale of woe to my vet who was, fortunately, well familiar with Stanley's cerebellar hypoplasia. To her credit, she never referred to Stanley as "that CH cat" but instead referred to him by her own made-up term of endearment for him.

"Well, hello there, Mr. Africa!" she cooed as she tenderly cleaned the bloodied fur. "Gotten into a fight then, have you?"

During that appointment, various causes for the aggression were considered and ruled out—toothache, stroke, seizures, brain tumor—and blood was drawn for testing. My cats all drank filtered water, so a mineral imbalance did not seem likely. I dared to hope this would turn out to be a simple matter, easily fixed by perhaps a change of diet. When the lab results came back, there was no obvious cause for the aggression there either.

Which just left the question of his original brain disorder.

"What's *causing* this aggression, doctor? Is it his CH?"

She hesitated. "Maybe." Another pause as she continued to study him thoughtfully. "But maybe not."

I groaned inwardly. It was taking all my effort to keep in mind the resilience and perseverance I had once learned from the wildebeest from my African childhood. Step by step. Certainly I would need this here.

"I have always known CH cats to have dominant personalities. Maybe it's a compensatory measure? But they've always been sweet-natured," she mused, stroking his fur.

Calming medications were considered, rubber claw tip

covers were halfway considered, and euthanasia was completely off the table. I similarly swatted away any suggestion of rehoming either cat.

I gulped and stared dully at the vet. "So now I have a cat with brain damage, and incontinence, *and* an aggression issue?"

My despondence was met with a warm, sympathetic gaze.

"I'm sorry." Then, "Can you perhaps keep Mr. Africa physically separated from Saba with a baby gate?"

Chapter 35
Cathyfromafrica

Africa is mystic; it is wild. To a lot of people, as to me, it is just home.

—Beryl Markham, *West with the Night*

Dar es Salaam, early 1970s

After so many years in Africa, it soon became a delightful surprise when I encountered anybody who could pronounce the *th* in my name correctly.

With a name like Catherine, this didn't happen often.

I was Catherine or Cathy almost exclusively in North America, but the consonant cluster *th* is present in fewer than 8 percent of all the world languages. In Europe or in Africa, I was often called Kotreen, Caffee, Caw-tee, Cassie . . .

Depending on which African was addressing me, and from which tribe they hailed, yet more name variations could result. The Maasai gave me the Maa name "Nashipai,"[55] and the Arabs named me "Seynabu Sekk." Depending on who was explaining it to me, it was either the name of a relative of the prophet Mohammed, or it meant "a bag full of gratitude."

---
55   Smiling

From an African elder, I could usually expect "Ah, my child." The simplest term of endearment I received came from Neema, to whom I was "Sistah."

Throughout our Africa years, we made periodic trips back to Canada for home leave, during which time the pronunciation of my name changed yet again. Or was it a nickname? My new label, all one word but six syllables long, was given to me by certain Canadian friends and used to link my previous residence to my identity.

"I want you to meet my new friend!" they would say, when introducing me to others. "This is Cathyfromafrica."

This thwarted my original hope to just blend in and quietly belong. There was more to the real me, I felt, than my childhood in Africa, but with some people those years eclipsed all else, and the real me was never investigated any further, even years after my time in Africa.

If I sat with *mzungu* kids during lunch at my Tanzanian school, it did not escape my notice that these fellow expatriates tended to use the exact same phrase that my mother used when falling into conversation with someone from another land.

"Where are you from, originally?"

We expat kids (we were also labeled as TCK, Third Culture Kids) had all experienced the confusion from being asked, "Where are you from?" since it usually wasn't clear whether we were being asked about our place of birth, where we had been raised, or where we were living now. Tacking on the additional word "originally" usually solved this awkwardness.

Sometimes the conversations descended into bragging matches as to who had had the most vaccines for overseas travel. Sometimes we lamented this hopscotching lifestyle of moving so much.

But we all, in body, despised the weekly malaria pill. The

tedium of airports and planes was another topic on which we all gloomily agreed. Air travel, our cross to bear, was sometimes my aerial classroom, often my portal to new experiences, and invariably the disruptor of my circadian rhythms.

My mother, my anchor incarnate, was always ready to commiserate with me when I felt destabilized from constant travel. She, too, had grown up overseas, albeit not the entire time in Africa, but with a considerable portion of her childhood in different European countries. I never got the impression, however, that she had any self-identity issues despite a life steeped in so much traveling. Indeed she cemented my self-identity. Somehow, she created stability for my childhood just by being herself. I would happily engage in hours of solitary play, secure in the bone-deep knowledge that if I needed her, she would be there. She would come unbidden to my side whenever I was sick or injured, and I was invariably given meticulous care and regained my footing in good time. Just by their presence, my parents created a sense of stability for me, whether they were by my side as we trudged through yet another airport, or singing Christmas carols together during the holidays. Singing Christmas carols in my head also helped me pass the time in those tedious airports, come to think of it.

Chapter 36
The Lion King

Certainly, no one said "hakuna matata" when we were there, at least not in that way. "Matata" meant fighting or a brawl or a screaming match or a riot or some sort of unrest, as in "There was a matata in the village last night, but it's all quiet now."

—Craig

USA, circa 1994

Disney's animated *The Lion King* came out many years after I had left Africa. Had it been released when I had been a child living there, my guess is I would have been too puzzled to enjoy it.

I wish I could have enjoyed *The Lion King* more, during my adulthood. I *did* enjoy it, I suppose, but the filmmaker's artistic license left me confused. I had walked into the movie, a thirty-something-year-old adult, happily anticipating lovely artistic animation.

"Ooh! Rhino!" I whispered delightedly to myself as the first animal appeared in the opening sequence. The rhino was then followed by a hartebeest in the movie (or perhaps that was a topi?). Then meerkats, and a cheetah. A marabou stork, perhaps one of the ugliest things in Africa, was followed by a glimpse of—was that Victoria Falls? Now, this movie that I had thought would depict Tanzania had transported us to the border of Zambia and Zimbabwe? Just as quickly, the film took us back to Tanzania as Kilimanjaro came into view. A reassuring parade of familiar Tanzanian animals continued, as guinea fowl pranced across the screen followed by a hornbill, greater kudu—perhaps one of the most beautiful things in Africa, Cape buffalo, and oryx. The camera lingered on a mandrill.

Why did the animators draw his tail that long?

Leaf cutter ants then marched across the screen. A flock of flamingo took flight. We were given a glimpse of a rhinoceros beetle and some sort of a rat.

"Shhh!" said my friend, next to me, when I delightedly recited each animal name out loud.

About an hour and a half later, once the movie had ended, the two of us left the cinema chatting agreeably. There had been plenty of wildebeest in this movie, which cheered me somewhat. My familiar buddies were featured in a stampede scene and the artistry there had thrilled me no end. But I was still disappointed. Artistic license in an animated movie is one thing, but in some places the artistic license was inconsistent too. Setting aside the trifling matter that these were animals that talked, danced, and occasionally burst into song, other aspects were puzzling to me. Lions and hyenas were working cooperatively? The herbivores were all delightedly cheering the birth of another carnivore? The names of the characters did not clarify things for me either.

Years later, I fell into conversation with a different friend who, like me, had been an expat and an animal enthusiast but, unlike me, had lived in India. We were on the subject of

Disney movies. Because of her childhood in India, she was well familiar with Kipling.

"I was somewhat annoyed watching *The Jungle Book*," she said. "There were so many inaccuracies."

I glanced at her sharply. Was this someone like me who had watched an animated movie about animals—animals who talked and burst into song, no less—and kept stumbling over the parts that involved artistic license? These weren't supposed to be documentaries, after all.

"Inaccuracies?" I ventured cautiously. "Like, what inaccuracies?"

"Well," she huffed, "there are no orangutans in India, to start with. And the story *is* set in India. And I lived there. For several years."

"So the monkeys were portrayed inaccurately?" I asked, thinking back to another film showing a particularly ridiculous tail on a certain African mandrill. Hopefully she would not notice that *monkey* had popped out of my mouth when I should have said *ape*.

"Well, monkeys were inaccurate in that movie too," she said. "But the orang is an ape, and we don't have any apes in India." Then, adding an afterthought, "Except gibbons. Anyway, the elephants were wrong too."

What was wrong with the elephants? I cast my mind back to what I had remembered about *The Jungle Book* and recalled only that the Asian elephants had been correctly depicted with their smaller ears and rounded backs.

"In India, the elephant herds are led by *matriarchs*, not by the males. But in that movie, a male was in charge."

All elephants have a matriarchal structure, a fact I knew full well. How could I have forgotten this, so soon after my error a minute ago regarding monkeys versus apes?

"You grew up in Africa, didn't you?" She turned to me. "African elephants are the same way, aren't they?"

I agreed that they were. "Do you know, I felt just as puzzled after *The Lion King*." The two of us commiserated for several minutes about Disney animations muddling with the animals we loved.

The movie also rankled in another aspect.

Whatever happened to the word *shida*?

When I returned to Tanzania in my fifties, on my first day back, I noticed this word had dropped off the face of the Earth.

"*Daaaaah!*" said a shop vendor sympathetically when I spilled my bottle of Fanta Orange. "*Hakuna matata.*"

Once the spill was cleaned, I pulled my driver to the side.

"Does nobody use *hakuna shida* any longer?" I asked him, very surprised. "*Matata* used to mean some sort of serious fight when I was here last." My jet lag from the trip over was still considerable enough that I thought I might have misheard. It has meant something along the lines of many unclarified issues, I had thought.

My driver confirmed my suspicion that *The Lion King's* catchphrase was now so cemented in the minds of *wazungo* that many Africans in and around the tourist industry soon began using it in place of *shida*. Later, I was told that either one is correct, and that the people from Pemba used it more than Tanzanians. I resolved to keep using the original phrase. For reasons both logical and illogical, that movie bothered me more than I cared to admit.

A staff member in the tourism industry confided to me they only begrudgingly used *matata* with the tourists, since it was the only Swahili word many of the tourists knew. "We blame Hollywood for that whole *hakuna matata* thing."

I also had to squash down my annoyance when people asked me whether a dog I had around the time of the Disney flick was named *Rafiki* "after that monkey."

Some days it didn't seem worth the effort to explain that, no, my little dog was my beloved friend and the name was chosen solely from my childhood years speaking Swahili in Tanzania.

So eventually I didn't bother to correct the people who thought my little dog Rafiki was named after the mandrill in *The Lion King*. It made them smile if I changed the subject to the film's main character instead:

"And I've seen lots of dogs named Simba too!"

Chapter 37
Cin's Dinner Guest

Dear Uncle Carlo,
That particular story of your father inviting the priest to dinner was one of my favourites. My mother often told the story to me.
Love, Cath

Montreal, circa 1970

"Pleased to meet you, Father. I am from Piedmonte, also."
This greeting from my great-uncle to a priest he had once met was a key turning point in a family story that my mother had told me. The story, which took place long before my birth, was a mainstay in my mother's rotation of bedtime stories. I begged for animal stories in particular (like *Born Free*). She instead enjoyed telling this one from her own family, especially because it involved food, which was one of her favorite subjects. Fortunately it also involved animals. Or rather, one particular animal.

"May we just skip over the food part?" I was lying on my back in bed in Montreal, age seven, and tried not to whine when making this request, but really the other parts of this story were much more interesting.

"I most certainly will not!" Mother would answer from her perch on the side of my bed. "All the parts of this story are important. Now shall I tell the story or not?"

"Yes, yes!" I would snuggle deeper under the covers in delicious anticipation. "One day when Uncle Cin was in Eritrea," I prompted.

"One day when Uncle Cin was in Eritrea," she began agreeably, and went on to describe how her Uncle Francesco DeRege (nicknamed "Cin," pronounced "chin") from the Manta, Piedmonte region of northern Italy, had been posted to Eritrea, on the Horn of Africa. Cin, a diplomat, had been serving in "the Horn," in the Italian colonial administration there at the time.

"And one day, there comes a priest in that part of Africa where my uncle was." Her phrasing of sentences in English was occasionally just slightly off, some of the very few times that it was noticeable that English had been a second language for her.

"So Uncle Cin invited him for a meal." I was failing to keep all traces of impatience out of my voice.

"But the *reason* he invited him," she gently chided me, "is important."

"So one day, there comes a priest in that part of Africa where my uncle was . . ." And she went on to describe that the two men met, exchanged pleasantries.

"Hello, how do you do, Father?" I gave my best imitation of Uncle Cin's voice greeting the priest, for which Mother pulled a face at me because I never did manage to get his vocal inflections quite right.

The priest happened to mention that he was from a particular region in the very north of Italy, near France, named Piedmonte.

"Pleased to meet you, Father. I am from Piedmonte too." We came to Cin's pivotal sentence. I resisted the urge to fidget with the edge of my blanket.

"So, anyway, go on" came out of my mouth before I could stop it. Mother kindly ignored it and continued with the story.

The priest was delighted to make the acquaintance of a fellow countryman all the way out here in Africa, and the two men happily conversed about their homeland, over two thousand five hundred miles away, Piedmonte.

"Which is where you are from too," I would say to Mother, who would nod, smiling.

Amongst the subjects they discussed was the food back home. Cin then informed the priest that he had a cook skilled in Italian cuisine, and would the good Father like to come to dinner perhaps?

Presently the time came when the priest arrived at Cin's house and found the dining room table all beautifully laid with an exquisite white silk tablecloth.

"A tablecloth that reaches all the way to the floor," I reiterated, significantly and carefully.

"A tablecloth that reaches all the way to the floor," Mother agreed, and went on in her unhurried pace to mention the lovely china and silver on the table.

As soon as the priest sat down, I would sit up, eyes shining.

The priest was quite delighted that, true to his word, Uncle Cin's Eritrean cook had prepared a beautiful, expertly prepared, utterly flawless Piedmontese meal. The grace was said, the meal blessed. With his salivary glands now geared up, and his face transported with joy and anticipation, the priest laid his linen napkin in his lap. He kept his eyes on his host.

I kept my eyes on Mother, who had a twinkle in her eye.

The priest couldn't take his first bite until his host took his first bite, and his host wasn't yet eating.

"The priest picked up his water glass," said Mother, and here I sat up straighter in bed, straightened my shoulders, stifled another giggle, and then pantomimed a man with one finger raised, about to give a very serious, very important instruction.

"And then . . ." Mother paused for effect. "My uncle said to him, 'Be careful, Father, be sure to—"

"—keep your feet very still!'" Mother and I recited in unison this cryptic instruction given by Cin to the priest, both of us giggling by now.

The priest paused with his water glass suspended above the mouthwatering Piedmontese risotto and breaded veal cutlets on his plate. At the most, he had expected "Don't burn your mouth, the food is very hot." But this? What a curious thing to say.

"Keep my feet very still?" His laugh was polite and slightly puzzled as he reluctantly lowered his glass, his curiosity piqued. "And just why, pray tell, am I to keep my feet very still, might I ask?"

"You must keep your feet very still," Uncle Cin reiterated, "because—"

And here Mother and I continued the sentence in unison once again: "—under the table, there is a lion."

Another bemused, polite chuckle from the priest.

Until he caught sight of Cin's deadpan face. His polite chuckle trailed away into nothingness. Cin was completely serious.

I bounced slightly in bed now, hugging my sides, and tittering.

"You mean . . . under the . . . ?" The priest pointed vaguely in the general direction of the tablecloth. The exquisite white silk tablecloth that reached all the way to the floor.

"Yes." Again, Cin's voice was utterly resolute. "Therefore, you must keep your feet very still." By now, I was drumming my feet under the bedcovers, a huge grin splitting my face.

Slowly putting down his glass, the priest studied Cin yet again, who by now had picked up his knife and fork. His host still hadn't begun to eat but reiterated the solemn and quiet instruction that one's feet ought not move. The dubious priest very cautiously lifted a fold of the white tablecloth that reached all the way down to the floor.

He scrutinized Cin once more.

Then he cautiously peeped into the shadowy recesses underneath the tablecloth.

A bone-chilling growl issued forth.

Here, Mother interjected her own passingly fair "grr-rrr-rr-rrrrrrr!" while I contorted my own face in my imitation of a lion's snarl, hampered by giggles, hunching my shoulders, and arching my fingers as though they were talons at the ready.

"Oh!" The priest stared.

A tawny face came into view.

Mother said, "It was a big, snarling—"

"—lioness!" I finished with a squeal.

Man and beast stared at one another.

The tawny, leonine face stared at the human face, which was rapidly draining of all color. The widening eyes of the priest met the luminous amber eyes of the young African lioness, her pupils huge and round in the dim light underneath the table. A snarl creased her golden face.

Two faces, maybe ten inches apart.

Another growl.

No more "oh" from the dumbstruck priest.

This second, louder growl came with a blast of putrid

breath from her open mouth, where her lips curled back to reveal four especially long, gleaming incisors.

The priest, who had been repeatedly and politely warned not to move his feet, then moved his feet, scraping and shoving his chair backward. There was a loud clatter as his chair toppled over, and his thrashing feet skidded upon his linen napkin, which had dropped from his lap.

"P-please excuse me, sir," his plea was stammered, with raspy breaths and a cracking voice, "I must be going." He stumbled and staggered his flailing limbs to the door, losing a shoe in the process. Cin leapt from his own seat in a bid to help his guest, and barely caught his chair before it too would have toppled backward.

The priest paused from his windmilling, for just an instant, in the doorway, his ashen face turned back to offer his thanks for the dinner invitation, succeeding only in babbling "Th-Than . . ."

Then he bolted.

The Eritrean cook skilled in Italian cuisine had emerged from the kitchen by now, hearing the commotion, and he and Cin ruefully gazed around at the disarray of the dining room.

"Pity," said Cin. "He need only to have kept his feet still, and she would not have bothered him."

I was rocking back and forth by now, clutching my sides, barely able to wheeze. "Don't . . . move . . . your . . . feet, Father! Don't . . . move"—gurgle—gasp—"your feet!"

Mother, too, was chortling with head thrown back, and stammering about all that lovely food! "Poor chap, that would have been scary. That face, ten inches away! I would have fainted dead away!"

Craig passed my bedroom doorway just then, on his way to his own room, but promptly doubled back after hearing snorts and gurgles from us.

He poked his head in the door and took in the tableau: his little sister convulsed in laughter and Mother wiping her eyes.

"Let me guess," Craig said. "The lion under the table?" He knew perfectly well that almost no bedtime story could leave me so convulsed as that one. A close second was Mother's stories of the goats she had seen up in trees in one town, during the years she had lived in Morocco. It made for a bizarre sight, yet these cloven-hooved animals did truly spend several hours each day up in the branches of argan trees.

Still, lions under tables easily trounced goats in trees.

After a while, Mother and I regained our composure, and she settled me back into bed.

"So, Mother," I asked, now that I could breathe normally, "how long was Uncle Cin keeping lions, then?"

Mother replied, as she kissed me goodnight, that he only did it for a few years. "But in the end, he had to let them go." Each of his lions was eventually released into the wild. The reason had nothing to do with legal regulations, nothing to do with monetary fines, and nothing to do with special permits needed to keep wildlife.

I asked what had been the reason, then.

She paused in my doorway, before turning out my light.

"Because they weren't exactly . . . *friendly*."

Chapter 38
FOMO Cat

Dear Catherine,
I can only imagine how he looks now. He must be so much bigger! Whenever you have time, can you send a recent photo? We really miss him. By the way, I've added your name to the TAWESO website under Friends and Partners.
—Dr. Thomas

Virginia, circa 2017

There was a sofa behind my computer desk with a cat bed on it. I had only to take one hand off the keyboard and reach behind me, and my fingers would then be softly licked by Stanley, nestled there. He would proceed to groom my whole hand if given half the chance. If I gently waggled his tipped ear, he would scrape my hand off his ear with one paw, and then my hand would be licked yet again.

During some portions of the day, he was barricaded in my kitchen behind a baby gate. Otherwise he was ensconced in this particular cat bed, complete with heating pad, on my sofa. My brain-impaired pet spent many peaceful and purring hours with me in this manner, mostly sleeping, close enough that I could dribble water into his mouth periodically throughout the day from a syringe—rather than carry him to his water dish, where he could drink, but it took considerable effort, time, and many attempts—and close enough that I could prevent him falling off the sofa. My rump-in-chair time stretched many hours each day, since I worked from home. Stanley loved this. With the exception of food and bathroom breaks for both of us, the happy time passed uneventfully.

If I remembered to bring him his favorite blanket, the peaceful hours would roll on with my two hands still occupied on the keyboard and his four paws with the white-tipped toes occupied kneading, kneading, kneading his blankie.

The serenity was abruptly shattered one day, when Stanley awoke, found me gone, and reached the unwarranted conclusion that I had slipped away to give cat treats to the others, utterly neglecting his own need for a treat. Stanley is *extremely* food-driven, to put it mildly.

Cue the panic attack.

At his very first indignant yowl, I came running back. He was already in full, frantic, flopping and flailing mode, still yowling, when I arrived on the scene.

"What am I missing? *What am I missing?*" was the message I heard from my thrashing cat. "Is there *food* that I'm missing?"

With barely a split second to spare, I caught him before he fell completely off the sofa. I half expected him to lick my fingers once again with his profound gratitude that I had saved him from a fall that could well have resulted in a possible injury, given his lack of bodily coordination from his brain disorder.

He sniffed my fingers anxiously for treats instead.

Empty.

The look of utter disappointment on his little face had

to be seen to be believed. Both ears went sideways, and all his whiskers drooped. A pair of plaintively blinking eyes gazed up into mine before he slumped in my arms with a despondent sigh.

It was obvious there was only one thing left to do.

I cuddled my little FOMO-afflicted friend closer in my arms, and we headed off to the kitchen for a treat.

***

Most of the time I worked from home, but occasionally I would end up traveling for work-related functions. There came a day when I had to drop Stanley off at a boarding kennel for a week, since I would be out of town for a work trip. This would be our first separation since he arrived in America.

"These are his food and water bowls," I said as I checked him in and handed over his rubber bowls, and a bag of his favorite treats. I explained his neurological condition and how he might chip a tooth if he were to be fed from metal bowls, due to the uncontrollable head tremors. "So only these rubber bowls."

And they reassured me he would sustain no chipped teeth. They cheerfully checked him in and bade me a safe and happy journey. I paid and I left.

Over the following days, I tried not to ruminate on Stanley. Was he missing me? What thoughts might be going through that little tabby cat head? It was, after all, his first separation from me after living cheek by jowl with me for many months. Was he upset in the unfamiliar surroundings? It took immense effort to concentrate on work and squash down the ache in my heart over how much I missed him. Would the staff remember that no metal bowls were to be used, so his teeth wouldn't chip?

Upon my return a week later, I found, true to their word, that Stanley's teeth had indeed remained intact. But to my shock, he had gained considerable weight.

"Sorry, but we did go through the entire bag," said one kennel worker, somewhat sheepishly handing me back the bag of cat treats.

"Wh-what happened?" I said, staring from her to the empty bag, then back again. She mumbled something about Stanley really enjoying the treats, but would not elaborate. Stan glanced at the empty bag as I settled him in his carrier for the ride home.

I could not shake my impression that he looked very pleased with himself and the way he had been treated. "Now *that* was a bit of all right, Mum!"

Days later, I brought in a different cat to the same kennel, which also offered grooming services. As the grooming staff detangled my long-haired cat, I probed whether they had heard anything from the boarding staff about Stanley.

"Oh, we all *love* that cat!" came the enthusiastic and immediate answer. "The way his head wobbles around is so *cute*!" They went on to say that they had not previously met a cat with his particular neurological condition and found it hysterically funny how his head would sway and wobble when they offered him a treat from a cupped hand. The story went on that the first kennel worker had been taken aback by the head tremors and could not stop laughing.

"Hey, Debbie!" she had said, "Watch this!" She offered a treat to Stanley, who finally was able to get it into his mouth after several long seconds of head tremors.

"Oh, that is *too cute*! Let me try!" said the second staff member, who gave Stanley a second treat and laughed just as heartily over his head tremors as the first staff member had done. To my cat's great delight, a third staff member then arrived on the scene, and she, too, wanted to try. A fourth staff member followed, and a fifth.

Stanley's treat bag emptied in record time.

Settling Stanley back in his bed at home, after his jolly little lark, he blithely ignored me as I reminded him we were settling back into normal life now.

"With only an occasional treat or two each day, now, mind."

This was, of course, in stark contrast to his view that the treats had been all well-deserved and long overdue. All the while, I was hoping the boarding kennel staff had not created a monster who now expected vastly increased portion sizes, or had wildly exacerbated FOMO otherwise.

As though brain damage, daily baths, and bouts of aggression were not enough, now I would have to sharply monitor his caloric intake as well.

Looking down at the contented cat in his basket, I did a double take.

He did, most certainly, look like the cat who got the cream.

Chapter 39
Fupi and Fupi and Fupi

Dear Dad,
When I bring my dog near the mongooses, they spit!
—Me, 8

Dar es Salaam, early 1970s

Two mongooses were bad enough. There would be no good reason to add a third.

For whatever reason, our family succumbed to the impulse of adopting a third mongoose, even though I wasn't much enjoying being bitten by the first two. Our third mongoose came to us when we were on a trip to Mafia, an island close to the Zanzibar archipelago famous for whale watching. A street vendor, who sized us up as shrewdly as Pravin had done, was able to persuade us in short order to adopt the mongoose he was holding along with the fruit we had originally intended to purchase from him. Our flight home from Mafia to Dar was a short flight, but in an unnervingly small plane, flown by a pilot who had the disconcerting habit of keeping all the aircraft windows open. We spent great effort on that flight keeping our facial expressions completely innocent, seeking to not draw any attention to a certain large, floppy canvas beach hat one of us was casually carrying upside-down, closed, and holding by the large brim. To our relief, the pilot either never suspected we were smuggling a mongoose onboard in a hat, or perhaps he purposely feigned ignorance.

Soon enough we were all back home again.

The introduction of "Fupi the Third" to Fupi and The Other Fupi went surprisingly uneventfully. Eastern banded mongooses are amongst the few mongooses who live in a colony. All three mongooses sniffed noses, then went scampering off to play in the garden. Now Alice would be spat upon by three mongooses.

"I must be bonkers," muttered Dad, watching them go. "Why did I ever agree to a third wild mongoose being kept as a pet?"

When Pravin knocked on our door the following day, and walked in carrying another *kikapu*, there was a chorus of groans from the family, and Dad rolled his eyes.

"No, no!" Pravin hastened to assuage our protestations. "This isn't another mongoose! I *remember* you said you didn't want another mongoose!" He nonchalantly opened the *kikapu* to reveal his latest present to us. We all peered dubiously at the undeniably cute and innocent baby squirrel inside.

Unlike Canadian squirrels, African ground squirrels have less pronounced ears and sparser tails, but still have coats with varying shades of brown and gray. These were new to me, and the first ones we saw in the game parks tended to run to underground burrows when threatened. I was used to Canadian squirrels, who ran up a tree.

Mother caught sight of the look on Dad's face. She hastily and gently took Pravin by the elbow, steering him into the dining room for a cup of tea because he was surely *thirsty* in this humid weather, before Dad could blast our generous, albeit misguided, benefactor about how wild animals are not meant to be pets.

This wild animal, however, soon was a fixture at mealtimes, to my delight. I might have been too entranced with the squirrel to marvel that Mother would even allow such a thing at table. This would have been unthinkable back in Canada. The tiny African squirrel pup would sit up on his little haunches, there on the table, nibbling at various tidbits we'd feed him from our plates.

Alice was not necessarily delighted, perhaps dreading another hostile reception. It was likely a relief to her that this small mammal did not spit on her. He didn't have the same manic energy levels as did our mongooses, and indeed the poor creature weakened with each day that went by.

He had barely been with us two weeks when he passed away. Once again, we were a household with three instead of four small pet mammals, and the ones we had left had very un-squirrel-like bad tempers.

Fupi the Third was the most irritable of the lot. Whatever honeymoon period we had had with "the dear little thing" was waning with each bite he inflicted on us. The mongoose bites had reached a frequency that our African friends began to offer fewer sympathetic *poles* and less tongue-clicking than in the beginning.

"You know, mongooses—" Dad would begin.

"—should not be pets." We could now finish his sentence perfectly, but with a bit more sadness each time.

***

Presently I noticed, with relief, that Pravin finally did stop bringing us any new pets. Indeed, his visits stopped completely. It was only during my adulthood, however, that I learned the real reason.

Assault.

Craig later explained to me that Pravin had gotten beaten to a pulp and ended up in a rickety bed in Muhimbili Hospital, barely recognizable. Now a dull hospital gown replaced his trademark vibrant attire.

His pulverized features did manage—just barely—to break into a grateful smile each time my nineteen-year-old brother visited him in the hospital—a smile that was often replaced by a grimace of pain.

One question remained unanswered.

Pravin waved one hand—heavily bandaged—in a dismissive gesture when Craig asked who had assaulted him. Ever the master of diversion, Pravin promptly—albeit feebly—joked how Craig never did sufficiently appreciate any of the mongooses, or the squirrel.

"Yup," Craig quipped right back. "Absolutely hated the little buggers."

A weak chuckle from Pravin, abruptly cut off by wincing as he reflexively laid one hand on his bandaged torso.

A nurse entered then, to announce that visiting hours were over. She might have brought the visit to a close rather reluctantly because Pravin had no family. Craig was his only visitor.

"I am . . ." Pravin was serious again. "I am incredibly grateful you came."

"Hey, just get some rest now, eh, *rafiki?*"

Jet-black hair rested on the dingy-white and stained hospital pillow, as much of a contrast as his small, thin, broken body in that enormous, rickety bed.

Months passed. Until a day came when Craig arrived for his regular visit and the rickety bed was empty.

We never did learn who had beaten Pravin.

The name of his assailant went to the grave with him.

Chapter 40
Man-Eater

And once they are man-eaters, you can't do anything about it.
—Mother

Northern Tanzania, circa 1971

The nun perhaps was unwise to adopt a man-eating lion.
   Then again, she wasn't a real nun. And perhaps he wasn't a real man-eater.
   It was a bright sunny day in northern Tanzania, about ten years post-Independence and a few months after my eighth birthday, as my parents and I pulled into the driveway of the nun's lodge. The long rains had just ended, and the scent of the cool red earth rose to meet us. We were far from the coast, with its sandy pale soil. Various birds that I could not identify called out from the nearby trees, whose leaves rustled as though a monkey had just jumped from one branch onto another.
   The lodge we would be staying at also featured a small side business for the last half dozen years or so rescuing wild cats. The wild cats were usually somebody's former pet who had outgrown the resources of an individual insufficiently

experienced with such animals.

A cat rescue? This delighted me. Mother listed a leopard, a cheetah and lion residing there, all former pets, and then added, with a slight shake of her head, that one of the lions was said to be a man-eater. This did not delight me; it puzzled me.

Man-eating big cats are a tragic and thankfully not very frequent fact, both in Africa and in India. I never did find one conclusive answer as to what causes a big cat to turn into a man-eater, intentionally seeking out humans as food. Amongst the many theories was that some lions turned to humans when their regular prey was not available due to disease like rinderpest or drought. Others developed into man-eaters after happening upon human corpses left out in the open as part of funeral rites or having died along a caravan route.

About seventy years before I arrived in Tanzania, just over the northern border in a Kenyan area named Tsavo, two man-eaters had spent almost a full year terrorizing construction workers, racking up a death toll of over thirty humans. The cause? Toothaches, I was told, which had made them irritable and unable to eat their traditional prey.

But regardless of the reasons for man-eaters pursuing humans, these lions were invariably hunted down and shot. One human death spelled out the lion's own death warrant, written in stone.

My brain could not absorb why a lodge owner would keep a man-eater, let alone on her business premises.

"He's killed people before, but not in *there*," Mother told me. "That's *why* he ended up in there." The story she had heard was that the lodge owner, a softhearted wealthy widow who introduced herself as "Sister Maria," wanted to give him a chance. The widow had once had a bit part in a movie as a nun. Since then, for whatever bizarre reason, she had clung to the title as her own. Real nuns who met her allowed her to continue her harmless eccentricity. We soon slipped into the pattern of referring to her as the "nun" or "Sister" too. Her funny moniker did set her apart from the hundreds of other lodge owners in Tanzania.

Mother theorized that perhaps the nun thought, "*dum spiro, spero.*"[56] Maybe the nun believed that while the cat was alive and still breathing, there was still hope. Maybe she hoped to reform him. "Otherwise he would not be alive. He had killed about five people before."

Five?

This was the point where Mother's story stretched credulity for me. It would have been unconscionable that such an animal was not instantly executed after *one* human death. Five human victims was unfathomable. Especially for a former caged pet who didn't have to be hunted down through the African bush for days or months on end.

A current man-eater who had not been euthanized?

Dad's assessment was perfectly blunt: "That woman must be barking mad, to keep that lion."

Sister Maria greeted us warmly at the front door of the lodge. She was of average height, with a beautiful smile and dressed in regular clothes despite self-identifying as a nun. Maybe I had expected her appearance to be eccentric, in keeping with someone who keeps a man-eater still alive, but she was instead quite normal-looking to me. Dad was perfectly polite during these greetings too.

She had just bidden farewell to a small group of chattering Tanzanian schoolchildren who were being shepherded back into their ramshackle little minivan.

I had barely finished my how-do-you-do when she smiled

---

56   While I breathe, I hope.

widely at me.

"Well, young miss," she said, gauging my height, "you are probably right around the age of those schoolchildren who come here to see my big cats! Do you like big cats?" Her smile grew yet wider as I nodded emphatically. "We have six big cats at the moment," she said. "A cheetah, a leopard, and some lions." She went on to explain that they had all been former pets that she had rescued when the previous owners had chosen to relinquish custody for varying reasons. Each cat was safely ensconced in sturdy cages, she reassured us, and posed no danger to her guests, adding *hakuna shida* with a laugh.

Sturdy cages? Firmly closed? Good.

Sister had run this guest lodge for several years, along with help from her brother, and her property consisted of guest cottages and the assortment of big cat cages (which the school tours referred to proudly as "our cats"). Unlike a common roadside zoo, this property was upscale and spacious. She stabled her horse and a pony on the grounds too, and the stable yard contained a large pen of donkeys as well. I listened with rapt attention as she recited the lengthy, very detailed history of the leopard, the cheetah, the lioness and the various orphaned lion cubs on the premises.

"Do you have an adult male lion also?" Dad asked, trying very hard to keep an innocent tone in his voice.

Mother shot Dad a quick look.

Sister blinked. "His name is Fire, and he came from Dodoma." It did not escape my notice that rather less detail was offered about him.

The leopard and cheetah were stunningly beautiful adults roaming in ample cages, where occasional sunbeams peeked through to illuminate the exquisite markings on their coats.

The rosettes on the leopard's coat smoothly flowed over rippling muscles as the cat quietly padded across his cage. The cheetah (to me, the most dog-like of all the big cats) lifted his surprisingly small head and gazed at me silently. The distinctive tear marks framing his muzzle, according to an African legend, were from the first cheetah, in the dawn of history, whose cubs were killed by their enemy, the lion. She cried to such an extent that she gained permanent tear marks and has passed them down to every other cheetah ever since.

I strolled over to the lion cage. Initially it looked empty, but upon closer inspection, I realized it was indeed occupied by four lions, all in varying stages of sleep or lethargy, their slumber not disturbed in the least by my presence. Unlike the leopard and cheetah cages, this enclosure was enormous and occupied pride of place on the grounds. No effort had been spared for these magnificent and impressive animals, who were clearly the crown jewels of this cat collection. Their sturdy wire enclosure bordered the main driveway coming up to the lodge. All cats love an elevated height, and this cage had been built around a tall basking platform on which these big cats could climb, bask in the sun, and survey their surroundings. Lions often especially enjoyed *kopjes*, small hills found in generally flat game park plains, or "these curious hill-heaps of rock" as Sir Henry Morton Stanley called them. Whoever had designed this cage was probably well familiar with how fond lions are of *kopje*, and this basking platform was then specifically created for their enjoyment.

As lions are the only social cat, this assorted little pride was all housed together without any discord. Two unrelated cubs were here, each an orphan brought here under different circumstances. The adult male and the adult female were brought here from different backgrounds as well. The cubs were sweet. The adult female was lovely.

And then there was Fire—either a rescued man-eater who had killed five people, or somebody's former pet, depending on your source. This lion, probably around five hundred pounds and nine feet long, was undeniably splendid, with a striking rich, thick mane.

This adult male, in full regalia, was reclining on his basking platform, dozing off from time to time when he wasn't gazing at the nearby cages of the leopard and the cheetah. Because he was not close to the wire, I couldn't catch his scent, but when he turned to stare at me, my brow furrowed.

This cat was inscrutable.

Was he a lion?

For a split second, I almost thought I was looking at some sort of demon or unknown spiritual entity. Was he lightning? Or thunder? Perhaps he was something else in a lion's skin.

Shaking my head slightly, I looked again at Fire.

The cryptic being that I thought I had glimpsed was no longer there, replaced by a regular bone-idle lion snoozing surrounded by cubs and lioness, all giving him his due deference. Now, once again, I was seeing a lion like all the others I had seen in game parks or like the ones I had seen in films or TV during my childhood in Canada. Like thousands of other children, I had enjoyed watching *Born Free* and laughed at the antics of Kitty Kat, the retired circus lion on the TV show *The Addams Family*. More endearing than Kitty Kat, in my estimation, was *Clarence, the Cross-Eyed Lion*, and I tried to never miss an episode. The lion tales recounted by Dr. David Livingstone had also been added to Mother's repertoire of bedtime stories once we learned we would be coming to Africa. Livingstone had described, in particular, how he had survived a lion attack, in thrilling detail.

Bang!

I felt a surge of annoyance at whoever had just made that sound. Did someone just set off a firecracker? Now all the cats were waking up and gathering at the gate to their enclosure, looking very expectant. None of them was facing me any longer. I lingered a few minutes longer after the crack of the stupid fireworks. There was nothing to see but leonine backs. As I turned to go, the rattle of a wheelbarrow with a creaking wheel approached the lion enclosure. It was heavily laden with several large cuts of meat, which I had no doubt the happy lions had smelled from clear across the property.

Chapter 41
Swept by the Roar

The sound of [the lion's] roar in my ears will only be duplicated, I think, when the doors of hell slip their wobbly hinges, one day, and give voice and authenticity to the whole panorama of Dante's poetic nightmares. It was an immense roar that encompassed the world and dissolved me into it.

—Beryl Markham, *West with the Night*

Tanzania, early 1970s

Up until now, the only roars I had heard were from lions very faint and far off, in a game park, or the MGM lion, who roars in the movie's opening sequence. But the MGM lion is only filmed during the roar portion of the sound curve.

When Mother and I heard Fire roar, it was different. In real life, it could be graphed out like a bell curve. It begins with some quiet introductory coughs and some low moaning, which builds to baritone roars. At the peak, it is maybe a half minute of full-throated roars, which descend back down into concluding grunts. As it concluded, I almost expected Mother to pipe up with the hearty line from Shakespeare's *A Midsummer Night's Dream*, "Well roared, Lion!" Instead, she seemed unnerved about how the sound carried.

The MGM lion never threw his voice. This was new to us. Mother and I had left the main dining room of the lodge and were walking back to our cottage, perhaps about twenty-five yards away from the lion cage. Fire was roaring, to reiterate ownership of his domain, I thought. The two of us exchanged wide-eyed glances. Each of us could have sworn on a stack of Bibles that the cat was right next to us.

Interspersed with Fire's roars, the female decided to pipe up too. The two voices rose and fell with their contrasting messages.

The female seemed to be attempting to politely ask, "Any other lions nearby? Are we the only ones? Answer if you can hear me!"

But soon she gave up as Fire continued to drown her out, still insisting that every other lion, far and wide should know, unequivocally, "This is *my* territory, it's mine . . . mine . . . mine . . . mine."

"*Hannibal ad portas!*" muttered Mother.[57]

The roar had such a large feel to it, so big and bold, that I could have easily believed it came from an animal twice as big. The word *thunder* fit this lion. I felt mildly surprised that the surrounding trees were not bent over from the sheer force of it. As the low-frequency roars continued, their pressure waves thudded against my body. These reverberations should have knocked me off my feet.

The volume increased, and I now felt the sound waves smashing up against my body. The full phenomenon of the acoustics of a lion's roar, and its ventriloqual effect, just begs belief. Craig had once told me what it felt like to stand next to a sound amplifier at a rock and roll concert, but he agreed that

---

[57] The conqueror Hannibal is at the gates, ready to kill you!

a lion's roar was yet more awe-inspiring. In fact, a lion's roar can reach over 113 decibels. In comparison, a thunderclap is 120 decibels.

"My chest!" I chuckled to Mother as a crushing sensation came against my sternum.

"Is he out?" Mother wasn't chuckling. Mother had one hand clutching her chest. She was darting nervous glances in the direction of the lion cage. "*Sfuggito?*"[58]

"No, no, the lion is still in his cage," I said, as the roars increased. "*Hakuna shida.*"

She certainly had a point, though, because the way he was throwing his voice really could have convinced you he was mere inches from us, as we walked on the reverberating ground alone in the dark. Decades before that night, Dr. David Livingstone had said that the majestic roar of the king of beasts was indeed well calculated to inspire fear, and Mother would have doubtless agreed with him.

"He's *out*!" she continued, her voice now shrill as she picked up the pace. "*Su! Su!*"[59] By now the volume was slightly stupefying me, and I felt too lightheaded and breathless to answer her that no, he was still in his cage.

Mother's rising panic was penetrating through my stupor, though, and I mumbled repeatedly that he was still in his cage until we got to the door of our cottage.

As she fumbled for her keys, Fire kept roaring.

Mother, violently shaking by now, tried and missed the keyhole. "He's out, I'm sure he's out," she babbled.

Still stupefied, I dully noticed that she had now dropped the keys.

"Hey, Mother, you dropped—"

---

58 Escaped?
59 Out

And then, to my shock, I felt her sweep me up into her arms.

"We die together, sweetheart!"

Her scream must have alerted the staff. One of the cooks found us right then. The tableau that his flashlight fell upon was a hysterical woman clutching a breathless, disoriented little eight-year-old girl, presumably before they were both mercilessly torn limb from limb by an incorrigible man-eater who was surely only inches away.

"Well, that's what I thought," said Mother, slightly defensively years afterward when telling the story to others.

"But," I chimed in, "the lion was in his cage the whole time."

"He could have had us both to eat," she continued, mildly indignant. Then, seeing I was about to mention the cage again, she begrudgingly added, "If he really was out."

Chapter 42
A Movie Star

Altogether twenty-four lions, lionesses and cubs were used in the picture. Apart from [my seven adults], none of the other grown lions could be handled, largely because they were kept permanently confined and given no opportunity to run free on the plains. I am firmly convinced that it is the boredom and frustration of captivity which makes lions dangerous.

—**George Adamson,** *Bwana Game,* **describing lions cast in** *Born Free*

A domesticated lion is only an unnatural lion—and whatever is unnatural is untrustworthy.

—Beryl Markham, *West with the Night*

Early in our visit, one of the lodge staff surprised me with a tidbit of impressive news about the male lion. Incredulous, I scampered over to find the nun straight away.

"Sister Maria! Sister Maria!" I came skipping into the lodge slightly breathless.

"I'm over here, Miss!" her cheery voice sang out from the direction of the lodge dining room. "Hello, Miss!" she said as I found her at the main table meticulously sorting paperwork, all painstakingly arranged in neat piles. "You look excited!" Her serene smile met my wide grin.

"Hullo, Sister!" I bounced slightly from foot to foot as she drew out the chair beside her, patted it, then turned back to her paperwork, still with a warm smile.

"Hey, Sister!" I said. "I heard about your lion, Fire!"

"Fire?" She dropped the paper she was holding and instantly turned her full attention to me, smile now vanished. Her voice continued in measured tones. "Fire? What about Fire?"

"I heard about him!"

"Did you, now?" She was still giving me laser focus and cleared her throat. "What, um, what did you hear?"

"I heard he was in a movie!" I was seated on the edge of my chair. This was the most exciting news I'd heard all day. "Is that true?"

"Is what true?" Still the laser focus.

"Is it true that your male lion, Fire, was in a movie?"

"Movie? Oh, yes." She fingered her cross, seeming not to notice that I was somewhat giddy about the idea of a movie star on the premises. "Yes, yes." She was gathering up papers rather hastily now. "A film crew was borrowing pet lions to use in a movie. Fire went."

"That is *so* neat!"

"Yes, well, if you will please excuse me, I'm needed in the kitchen now."

"Please, Sister, may I ask one more thing?"

She paused in the doorway, with a tight smile, but eyes fixed on her papers now all in one haphazard pile clutched to her chest. "Yes, miss?"

"What was the name of the movie he was in?"

"*Born Free.*"

Oh . . . my . . . word.

A Billion Blue Wildebeest

***

"Yes, I did hear that," said Mother, when I reported to her excitedly that Fire had been in *Born Free*. Back in Canada, she had taken me to any animal movie she could find, and I had been enraptured in the true story of Elsa the lioness. Just over the Tanzanian border lay Kenya, where the real-life couple, George and Joy Adamson, had raised the orphaned lion cub to adulthood and successfully rehabilitated her into the wild. It had become a bedtime story I had repeatedly requested when growing up, and scarcely had we landed in Tanzania than I was begging my parents to take me to meet the authors. Such a meeting never did come to be, alas, and Elsa had already passed away by the time we arrived in Africa.

It turned out that Fire and the adult female here at the nun's lodge had been amongst the dozen or so pet lions borrowed for use as film extras. Had I already unwittingly watched Fire himself on the big screen?

Mother looked down at my beaming face and hesitated.

"What?" I said, as I noticed her pause. "These two lions *were* in the movie, right?"

"What I was *told*," Mother continued, haltingly, "was that the female behaved beautifully for the film crew, but the male was, well, you remember. I told you he was a man-eater. And once they are man-eaters, you can't do anything about it."

"But, Mother, if he *really* had been a man-eater, he would have been shot by now," I reminded her, only barely not rolling my eyes. I wasn't fond of Fire, particularly. Even if he were a movie star, I wasn't desperately wanting him to be innocent. But a man-eating lion must be shot to death as soon as possible—that was to me as basic as the laws of gravity.

"Well, that's what I was *told*," she said, again not divulging her sources. "Anyway, the male, I think they only used once, in a group scene, and the camera crew mostly filmed his scenes by having the humans inside cages, with just their camera lenses protruding out. Nobody was hurt, but that male was returned very quickly to Sister Maria."

George Adamson, coauthor of *Born Free*, still had three of the lions that been used in the filming, but his favorite was Boy, a nine-month-old male lion previously named Fortior. George poured endless effort, years after year, into the rehabilitation, back into the wild, of the young male, rather than see him go back to captivity.

Boy transitioned well from his beginning as a battalion mascot in Nairobi to eventually living free in the wilds of Kenya.

Until recently.

That evening, at dinner, one of the guests said, "Did you hear that George had to shoot Boy?"

All breath left me. I guessed instantly which "George and Boy" she was referring to, but surely this wasn't true?

Surely I had misheard?

Boy?

A cold flush went down my whole body, and I still couldn't gasp because my throat had closed up. Boy? I could not fathom why George Adamson would have had to shoot one of his most beloved lions.

The guest went on to tell her spellbound audience that Boy had bitten a *mzungu* boy named Mark Jenkins, and had bitten Muga Bocho, one of George's staff members. George sent Muga Bocho to Garissa Hospital and covered his bills. But Boy conclusively signed his own death warrant on June 6, 1971, when he attacked and killed Stanley Murithii, the Kenyan who was perhaps closest to Boy.

A Billion Blue Wildebeest

By now I was in tears. Stanley Murithii, from the Meru tribe, had been working right alongside George Adamson, meticulously caring for Boy for over seven years and even spent considerable effort nursing Boy back to health after the cat had sustained an injury.

Then came the day that George heard Stanley screaming and ran to his aid. George found Boy with Stanley in his jaws.

George later described the scene in his book:

"As I rushed toward him, shouting, Boy dropped Stanley . . . Stanley was left on the ground, covered with blood. I strode past Stanley, raised my rifle, and shot Boy through the heart. Making certain that he was dead or dying, I turned back to Stanley. As I started to examine the wound on his neck, Stanley died. He had bled to death in less than ten minutes from the moment he had first cried out."[60]

I wiped my eyes. The shock of Stanley meeting such a horrific death seared my soul. Also, my brain was trying to absorb the fact that George had shot his dear lion friend of seven years, stone cold dead, right then and there. In later years, I read how George was never able to talk about the two deaths without his voice breaking. I heard conflicting reports that the Murithii family had buried their young son, only twenty-eight years old, when he was killed, near their village, many miles away, or that no family had been found and his remains instead were placed in a common grave. George Adamson made the firm request that his own remains were to be interred alongside Boy, when the time came. At the time of his passing about eighteen years later, George's grave was placed near Boy, just as he had requested.

During my adult years, I purchased a copy of *Born Free* and meticulously freeze-framed every scene I could find that

---

60   George Adamson, *My Pride and Joy*, 1987.

featured an adult male. I scrutinized these endlessly. Was that Boy? Was that Fire? Wasn't his mane darker? It might well have been neither cat, for all I knew. YouTube did have, I found, videos of George and Boy but these invariably brought me to tears after only a few seconds.

But back on that night, in the early 1970s, I was just a little girl who had learned of two horrific deaths, and I was barely absorbing the conversations swirling around me. There were some sympathetic murmurs going around the table, along with "Quite right" and "Poor Stanley."

"Once they are man-eaters," Mother chimed in. "You can't do anything about it."

Sister abruptly got to her feet and began clearing away our plates.

"So Boy was in *Born Free*? Didn't you say your male lion was in *Born Free* too, Sister?" Dad asked.

Mother kicked him under the table.

Our hostess muttered something along the lines of "Yes, well, Fire would never be like that" as she quickly left the room.

I was not able to resist the temptation to shoot a triumphant look over at Mother.

Yes, Fire would never be like that.

Chapter 43
Limpy Lou

"I didn't visit the donkeys after that."

—Me

Tanzania, early 1970s

A stable was always a delight for me. Here at the lodge, the nun had a pony stabled as well as her own horse. Regretfully, I remember next to nothing about the pony. The poor thing was utterly and completely eclipsed by the nun's magnificent mare. Queen of Diamonds was a beautiful gray mare with an expressive and lovely face. David, the *syce*[61] there at the stables, was delighted that I was a horse enthusiast and regaled me with tales of the mare's many admirable exploits.

We had already become David and Missy Caffee to one another. David was an accomplished rider but said Diamond was off-limits to anyone except Sister, and that even when walking the horses to and from the grazing pasture, he remained on foot beside them the whole time. "Rules are rules."

David's duties varied widely. "Basically anything except

---
61 groom, stablehand

the cats" was how he put it. The lion's share of his duties, he said, was his stable yard duties pertaining to the donkeys and horses here. The pun worked just as well in Swahili.

"I heard that Sister goes into the lion cage to visit Fire unarmed," I said to him one day, while the two of us were grooming Diamond. *Foolhardy*, I thought. "And she goes without even a *panga*[62] or a *rungu*."

"Or *this*," the *syce* said, and patted his holstered pistol before taking the curry brush from me and handing me a comb instead for her mane.

"Perhaps God is giving her special protection?" he suggested. "She's the only one who really loves him. She prays he will become gentle. He has never hurt her. She tell us *hakuna shida*,[63] but the staff who have to do his feeding and the cage cleaning only go in when they are armed." A pause. "I'm glad my duties are not with the cats."

"Please tell me," I said, combing out a tangle in her mane, "do you suppose I may ride Diamond, perhaps?" I tried not to sound too beseeching. The mare was incomparably beautiful and had almost a balletic gait.

"Nobody rides Diamond except Sister." The *syce* laughed, seeing my exaggerated pout. But we lamented together, since he would have also loved the chance. But rules were rules.

One rule I couldn't understand involved the donkeys.

During my visits to the stables, I was frequently, and gently, and consistently, steered away from spending any time with the ragged assortment of donkeys in the large pen. If any lodge staff member found me at the donkey pen caressing one of those velvety noses, he would abruptly summon me away to help groom the horses. If I were found stroking the

---

62   machete
63   no worries

chocolately brown stripe, in the shape of a cross, found on the donkeys' shoulders, someone was sure to thrust a broom in my hands and say, "Let us now sweep the stable yard together." I soon learned to stop singing little songs to the donkeys, because the staff would find me sooner and divert me away quicker. Whispering little lullabies stealthily into those absurdly long and furry ears usually didn't draw too much attention, happily.

Several of the donkeys were in their dotage. Others were limping, I noted with concern. If either of the horses had even the slightest scratch, the veterinarian was summoned without delay. He was also called when any of the big cats needed attention for any medical matter. But the donkey pen had several occupants with various afflictions, and none of these generated a call to the vet. My queries about when the vet would turn his attention to them went unanswered.

I found David walking to the donkey pen one afternoon and caught up to him as he began leading one donkey out of the pen, Limpy Lou.

"Oh, hooray!" I called out to him. "Is this one finally headed to the vet?"

"Aah!" David recoiled, spun around, and stiffened, staring at me wide-eyed.

"Aah!" said another staff member behind me, Matthew, who exchanged glances with David. This time I was gently shooed out of the stable yard completely, all the while complaining to Matthew about being constantly thwarted or foiled in my efforts to be with Eeyore and company.

Flinging my arms wide in exasperation, I couldn't seem to make Matthew listen to my bitter, indignant but very legitimate complaint. "Hey! Hey! David just dodged my question! All I wanted to know was whether the vet was—"

Bang!
Matthew stopped. I came to a standstill.
Firecracker?
No, that was a gunshot.
I gave a sidelong glance to Matthew.
Limpy Lou is probably startled and needs to be comforted. If I bolt quickly enough, I can make it back to the stables before he can catch me.

"Ah, Miss! *Hapana! Hapana!*"[64] Matthew shouted uselessly as I ran straight back to the stables. I found David behind the main stalls.

Limpy Lou was collapsed on the ground in front of him. She was lying on her side, one hind leg kicking with increasing feebleness.

For several seconds, nothing moved except that one convulsing leg.

It wasn't even her limping leg.

I looked at David, who had heard my gasp and met my wide eyes with profound grief, his shoulders heaving as mine were. Her leg stopped moving, and I looked at the donkey carcass. That was all she really was now.

David carefully put his firearm back into his holster.

The slight cloud of gunpowder was dissipating, but the scent still hung in the air.

As I fled the stable yard, my feet winged by horror, I almost knocked over Matthew coming back in. This time he wasn't trying to steer me away anymore. He was avoiding my eyes and pushed an empty wheelbarrow.

A wheelbarrow with a creaking wheel.

I ran past the man behind him, who was carrying two *pangas*.

---

64   No!

I ran past the gate for the lions' enclosure, where they were all assembled, all alert and expectant.

I ran back up the driveway that no veterinarian would travel on their way to administer donkey care.

It wasn't long before Dad found me seated at the foot of my bed in our room, sobbing and rocking, tears streaming onto the pillow I clutched tightly to my chest. I shook my head mutely when he asked anxiously if I had been bitten or hurt. Still mystified, he then sat beside his keening daughter, drew me into his arms silently, and we rocked together as I cried.

"Sweetheart . . ." Dad took me by the shoulders and searched my face tenderly. "What is it?"

One of his hands gently stroked the hair out of my eyes, bumping into my own raised hand. My tremulous hand was up at the level of my head, thumb extended to the ceiling and first finger extended, pointed to my temple.

"Gun?" he asked, uncomprehendingly.

I nodded mutely, my constricted throat slowly loosening, and drew a deep shuddering breath. Then I told him about the *raison d'etre* for the donkeys.

"Oh, Dad, why does a carnivore have to be a carnivore?"

Dad just held me and rocked me some more.

Chapter 44
Feeder Fish and Donkey Hides

Ejiao can fetch around $400 per pound.
　　　　　　　　　　　　　　—*The New York Times*, 2018

Dear Catherine,
The families were broken because of poverty, and children were the most affected. As a result, they had to be taken to other relatives. There are situations where the children went to cities to become beggars.
　　　　　　　　　　　　　　—Dr. Thomas, TAWESO

Tanzania, circa 2017

As a result of my African childhood, I had begrudgingly accepted the unassailable fact that something needs to die for a carnivore to eat. However, sometimes the opportunity comes to snatch a would-be victim from the jaws of another creature. In later years, I often found myself walking out of pet stores with odd purchases.

"You want to buy a feeder fish? As a *pet*?" a store clerk asked me one day.

"Yes, that's right."

"Um." The clerk was clearly puzzled. "People usually buy

our feeder fish to be fed to . . ."

"Yes, that's right."

He held my gaze for a few seconds, then returned my smile as he shrugged and rang up my purchase. He was still smiling as I left the store with my new pet.

Even so, it wasn't until I returned to Tanzania in 2017 that I learned of the other details regarding the death of Limpy Lou and the other donkeys at the nun's lodge. It turned out different parts of those carcasses went to different destinations.

This, I learned during a conversation with Dr. Thomas. The two of us had been discussing the details of the adoption of my cat, Stanley. I was surprised to learn that Dr. Thomas had perhaps only a dozen rescued cats and dogs available for adoption in his entire animal welfare organization.

"Why so few?"

"Donkeys." He shrugged with a smile, and explained a large percentage of his time was spent out in the rural villages, focusing on donkey welfare. "We have to help stop the donkey skin trade."

It was from him I first learned that a global trade in donkey hides existed, and that donkeys were possibly the most trafficked animal in the world. From around 2015 onward, over one million donkey skins were being traded per year. A vast percentage of these were from Africa.

A vague memory flitted across my mind. There had been an Asian gentleman who made regular visits to the nun's lodge. He always departed with one or more rolled-up donkey hides on his bicycle, and I had never thought to ask why.

When I asked Dr. Thomas what the donkey hides were used for, he explained that once the hides were boiled, a gelatin was extracted, which is a prized ingredient in Chinese traditional medicine.

"*Ejiao*," he said, a name that sounded like "uh-jee-ow" to me. This *ejiao* was sought after by many Chinese as an antiaging substance, which was purported to also increase libido. It was often sold for over three hundred American dollars per pound.

"Not just *sold*," he clarified. "Donkey hides are in such high demand, the hides are . . ." A pause for emphasis. —"being *stolen*."

Now that I was suitably shocked, he proceeded to unfold the full horror for me. The theft of donkeys was rampant across Africa, he said. In several instances, rural villagers in Tanzania had woken to find the carcasses of every last donkey in their village, stolen, killed, and stripped of their hides overnight. Donkeys who had drawn their plows, carried their water, pulled their carts, and served as their pack animals. All dead and skinned.

Every last one.

Without them, the entire village was doomed. It fell to the humans to undertake the labor previously supplied by the donkeys. Humans then carried loads on their own shoulders to and from market, hauled water and firewood, and used hand hoes in their farming. It was untenable, and their previous critical level of poverty descended yet further until families actually broke up. Children, if they were lucky, were often sent to live with relatives in villages who still had donkeys, and adults often migrated to cities to seek employment. Some sold their land. Girls lost their opportunity for education overnight, since the school fees could no longer be paid. Without education, skills or money, these rural villagers arriving in the cities joined the already oversaturated ranks of the urban street peddlers and beggars. Frequently the women became *mama ntilie*,[65] selling prepared food or sugar cane on the street, especially porridge, and the men turned to petty trading, as hawkers or street vendors, nicknamed *machinga*. The children begged while walking between cars stopped at each red traffic light. By the end of each day they all fell under the label of *walala hoi*, explained to me as "hard labor, the people who go to sleep exhausted and hungry." My own personal memories contained multiple instances of street vendors selling me handfuls of roasted peanuts for almost nothing, which I would receive neatly contained in a paper cone made from sheets of newspaper, cones created deftly by them in mere seconds.

The children's nursery rhyme "The kingdom was lost, and all for want of a horseshoe nail" came to mind as I was being told the grim donkey-related facts. Farms gone to rack and ruin. Thousands of rural Tanzanian families, plunged into poverty overnight, having been so cruelly robbed of the basic instrument of their livelihood—one simple donkey.

TAWESO spends considerable time petitioning lawmakers to create protective legislation to thwart the donkey hide trade. This is, of course, a moot point for the villagers already bereft of their livestock. However, some rural villages do still have some of their donkeys left, and in these cases, TAWESO pours massive efforts into safeguarding these remaining animals from theft and improving their condition. Sturdy enclosures are built, hoof overgrowth is tended to, neck wounds from ill-fitting yokes receive care and frequently the model of the donkey carts is changed to a more efficient design. All of which has a direct positive effect on the farmers, who can then get their work done more efficiently and feed

---

65   Women who sell food or sugarcane on the street. Literally "Mother, put it on my plate!"

their families.

While the rescue of a companion animal may bring pleasure, to rescue an agricultural animal has the additional benefit of aiding the livelihood of the animal's owner.

And the livelihood of many African farmers is tenuous at best, to begin with. In many cases, these same farmers are also feeding their desperate donkey-less relatives, who have now come to live with them. And the unscrupulous donkey hide trade is still happening all across the world, in various developing countries.

When I asked Dr. Thomas if the demand for hides could be met by creating breeding farms instead, he replied somberly that it would still be impossible to keep up with the demand for hides, because donkeys only foal once per year on average. Very little legislation existed to protect them.

"The situation could not," he said, "be more dire."

Chapter 45
Seven Stumped Vets

Dear Dr. Thomas,
Stanley is still a bit mkali sana[66] *so I keep him locked away from Saba.*
Catherine

Virginia, USA, circa 2017

Still unresolved was the issue of Stanley's periodic episodes of aggression toward Saba. My vet had ruled out all the most obvious possible causes and was stumped.

"Perhaps," she suggested, "a baby gate could be used to separate the two combatants?"

So a baby gate was begrudgingly purchased, and my newly barricaded kitchen was given over to Stanley. Thankfully Stanley, with his diminished brain and physical impairments, could not scale a simple baby gate. Meanwhile, Saba, lithe and limber and in possession of a full brain, wisely chose not to scale the simple baby gate and avoided the area.

I turned once more to the mystery of his aggression. I owed Saba a secure and safe home. Stanley too. But how did

---
66   fierce

one solve a mystery with so few clues?

That crushing despair I felt when I first realized, months ago, that this cat had brain damage had returned. Now that I was faced with the additional problem of irregular bouts of aggression, I was completely despondent. Sometimes all I could do was to join Stanley on the kitchen floor, hold my cubbie in my arms, and rock him while I prayed for a solution.

My vet's suggestion to seek a second opinion seemed to be a reasonable place to start. I launched on a desperate tour, scouring the landscape for any clinician who might help. I begged, wheedled and cajoled, and quite rapidly Stanley's dance card was filling up with multiple veterinarian appointments.

The vets all initially seemed delighted to try to tackle this challenge. But invariably, every last one of them was stymied. Some would start to explain to me aspects of CH of which I was already familiar. I only barely managed to squash down my childhood habit of "So, anyway, go on" and listen patiently instead.

The endearing whimsicality of Stanley's character was on full display, so my recounts of vicious fights might not have sounded credible. My conversations with them would always come back to the same subject: "Is it his CH that is causing this?"

"Well, yes, he has a cranial anomaly," the various vets would say, "but not all CH cats have aggression issues, and lots of normal cats do have aggression issues. For instance, have you ever seen that TV show called *My Cat—*"

"—*From Hell*, yes," I continued icily, "but my cat is not from hell."

"Well, perhaps your other cat, Saba, thinks otherwise."

Off I went to make more appointments.

A veterinary behaviorist was the next in line, since I wanted to see if his CH was masking a behavioral issue. This new vet made a home visit, and we made polite small talk as I moved piles of Stanley's freshly laundered towels and pee pads off the sofa. Soon the two of us were seated there with Stanley, with the vet scratching my cat behind the ears while I described the fights where Stan would assail and assault Saba. During the entire visit, my "vicious" cat was instead in one of his purr-purr-purr moods, meek as a lamb with paws demurely folded, and to my frustration I could see the behaviorist was probably underestimating the severity of the problem.

I told him that Stanley had repeatedly attacked Saba.

"It's perfectly normal for cats to have an occasional falling out."

I told him that Stanley had actually caused wounds to Saba. Wounds that required vet care.

"That's different. That's bad."

"Right."

Next the lab results were reviewed.

"Ah, yes. The thyroid levels are normal," he said. "I'm seeing no adrenal dysfunction, and we've ruled out toothache. And it's not play aggression. And it's not territorial aggression."

Nothing new here yet . . .

If only this aggression *had* been caused by one of these factors, a solution would have been so much more readily available. It was the not knowing that was killing me. We each absent-mindedly stroked the relaxed cat between us. Stanley contently groomed himself.

I feebly joked that perhaps my cat was auditioning for that TV show about aggressive cats.

"Yes!" This got a burst of laughter from the behaviorist, who added, "I wasn't sure if I could mention *My Cat From Hell* because I didn't want to hurt your feelings."

In the following days, I filled the prescription for anti-aggression tablets that the behaviorist had recommended but continued with more appointments with more specialists.

"Don't bother taking that CH cat to any neurologist," I had been told. "Why bother? It's not like they could give him back the missing part of his brain."

So off I went to a veterinary neurologist with my incorrigible cat.

We soon found ourselves in a typical neurology office, where cats, mostly seizure cats I guessed, were treated.

"Does your cat ever have seizures?" was the first thing that the vet tech wanted to know, glancing at my yawning cat. The front desk receptionist had already asked me the same thing. Stan paid no attention as he groomed his white-tipped paws. Within minutes, the neurologist himself strode in, also inquiring very earnestly whether my cat had ever had, perhaps, any seizures that I might know of, by any chance? I answered each one politely, but then I noticed something.

Stanley was now up on the examining table.

And now my cat's tone of voice had changed.

No longer was I hearing his customary peevish little meows that he regularly voiced with all previous vets.

Today he was growling. A low, deep, menacing growl.

"Really, Mother?" his eyes said. "This is the *sixth* different vet you've brought me to. *Really*, Mother?" My poor cat had already been poked and prodded by so very many different veterinarians.

Stanley had borne it as long as he could. There comes a limit. I had hoped he would be cooperative today.

He wasn't.

Today his thinly veiled threats were no longer quite so thinly veiled. He glared with flagrant fury at any staff member who came near him, his growls rising to an ominous pitch. This did not bode well. The vet stepped toward Stan, thermometer in hand, but hastily stepped back again as Stan, no longer saber-rattling, attempted to lunge at him, teeth at the ready.

"Oh." The vet was taken aback, and exchanged knowing glances with the vet tech, who abruptly left the room.

"Your cat is saying," he said, chuckling with forced nonchalance, "he's a teensy bit upset."

The message I instead heard in my mutinous cat's yowls was: "Right. The first one of you to touch me had jolly well better summon a hearse."

"Ha, ha," the vet continued, feigned cheerfulness still in place. "Now, if it's okay with you . . ." Two vet techs entered the room. "We will just take him in the back and finish our examination of him there." The two vet techs advanced upon Stanley, who was now screaming blue murder, whirling to face them, incandescent with rage, while I peeked through fanned fingers. They deftly wrapped him in a big blanket and left the room with their struggling, screaming bundle.

Screams that were admittedly slightly muffled by the blanket but seemed as clear as day to be "I am *fed up* with you lot! *Fed up, I* say! Let me *go*!"

All this white-hot fury from Stan, and for once, Saba was nowhere around. This neurologist now earned the dubious distinction of being the first vet to be left in no doubt as to my description of Stanley's rages, nor his ability to rain hellfire down on Saba.

The vet followed his two technicians out the door, tossing one last remark back over his shoulder at me.

"Your cat seems to think he is a star on that television show called—"

And the door slammed shut.

It was a safe bet he wasn't referring to the *Annual Kitten Superbowl*.

About a half hour later, Stan and I were back in the car on the way home. This vet had been the sixth who had been unable to tell me a cause for the aggression, although he had taught me a new word. My cat's staggering was clinically known as a "titubar gait." This vet also added the crushing verdict that "there is nothing we can do for him neurologically, but, by the way, did you know he can't see very well?"

I was thunderstruck. Barely in time, I stopped myself from asking, "Truth-Truth, doctor?" None of the previous vets who had assessed this cat had ever mentioned any vision issues. Not one.

I wiped away many a tear during that car ride home that day. I was the owner of a cat who had the staircasing issues of brain damage, needed strict caloric monitoring, needed daily baths, had aggression and a titubar gait, and now he needed an eye appointment.

Days later, I lifted my cat onto the veterinary eye specialist's examining table with some trepidation about whether he would behave as abominably for this vet as he had done for the last one.

The remaining portions of Stanley's brain reached the firm but unwarranted conclusion that his life was under dire threat from the eye veterinarian, so the cat behaved correspondingly. Stan was in full cry once again. His shrieks, screams and struggles were heard throughout the entire building. The staff were polite about Stanley's outburst, although clearly relieved when the exam was over.

"Oh, yes, poor vision. Very poor vision," came the brisk diagnosis, and Stan was once again bundled back into his carrier. The laden carrier was gingerly handed back to me. They laughed politely at my feeble quips that if Stanley kept fighting with Saba, I would end up with two crossed eyes, compounding the one crossed eye I had from birth. My stammering attempts to joke about *My Cat From Hell* were similarly only met with more forced smiles. I paid and hastily left.

The other new, hurtful word I heard that day attributed to my beloved and blighted cat had come from an offhand remark from one of the vet techs who could not offer an answer about the aggression either.

"Maybe your cat is just a turd."

Chapter 46
La Luna

Dear Dad,
At night the moon is full, it is so light, it shines on the ocean.
—Me

"The moon rained molten silver over the dark foliage of the wild palms, the stars were as golden lamps suspended in the limpid air, and Venus glittered diamond-like upon the front of the firmament."
—Richard Francis Burton, Pangani River, Tanzania, 1856,
The Life of Captain Sir Richard F. Burton

Dar es Salaam, early 1970s

Fins, feathers and fur had all been woven into my childhood. Now I could add hooves.

I rode for several hours each week at an English riding school fondly known as "the Ranch," and featuring a neighing, whickering and whinnying medley of bay, white, black and chestnut horses.

We girls, African and expatriate, forged friendships with each *syce*, along with each *farasi*.[67] We'd been instructed to

---
67   horse and pony

mount our horses from the ground up, no mounting block allowed, but frequently when the owner, Ms. Voss was looking the other way, the *syce* would cup his hands, with fingers laced together, and surreptitiously give us a leg up.

"*Pole, Madam!*" he would apologize if Ms. Voss caught him out. "But is little girl! Is big horse!"

Our rides took place in either a paddock for lessons or a bush ride, all on soft ground that muffled the hoofbeats. It was only when I rode at other locations that I would then hear the clip clop of hooves, and it struck me as such a novel and delightful sound.

No bush ride was more eagerly awaited, however, than the midnight ride. Once each year, Ms. Voss organized a ride to take place in the middle of the night, and each year, two dozen little girls, giddy with excitement, descended upon the stables far, far, past their bedtime and usually in fits of giggles. There was usually such a great emphasis in Africa to be safely indoors before nightfall that this midnight ride was an extremely unusual treat.

We rode under clear, starlit skies made yet more clear by the lack of pollution in the African air. We rode in squeaky old saddles over hard-packed earth and barely dodged tree branches hanging in our path. Our excitement must have been contagious, because every horse on that ride had an extra spring in their step. No galloping was allowed on those rides, but we'd jump our horses over every fallen log we found.

These midnight rides are amongst the happiest of all my African memories.

On the night when I had my very first midnight ride, I was still smiling, still imbecilic all the way home in the car. My family at home would all be sensibly fast asleep, whereas I was still wide awake, ruminating over that ride with delight.

And one more happy event awaited me; Tomorrow morning I would have the chance to relive and savor every moment of this ride. Nonna was here visiting us from Italy, and she was perhaps my most ardent supporter in my rabid enthusiasm for all things horse-related.

Nonna had been a keen and accomplished equestrienne. She would listen, enraptured, to my childish warblings about any ride, eventful or not, and had the grace to pose questions to her small granddaughter as though I were a peer. Had I ridden in a Pelham? she'd want to know, validating her small granddaughter whose legs were barely yet the length to reach particularly far down a horse's barrel. Had I been careful to rise the fewest inches possible during a posting trot? Did the horse have a smooth gait? How I looked forward to seeing her tomorrow morning!

However, upon arriving home, a pleasant surprise awaited me.

"What do you mean, Nonna is still awake?"

Mother shrugged. "She's still awake. Upstairs, on the terrace. She stayed up, wanted to hear about your midnight ride."

I scampered upstairs, as Mother called out after me, "Mind you don't keep your grandmother up, it's almost two o'clock in the morning! The both of you ought to be in bed!" She muttered to herself how these midnight rides were such a ridiculous idea. "At this hour!"

I found Nonna on our terrace, where a single candle flickered beside the remains of a mosquito coil long ago burned out, the dropped ash still holding its spiral shape. In the dim light, Nonna was leaning on the railing and stargazing so intently that she only turned her eyes from the skies upon hearing the clomping of my riding boots as I crossed the floor.

"Ah, Cathy dearest!" Turning to me, she beamed with delight. She reached out a slender arm from under her shawl, drawing me to her side. I sighed with immense satisfaction, settling myself to stand beside her at the balcony railing. A feeling of delicious anticipation enveloped me—I now could discuss horses to my heart's delight with my favorite fellow horse enthusiast.

"Ah, Cathy dearest," she repeated, her eyes gazing up at the stars again. "You are so... . How you call it . . . ?" She searched for the words in English. "You are so fortunate to see the stars upside-down!"

Stars? She wants to discuss stars? Ask me about my ride!

Blinking hard and holding my tongue, I cast a quick glance at her. My beloved grandmother always lovingly and selflessly asked me copious questions about subjects I liked. I knew, somewhat crestfallen now, that I could do no less.

Squaring my shoulders, I dutifully joined her in gazing up at the inky black African sky with its brilliant stars. Being so enthralled with the fauna of Africa, I had barely paid any attention to the sky. Though I had vaguely noticed that the stars in the African skies were very bright.

It had been a matter of no consequence to me, aged eight, that these were the skies gazed upon by earliest humans, millions of years ago, and that these were skies of unparalleled beauty.

But what she had said baffled me. Head tilted slightly to one side, I said, "The stars are upside-down, Nonna?"

"No," she said. "Is . . . is not the *stars* which are upside-down." Her hands made a corralling motion as though she was gathering a group of items together. "Is not the stars. Is the *constellations* of the stars! *La constelli* . . . You see, it is *they* who are upside-down!"

She spoke haltingly as she stared up at them, eyes glistening in rapt fascination. "You see, in my gardens, at home, in Italy, I am above the equator. I see only the Northern Hemisphere sky. And when you are home in Canada, my darling, you, too, see only the Northern Hemisphere sky." More murmurs of delight from her. "But here! Here you are *below* the equator! Now you have all the beauties of the Southern Hemisphere sky!" She ended with another rapturous sigh.

I opened my mouth to blurt out the polite observation that she probably saw these same stars all those years when she lived in Eritrea, but I quickly closed it again when I remembered, just in time, that Eritrea was also above the equator. Successfully having withheld The Blurts tonight filled me with relief.

"See! See there, *Il Cacciatore*," she said, lapsing back into the habit of mixing different words from different languages in the same sentence. "The Hunter?"

Loath to reveal my abysmal knowledge of astronomy, I nodded with a wavering smile in the general direction of Orion.

"His head is down toward the ground, instead of standing up!" She laughed. "Here in the Southern Hemisphere, I must relearn all the stars."

I stared down at my riding boots, hoping against hope she would come around to the subject of horses.

Nonna, however, was freshly invigorated, pointing out Alpha Centauri and the Southern Cross. "Is just there . . . There, you see?" She pointed with her arm fully extended, almost on tiptoe. "Is very small. You see?"

"*There*, Nonna?"

"No, not that one," came her gentle correction, when I pointed out the False Cross instead of the Southern Cross.

"That one is *la falsa croce*."

Soon it became painfully evident to her that I couldn't find the real Southern Cross either. I nodded politely, my fingers twirling the braid in my hair and shifting my weight from foot to foot. Perhaps it was becoming painfully obvious to her that my knowledge of astronomy was tenuous at best.

Ever the diplomat, she graciously turned to more familiar subjects.

"*La luna!*" she said brightly.

"Yes!" I was immensely grateful that she was now directing her attention to the moon, the one celestial body I could reliably identify. Grasping for any comment I could contribute, I started jabbering about everything I had been told about the moon landing of 1969, just two years ago. The thought of man walking on the moon was almost too much for my brain to absorb.

"*Ecco, allora,*" she went on, brows furrowed in concentration. "The waning crescent moon—see now, because we are *below* the equator, it is the *left* side that is dark. You see? And when it is a waxing moon, then the *right* side is dark. Is the opposite of what I see in Italy."

"Mmm." I found I could suppress the urge to drum my fingers on the terrace railing if I rummaged through the pockets of my riding pants instead.

"You see the *mare?*" She tried to show her earnestly squinting granddaughter a tiny dark splotch, which was one of the oceans of the moon. "If we had a telescope, I think we would see that it is now is at the *bottom* edge of the moon, instead of above."

My fingers came across a round object in my pocket: small, round, unrecognizable. I stared uncomprehendingly at it for a few seconds.

"Is a seashell?" asked Nonna, following my gaze, also puzzled.

"A carrot!" we both exclaimed simultaneously. She and I always carried them for horses when we rode. Nonna emerged from the mesmerizing African night sky's enchantment, and we laughed as we gazed at the carrot morsel and passed it back and forth. How could I have failed to remember to give my horse his treat?

"Ah, my dearest," Nonna said now, turning to me with her full attention. "You went riding! *Dimmi tutto!*"[68]

With her arm around my shoulders, we left the railing and made our way to the terrace bench, where she sat down and patted the seat beside her. The candle on the nearby table was now almost burned down. She wrapped me in a fold of her shawl that wafted Chanel N°5, cuddling me close.

And so, there under the Southern Hemisphere stars, which had gazed down upon earliest man, I recounted to her every last detail.

Years later, my mother told me that she had come to the terrace wondering why I wasn't in bed yet. She had been intending to admonish her mum to stop chuntering on about stars, and she planned to firmly whisk me off to bed.

However, upon catching sight of the magical little tableau—a rapturously delighted little girl, up far, far past her bedtime, reveling in the deliciousness of a long-awaited, horse-saturated discussion in the encircling arms of the enthralled wise, older equestrian, also up far past her bedtime—Mother tiptoed silently backward away.

---

[68] Tell me everything!

Chapter 47
Regrets and Mongooses

They strayed into one of the neighboring yards, one of the houses behind us, which would have fronted Toure Drive. That gardener thought they were wild.

—Craig

Dar es Salaam, early 1970s

Within the first two years of my childhood in Tanzania we had become the owners of three mongooses. Dad's repeated warning that mongooses should not be pets was being borne out. To my disappointment, I soon learned that Fupi the Third (our mongoose from Mafia Island) was even more prone to biting than the first two had been. Worse yet, all three animals would frequently bite the ankles of the staff serving us at the table. My own ankles were strangely ignored. Instead, my hands bore the brunt of their needle-sharp little teeth. The frequency was more annoying to me than the depth of their nips. The only pattern as to when they'd bite me was when they felt peeved. Their capricious irritability manifested itself whether I was raiding their nest for stolen items or merely walking past them.

The final straw, however, came when Fupi the Third inflicted a severe bite on Craig. He had found the mongoose in his room, rummaging underneath his bedside table, and he reached in to haul the mongoose out.

"He slashed me with his teeth," Craig said. "It was very fast and like being cut by a razor." Thankfully this wound was successfully treated at home. But it didn't do any good to the relationship between Craig and the mongooses. From that point on, his bedroom door remained firmly shut, off-limits to all mongooses, at all hours of the day or night.

The other result of this incident was that now the Mafia mongoose was mostly banished to his cage until we could come up with a suitable plan of where and when to release him back into the wild. This was becoming the increasingly obvious choice, since being caged only heightened his irritability as time went on. At one point, he escaped from his cage and had a short-lived reign of terror over our household. Craig was bitten again, souring the relationship yet further, if such a thing was possible. Finally, someone caught the animal and stuffed him back into his cage. Any further escapes were thwarted as the cage holding the bane of my existence was then reinforced with stronger wire.

Fupi and the other Fupi, meanwhile, were roaming further and further afield with every passing day, in their exploration of our garden and surrounding neighborhood. Wisely, they avoided cars and motorcycles. The sound of Craig roaring down the driveway on his chrome steed was enough to send them into hiding for hours.

They would return to the house for meals, but even those visits were becoming fewer.

Our cook was just as pleased to have fewer requests for eggs now. The requests usually came from me, spoken timidly from the kitchen doorway, until Nonna learned I was giving the eggs to the mongooses.

"My granddaughter wants an egg," she would announce to the cook, as she strode right past him and took an egg from the refrigerator herself. She would march past him on her way back out, as he hastily stood out of her way with his back pressed up against the wall, and she'd find me just outside the door, gawking in admiration. She'd hand over the egg to me with a wink, and Dad was none the wiser.

The household spoons were being stolen with less frequency now, but I still had days of finding one or two in their nest. Instead of thrice weekly raids, I now visited their nest perhaps only once each week. Invariably the nest would also contain miscellaneous items from each member of the family. There might be a silver foil wrapper from Mother's cigarettes, or a pen to be returned to Dad.

"I've been looking for that! Far out! Where was it?" Craig was delighted when I handed back to him one of his guitar picks from the mongoose nest. The mongooses would steal my little rubber Pokey and Gumby toys, which would be mixed amongst my old Rowntree fruit gum wrappers, which in turn would be amongst maybe a couple of Barrel of Monkeys figures interspersed with Jelly Babies packets, Polo sweets, and Mackintosh toffee wrappers.

Perhaps *nil desperandum*[69] was part of their mongoose credo, because they stayed on task. No matter how often I cleaned out their nest, they continued to steal.

Over time, our life with three mongooses settled into a slightly smoother pattern, with fewer bites, what with two away from home so often and the third safely caged.

Our property backed onto another property that faced

---

69 never despair

Toure Drive. That family happened to have a very dedicated gardener who was meticulously careful to control the rat population, keeping a careful watch, day and night.

Our gardener approached my mother one morning, our neighbor's gardener behind him. "*Madam?* May I speak with you?"

"I was so glad you were at school," she told me later, shaking her head slightly at the memory. "You didn't need to see that."

Our gardener wore a solemn expression. The neighbor's gardener was openly sorrowful. He was carrying two dead mongooses in his hands. The poor man could not have been more grief-stricken had he been King Lear carrying the corpses of two dead Cordelias in his arms. Fupi and the other Fupi had been mistaken for rats the night before, in the dim light of his lantern, and had been summarily dispatched. Upon closer inspection of the corpses, however, he saw to his horror that he had actually killed the pets of his *mzungu* neighbors.

Mother requested that the little bodies be hastily buried, before her daughter came home from school. Mother had become decreasingly fond of all the mongooses once they grew into adults prone to biting but still was very sorrowful about the deaths. She also spent considerable effort trying to comfort the nearly inconsolable and deeply remorseful next-door gardener.

"*Daaah! Pole sana Madam! Samahani sana!*"[70]

In the days that followed, our family grieved the two departed mongooses and pondered the fate of the third. Reluctantly, the entire family soon came to the agreement that Dad had been right all along and that keeping a wild animal was untenable. And, we sadly admitted, in all the time

---

[70] I'm so sorry

we had mongooses, we never once witnessed our little snake-killers actually killing a live snake. Fupi the Third was last seen scampering out of his cage as we released him in a large sisal field.

In the days that followed, I wrestled with the conflicting feelings of relief that peace was restored to the house and grief for the lost pups. Alice had no such conflicting feelings and was grateful to no longer be spat upon. Still, the house was strangely quiet, with a complete absence of squeaking and chittering and churring. All thievery stopped. Our spoons stayed in their proper drawers, my toys stayed in my room, and my candy wrappers stayed in my wastepaper basket.

Decades later, when I returned to Tanzania as an adult, I did catch a glimpse of a mongoose on one occasion, in a game park, though it wasn't banded.

"I had the banded ones as pets!" I whispered excitedly to my guide while trying to get a picture.

"Oh, *Mamma*," he said, frowning slightly, "none of the mongooses make good pets." Before I could reply with "So I learned," this particular mongoose disappeared back into the bush.

I lowered my camera and slouched back down in my seat. As the driver proceeded along, I gazed at the one mongoose photograph on my camera that I had managed to snap.

Nope, not as cute as mine had been.

I caught him glancing at me with sympathy, and to my surprise we soon stopped at a public rest stop within the game park.

"Come, I will find banded ones for you," he said, gesturing me to come sit on a bench that was unpleasantly close to a rather overflowing garbage can. As we walked toward the trash receptacle, a small colony of mongooses did—as he must have known they would—appear from within. *Banded!* They skittered away as we approached. There had not been enough time in this instance, either, for me to snap a picture, but at least we returned to the car with the satisfaction of a sighting—albeit very brief and at a distance—of banded mongooses.

After I moved back to North America, I often sought out the mongooses in the zoos I would visit. But sometimes an ordinary trip to the zoo felt like a bizarre experience. It was comforting to see African wildlife again, but incongruous to see my beloved old free-roaming friends now ensconced in enclosures. It was also an uncomfortable reminder that I knew far more about African animals than those from Canada.

For whatever reason, most zoos I visited tended to keep Indian mongooses. It took me a while to find the familiar African ones. Finally came the day when I had found a zoo that proudly announced that they had East African banded mongooses on display. I peered into the glassed-in enclosure hopefully but only saw one small, furry, indistinguishable little rump hidden in his den in the far reaches of his cage. Daring to hope he would emerge to give me a better look, I resolutely stood in front of this one particular cage and waited. The mongoose slowly started to venture out. A thrill went through me as he came closer to the glass, and I got a clear look at the brown bands of darker brown fur crossing his brindle back. Yes! Exactly as I had remembered! For a split second, various memories flitted across my mind. I could see Pravin walking in with the basket. I saw Mother fawning over the tiny pup, and how I would bring the pups with me up into my tree house. The memories of the three Fupis and their egg trick or spoon theft brought a wistful smile to my face. I now dared to hope that this animal would come close enough to the glass that I might see that characteristic little pale nose, and if I was lucky, maybe the horizontal pupils as well.

He was heading right toward me.

I held my breath.

Only a few more feet.

Then: *Bang!* A little boy next to me smacked his palm hard on the glass, and the startled mongoose fled back into its den.

The boy laughed hysterically. His mother yanked him hard away from the glass, and I left the building for fear that my barely squelched rage might instead burst forth. An hour later, fury abated, I crept back to visit the mongoose once more. The annoying child was out of sight, but sadly so was the mongoose.

Someone later told me that the African mongooses have been replaced with Indian ones. I never went back.

Fupi, Fupi and Fupi will never leave my memory. I miss hearing their chittering throughout the house, and my mother would frequently tell the story of her lit cigarettes being stolen from her lips. I'm reminded of them when I watch the antics of ferrets for sale in an American pet store. Certain candy wrappers now bring me right back to the times I had to extract these from the mongoose nests.

I miss the mongooses.

But I don't miss the bites.

Chapter 48
Two Empty Cages

No animal, however fast, has greater speed than a charging lion over a distance of a few yards. It is a speed faster than thought—faster, always than escape.
                        —Beryl Markham, *West with the Night*

Tanzania, early 1970s

Sitting in the back seat, I squared my shoulders as we passed the lion enclosure at Sister's lodge. Several months had elapsed since our last visit to northern Tanzania. This afternoon, the lions were in the middle of a meal, and the wheelbarrow with the creaky wheel had delivered another carcass all chopped and quartered.

Ever since our last visit, my brain had attempted to compartmentalize the logical fact that something has to die for a carnivore to be able to eat. But when a little girl grows fond of donkeys, the prey animal that is destined to—

Oh, it was just still too horrible to think about.

With a steeling breath, I quickly looked away and was able to compose my face just in time before our car pulled up in front of our smiling hostess at the front door. All the buildings looked the same, and the nun's warm hospitality had not changed. The horses, I knew, would be a comforting sight, and I resolved that stepping back into the stable yard, even with the donkey pen nearby, would be a healing moment.

Soon after settling our luggage in our room, I headed back down to the stables that still housed Diamond, who I hadn't had the chance to ride during my last visit. Those rules hadn't changed either.

I walked past the lion enclosure. Fire, now sated, was reclining on his basking platform, the lioness in the small den, and the two cubs swatting a vertebrae around their yard with clumsy paws.

Passing the cages of the leopard and cheetah, I called out a greeting to Chui and Duma as usual, but then did a double take and peered back into the cages.

These two cages were empty.

Chui and Duma had been keenly sought attractions for each school tour that visited here. Those schoolchildren were frequent visitors and were enthralled by the cats. I remained at a standstill in front of the two empty cages, at a loss, until Matthew walked past carrying gardening tools.

We exchanged warm greetings, and finally I was able to get past all the customary preliminary remarks and bring the conversation to the two empty cages.

"Matthew, where are Chui and Duma?"

"Gone, Miss."

"I see they are gone. Where have they gone to?"

I recognized the same evasive look that Matthew'd had when he had hidden the truth about the donkeys from me. He hesitated slightly, then mumbled that the leopard and the cheetah were not here because they had been rehabilitated successfully into the wild.

Rehabilitated?

"Please, Miss, if you will excuse me, I am needed in the s*hamba.*"

I watched his retreating back, still rooted to the same spot in front of the two empty cages. The cheetah had been a former pet, as had been the leopard. It would have been a massive undertaking to rehab a former pet. And cheetahs are notoriously difficult to rehab, since they take to domestication perhaps more readily than any other big cat. If not rehab, then what? Sister would never have agreed for two cats to be shot and quartered as dinner for the other cats, no matter how elusive Matthew's eyes had been.

I shuffled into the stable yard, so deep in thought that I had forgotten to call out "*Hodi.*"

"Ah, *karibu*, Miss! You're back!" came the warm greeting from David anyway, who then wagged a finger at me and delivered a mock lecture. "I am glad you are back, but I still cannot allow you to ride the Queen of Diamonds."

In Tanzania, it would never do to skip greetings or to rush through them. With great effort, I restrained all impatience through all our preliminary greetings until, as with Matthew, I could introduce the subject on my mind. But unlike how I had broached the subject with Matthew, I decided to try a somewhat circuitous route instead.

"David, you and me, we are *marafiki*, yes?" I gave him a steady look.

He blinked at first and cast a quick sidelong glance at the donkey pen.

"David," I repeated, forcing his eyes back to me. I cast a significant look at the donkey pen, then I looked back at him calmly. "David, we are *marafiki*, yes?"

I forgive you for withholding the truth from me before, about the donkeys. I understand now. Hakuna shida.

The *syce* took a deep breath, apparently knowing full well what I was implying. He returned my steady look. "Yes, Miss Caffee." He paused. "Yes, you and me are *marafiki*."

"And a *rafiki* will always tell truth-truth, yes?"

"Yes," he agreed. "A *rafiki* tells the truth."

"Truth-truth?" I emphasized, scrutinizing his kind face.

"Yes, Miss Caffee." Now that I had underscored to him that I knew full well the difference between truth and truth-truth, he smiled openly and repeated, "Yes, truth-truth."

"Good. Now, what happened to Chui and Duma?"

"Ah." He hesitated. "Come, we groom Diamond together." He handed me the same curry comb as last time, casting furtive glances as if he did not want his words overheard. "Come."

We shut ourselves in together in Diamond's stall, and he faced me squarely, still hesitating.

"Truth-truth," I prodded him gently.

He heaved a deep sigh and asked if everyone had been telling me the cats were rehabbed. He asked if I remembered Ahmed, a staff member who had been fired over a wage dispute since my last visit here. I nodded vaguely.

Diamond glanced sharply at David, who was brushing her tail too vigorously, his jaw clenched and his head shaking slightly from side to side.

According to bush telegraph, he said, Ahmed had been incandescent with rage over being terminated and swore retaliation. "A few days later, on a day when no guests or school tours were present and all the staff were in the lodge or the *shamba*, we heard screams, so much screams." They came from the far end of the property, where the big cats were housed.

For two seconds, everyone was paralyzed in horror. Had

a cat escaped? Then everyone was running. Some for shelter, some for firearms. Young children were scooped up and flung into the nearest rooms that could be safely locked. Several men ran to where the screams had been. They were horror-struck to find the cheetah, outside his open cage, dead.

"Ahmed killed Duma?" I was thunderstruck. But this did not explain Chui's absence.

"No, Ahmed did not kill Duma. Fire killed Duma."

Fire!

David paused, then said, "Truth-truth, it was the lion, Fire." He continued to describe a day so horrific that I ended up aborting any grooming efforts and simply sat agape on an overturned bucket to hear the rest of the story.

Ahmed had crept back onto the property that day and stealthily opened each one of the big cat cages. It had been his intent that with all cats escaped, the loss of revenue to the lodge would hurt Sister as badly as his termination had hurt him. The plan tragically backfired, however, when Fire used his first few minutes of freedom to attack Duma. This was later learned from what Ahmed had told the police, as he watched the horror unfold from his hiding spot. Almost completely defenseless, the cheetah had frozen in shock as the lion came at him. Then, with the diagonal path of a bishop on a chessboard, Duma leapt. He tragically underestimated the lion's ability to be the queen on the chessboard, however, and "Queen takes Bishop" soon played out. With the cheetah now dispatched, Fire then turned his attention to Chui, who had no intention of going gently into that good night and fought back with equal ferocity. It had been these screams that drew everyone to the scene, at which point Fire wisely scooted straight back into his own cage, trying very hard not to look like a lion who had just run amok.

Sister hastily secured the door of the lion enclosure and then joined everyone else who was gathered around the leopard lying on the ground. Chui had sustained horrific injuries and ended up being put out of his misery that same day by the hastily summoned veterinarian. Sister was now left with two empty cages on her property, and the local village jail had a new occupant in their cells.

"So the school tours are being told . . . the cats were rehabbed?" I asked David.

"*Everyone* is being told that the cats were rehabbed."

David and I both drew a collective breath and shook our heads. We continued our halfhearted attempts of grooming Diamond for a moment longer, then the two of us emerged from her stable.

While we had been sequestered in the stall, we'd missed the Asian gentleman finishing his regular business transaction. He was now pedaling past me, leaving the stable yard with his purchases. David saw me turn away, then my eyes met his as I gave a slight snort and shake of the head.

"It's good money for the lodge." His tone was dull and resigned as he watched the load of donkey hides going away. "And he's delighted with these sales."

"I'll bet he was especially delighted to buy the pelts of Duma and Chui too, wasn't he?"

David dropped his eyes. I had never addressed him with this level of bitterness, disrespect or anger before and clearly it stung.

"Miss, the pelts of Duma and Chui were not sold to him," he muttered, while I stared at him with hands on hips and eyes blazing. "Those pelts were too . . ."

"Too what?"

A long silence from David, then a gulp. "Those pelts were

too damaged."

My anger evaporated, and my whole body slumped. David and I just stood together in that stable yard for a few more minutes. There, in the silence, we were just a Tanzanian *syce* and a little *mzungu* girl, mourning a beautiful cheetah and a splendid leopard who had met such a violent, unfair death from Africa's apex predator.

"David," I whispered, "*pole*."

"*Hakuna shida*." His warm eyes met mine.

Later that evening behind closed doors, I told my parents the truth-truth that David had confided to me. Mother revived all her previous "man-eater" accusations, which to me had no bearing here since Fire had killed the exact same animals that he would have killed had he been wild.

Dad declared that Fire was a ticking time bomb. "It will come to a bad end."

Chapter 49
Rearing Queen of Diamonds

The shock produced a stupor similar to that which seems to be felt by a mouse after the first grip of the cat. It caused a certain dreaminess in which there is no sense of pain nor feeling of terror, though quite conscious of all that was happening.

—Dr. David Livingstone, *Missionary Travels*

Tanzania, early 1970s

Nothing ever escaped David's notice.

I arrived in the stable yard one afternoon, still wiping my eyes after passing Chui and Duma's empty cages. Of course, happy rehabilitated big cats are not to be mourned, now, are they? My family all dutifully maintained the fiction.

"Come with me, Miss Caffee." The *syce* knew full well I was still grieving the leopard and the cheetah that Fire had so ruthlessly killed. "Come, let us go collect the horses."

So I trailed after him on the daily task of collecting the horses from the grazing fields across the road and bringing them back into the stables. The thought of seeing Diamond again cheered me up somewhat, and I would at least be allowed to lead Sister's horse back to the stables. David, too, had a cheering effect on me and was soon able to nudge me out of my grieving and get me laughing at his jokes as we walked along.

"Well, someone's in a foul mood," I remarked as we walked past the lion enclosure, where Fire was glowering and prowling more restlessly than usual. With one paw up on the wire of his cage, the simmering cat turned and gazed at me through the wire with an especially disdainful look. "We would be done for, if that cage wasn't locked." I giggled.

"It is locked."

The mercurial cat bared his big yellow fangs in a low growl at us before contemptuously turning his back and bounding off to settle himself on his basking platform.

"Whew!" I said, fanning my face. The putrid breath of big cats was something I never got used to. I joked that there should be a toothpaste for lions. David laughed and countered that nobody could be persuaded to apply it to the patient, even if such a thing existed. And by then we had reached the horses.

David probably heard my rapturous sigh upon seeing the tall and beautiful Diamond once again. He probably noticed my little hands running adoringly over her coat as I slipped her halter on that face. It was a face, I was convinced, that surely rivaled that of Helen of Troy.

"Didn't you say you've ridden bareback?" he asked.

I nodded politely, never taking my eyes off that incomparable face and hoping he wouldn't ask for her lead rope, because I was determined to be the one walking this ethereal creature who floated rather than walked.

Then he said, "*Njoo*."[71]

He gave me a wink and a conspiratorial smile, lacing

---

71   Come.

his fingers together and holding them down at the level of his knees.

I stared uncomprehendingly at his cupped hands. Really?

"What if Sister finds out?" I whispered somewhat unnecessarily, since we were the only two people in that entire field. He whispered back that nobody would find out, since everybody else was at the other end of the property at this time of day.

I mounted hastily before he could change his mind. Never had I surrendered a lead rope more happily.

I was on Diamond.

I was actually on Diamond.

I was on the horse that absolutely nobody was allowed to ride except Sister. I thought I would die of joy.

Now up here on her broad warm back, I ran my hands over her neck and shoulders. With no reins to bother with, I rested my palms on my legs when I wasn't happily trailing my fingertips through her mane. David's grinning face was now far below me, closer to the level of my skinned knee and sandaled feet. With no saddle to bother with, there were no creaking, squeaking, leather sounds. Her back warmed my bare legs, clad in shorts. Both arms had already erupted in goosebumps.

I'm actually on Diamond!

For the first time, I was feeling her floating gait rather than only admiring her while on foot.

Another growl.

I'd lost track of time and hadn't realized we were already halfway back to the stables and approaching the lion enclosure. Fire was still in a foul mood.

Oh, no, you don't, I thought. The lion looked angry enough to charge and spook my horse, which would spoil my ride.

This was surely my one and only chance *ever* on Diamond, and the thought of Fire spoiling this for me rankled.

"Now see here, Fire! *Sio punda hapana.* My horse is not one of your donkey dinners!" I called out to the cat sharply.

Up on his basking platform, the lion barely glanced at the scowling little girl on the horse, with hands on hips, wagging a scolding finger at him. He growled again. David kept his eyes on the lion. The lion I had sternly bidden not to be a bother. Up here on Diamond's bare warm back, I was roughly eye level with the lion.

Fire glanced at me with lip-curling contempt, then turned his attention back to my mount and got to his feet.

Now, Fire, stay right where you are. Don't be tiresome.

My inward grumblings continued as I saw him contemplate whether to descend from his platform. I was about to whine to David that Fire seemed intent on spoiling my ride when Diamond began sidestepping. Because I was bareback, I could feel her slightly quivering, leaving me mystified as to why she was feeling spooked today when she had passed this lion's enclosure hundreds of times before, uneventfully. David shifted his grip on Diamond's lead rope and murmured soothingly to her.

"That will *do*!" I barked at the cat, who really did seem intent on being a nuisance to the poor mare.

Another growl as he slinked off his platform, then crouched at the far end of his enclosure.

Fire then locked eyes with me.

Diamond didn't exist anymore. Neither did David, nor the lodge.

It was only Fire and me.

Just an adult male African lion and a scrawny little white girl locked in one another's eyes. My annoyance had been replaced with a sort of paralysis. My disassociated brain now regarded the unfolding scene rather like a dreamy landscape that was devoid of time or sound.

The lion kept his death stare riveted on me as he began his charge, intent not on being a mere pest but on actual murder.

He is charging at me. He is flowing. Why is he flowing? Why isn't he leaping? I was expecting a bounding motion. Another thought that went through my spellbound head right then was that I realized: So this is what Dr. David Livingstone was talking about.

Yes, yes . . . Now I see. Even in my stupor, I still marveled at the depth of this paralysis. *Am I floating?* I was vaguely aware of my horse becoming increasingly frantic. I could not tear my eyes away. *Is he going to stop before the wire fence, or is he going to try to pounce on us? Do you know, I don't even care anymore if the wire holds.*

He pounced.

There was a rattling, clanging sort of sound as the lion slammed into the fence that he'd forgotten was there. Diamond must have forgotten the wire fence was there as well. She had borne it as long as she could.

Now the mare reared, tearing the lead rope from David's hands.

There are those yellow fangs again, I thought, still in a trance, and dully noticed that the wire fence was swaying back and forth from the weight of about five hundred pounds of enraged lion. His inch-long claws were hooked through the chain links, the massive pads of his paws pressed up against the wire. Another blast of putrid breath came forth as the thwarted cat roared in fury.

The mare finally came back down on all fours, and David grabbed her lead rope before she could get any further ideas of doing any more little cowboy horse imitations.

Eventually we were back in the stable yard. Fire had slunk back onto his basking platform. Diamond had remained on all four feet, and my daze was wearing off.

"Ah, *pole*! Miss Caffee, *pole*!" David said breathlessly. Neither he nor I could figure out what had gotten into that lion's head just now.

"Have they not *fed* that lion yet today? What just happened?"

Parts of my body still felt numb, and I could already picture what my mother might have said just now: "If Fire had been human, he would have been facing charges of attempted murder."

Time was no longer frozen, and real life was slowly reentering my consciousness. The "peculiar state" Dr. Livingstone had described had dissipated. My annoyance at the lion, however, remained firmly in place.

"What just happened?"

Perhaps by asking questions, I could delay the moment that I would have to dismount from this beautiful horse. "Is there a full moon? Did *that* affect him?"

David looked up at me, shrugging. "But"—he grinned now, motioning for me to dismount—"now is time."

Giving her one last hug while astride her, I reluctantly slid off. "Hey, Diamond. You're not the cowboy horse, Trigger." I delivered my mock scolding to her while delivering kisses on the soft pink nose. "And I'm no Roy Rogers. So no more rearing, eh?" Another kiss to the mare, while I answered David's questions as to who Roy Rogers and Trigger were, before turning back to the horse. "What if your neck had smacked into my head? You would have given me a nosebleed, you naughty girl."

The Queen of Diamonds did not look particularly contrite and snuffled through my hands instead, expecting carrots.

"I told you the cage was locked securely!" David smiled at me over his shoulder as he led the horses into their stalls.

"Indeed it was," I said. I stopped myself just in time before I pouted about Fire having spoiled my ride and recited instead another thing for which I was grateful: "And Diamond didn't give me a nosebleed."

"And . . ." David's tone turned serious, and he gave me a significant look while clearing his throat. "And you *have never* ridden Diamond. Right?"

"Oh, no, indeed," I reassured the *syce* on cue. "Me? Why, nonsense. Nobody rides Diamond except Sister."

Chapter 50
The Magic Circle

There is a lot of witchcraft here among both Whites and Blacks. Mother met someone who she thought was an alcoholic with wet brain, but it turned out that he was bewitched.

—Craig

Dar es Salaam, early 1970s

I found it very reassuring that we had a *kuzindika nyumba*[72] around our house.

No harm could ever come to us or our belongings because our whole property was carefully and meticulously surrounded by that nice, strong magic circle, and this comforted me.

Early in our first two months or so in Africa, as we settled into our new home, Mother came upstairs to my bedroom one afternoon with two handfuls of my little plastic farm animals.

"Beloved . . ." She opened her hands to show me toys that I should not have left lying about the living room.

"Oops, sorry." Embarrassed, I quickly grabbed a small tin box she could dump them into. "I wouldn't have wanted to lose that."

---
72   magic circle

Mother hesitated in the doorway. "By the way." Her voice sounded slightly off.

"Yes, Mother?"

"You won't have to worry about losing that . . . that thing, or anything else at all, for that matter, because . . . because I think you should know, we have a magic circle now. It's around the whole property."

"When was this done? Was I at school?" I didn't ask *why* it was done. A magic circle was a reasonable safety precaution against harm or theft in Tanzania.

To have missed seeing a witch doctor on our property, in full regalia, disappointed me somewhat. Often they are dressed head to toe in assorted animal skins and clothing of red, black or white, with a pouch of magic herbs about their necks. Crow feathers in the headdress are a frequent sight, and sometimes their fathers will have passed down to them peacock or ostrich feathers. Each bracelet and armband would also hold special significance. The entire image is undeniably stunning.

Magic, in Africa, could be a bad thing or a good thing. But magic itself was not disputed. Many Tanzanians often consulted native medicine men, sometimes called witch doctors (*babus*, nicknamed "Grandfathers" since most were very old—in fact, the older, the better), and many placed enormous importance on the concept of spirits and ancestors interceding for the protection of current generations.

Mother slowly came back in and proceeded to busy herself with her back to me, straightening my tidy bedsheets and plumping my already plump pillows.

She told me that a chicken had to be killed for the *kuzindika nyumba* ritual the *babu* did. "And that would have upset you. So naturally we had to have it done when you weren't here."

"Oh, yes." I nodded, staring at the floor and feeling a deep pang of sympathy for the chicken. "Yes, of course. Quite right. I wouldn't have wanted to see that." More questions, however, began to come to me. "So, wait, when did you decide to get this done? Where did you find a *babu*? Tell me everything from the beginning!"

"There's, um, not much to tell." Mother's open palm was briskly smoothing nonexistent wrinkles on my sheets. "Dad arranged for a *babu* to come here on that day when all the servants had the day off. And, um, and you were gone too. And the *babu* walked around the perimeter of the property twice counterclockwise, chanting, with the chicken, dripping its blood, and now we have a magic circle."

"That's pretty neat! So what did the servants say when Dad told them?"

"Oh, they're very pleased," she said, a natural tone back in her voice. She straightened up, facing me smiling and made eye contact with me again.

"All the servants are delighted. And actually"—and here she chuckled slightly—"they were only slightly disappointed that the *babu* didn't come from Lake Tanganyika, because all the best ones come from there."

"Where *did* this *babu* come from, then?" I was half expecting her to mention Gamboshi village, which is well known for its practitioners of magic. I had been told these villagers were equally skilled at good magic, *kutambika* (calling rain for crops, etc.), and at evil curses, *uchawi*.

"Beloved, I'm heading downstairs now." She gave me a quick kiss. "We'll talk more about it some other time. And please keep your toys out of the living room!"

"Yes, I will!" I called after her. "Sorry about that!" I walked over to my window and gazed out at our back garden. A back garden that was now safe, along with our whole property. Safe and protected. If I were Tanzanian, I might well have yelped out a "*Khaaa!*" of delight.

We have a magic circle now! That is so neat! Wait till I tell everybody!

***

Several years after we left Tanzania, over dinner back in Montreal, our "remember-when" conversation took a surprising turn.

Dad and Mother and I hadn't started out talking about dogs being poisoned, but the conversation had drifted in that direction after we had begun reminiscing about our years back in Dar es Salaam.

"It was the neighbors on both sides, wasn't it?" I asked. "Each one had a dog that was poisoned, didn't they?"

My parents nodded sadly, somewhat preoccupied with the meal.

"Good thing we had that magic circle around the house in Dar," I continued. My eyes were focused on my plate, and I almost missed the fact that Mother and Dad stopped eating and locked eyes with one another.

"That was a comfort," I said, pushing some rice onto my fork. "And it's why none of our dogs was ever poisoned, and our house was never robbed. All the years we were in Dar. The whole entire time."

"You still haven't told her?"

I looked up to see Dad gazing at Mother reproachfully.

"Beloved . . ." Mother had laid down her fork and knife. She looked directly at me. "Beloved, there was no magic circle."

Now my fork and knife went down. I stared at them.

"There was no magic circle," Mother repeated, regret in her voice.

My thoughts reeling, I began to stammer about all the crimes in Dar, how every single house surrounding us had had something happen to them, how their dogs were poisoned, or my friends' bicycles were stolen, or the houses were robbed, but nothing had ever happened to us.

"I know."

"But . . . So you mean . . . Why?" The seconds ticked by in awkward silence.

"We did it because—" Dad began.

"So we *did* have a magic circle?" I was utterly confused.

"No, I mean, we made up the story about a magic circle. Remember the Smiths?"

I nodded, still baffled.

Dad went on to recount how back in America, the Smiths had very credible signs and stickers placed on the doors and windows of their house saying their house was protected by a burglar alarm, when they actually didn't have one. "So in Dar," Dad went on, "the Smiths pretended to their servants that they had had a magic circle created by a witch doctor."

"When they actually didn't."

"When they actually didn't." Dad nodded. "As you remember, the *babus* had enormous credibility in Tanzania."

I gaped at Dad.

Mother picked up where he'd left off. "We gave all the servants the day off so nobody was home. Then when they all came back, we told them—and it was the only lie we ever told them—we told them the story that while they had been gone we had had a magic circle created by—"

"—by a *babu*," I intoned, somewhat dazed, "who walked

the perimeter of our property twice"—I waved one finger in vague counterclockwise circles—"with a dying chicken dripping blood."

"Yes."

"The servants were all delighted." Mother said, with perhaps a tinge of guilt. "Delighted, except—"

"Except for the fact that the *babu* didn't come from Lake Tangan . . ." My voice trailed off. "But there *was* no *babu*."

"No."

By now I was fighting back tears. "So you told *me* and the servants the same story, because if I had known the truth instead, I might have—"

"Beloved, you do blurt so," Mother said softly, sympathetically.

Later that evening, washing the dishes alone in the kitchen, I mourned, not for the first time, my own gullibility, and my blurts, and I mourned the magic circle that never actually existed. The fictitious magic circle created to preclude all harm.

I tried to remember if I had felt this same sense of betrayal and disillusionment about Santa Claus or the tooth fairy.

No, I decided. This was different. Did it feel different to me because a *babu* would have been far more credible than a jolly fat man with reindeer? Because African magic held greater everyday credibility than Santa traversing the entire globe in one night? Christmas presents had been brought by either Santa or by my parents. And our house had been protected either by the magic circle or it had been protected by . . . what? That was the factor that made this different in my mind.

It still stung that Mother had lied to me that day. Her apology only slightly lessened the pain.

Catherine MacLaine

My parents patiently answered all my questions that night about the once-so-comforting magic circle. All but one:

If the magic circle wasn't real, then why had we been the only ones who had never experienced any crime?

They were never able to answer that.

Chapter 51
Animal Communicator

I was getting propane with a friend. There was a witch doctor sitting on the ground by the entrance when we drove out with our newly filled tanks. He looked right out of Hollywood Central Casting. All his clothes—hat, loincloth, top—were made of wild animal furs.

—Craig

Virginia, circa 2017

Seven vets were enough.

I now had new information that Stan had a non-congenital vision problem, but no idea whether it was even a factor in the aggression.

The vision impairment had been the latest addition to Stanley's cascade of imperfections, discovered after the brain damage: the incontinence, frequent falls, strict diet and the aggression.

I had tried Feliway diffusers in the house for his aggression, collars with calming scents, rubber claw tips, and several strong anti-aggression medications. A friend had placed healing crystals and shungite under his bed. No change.

Euthanizing Stanley remained completely off the table. Ditto for declawing. Seven vets had now touched this cat. Seven vets who were all stumped and stymied.

And I wasn't about to risk encountering one more exasperated, drained and frazzled staff member calling my beloved cat a turd.

That stung more than I cared to admit.

***

I'd underestimated Stanley's strength. It wasn't long before he figured out how and where to push on the baby gate before it fell. Back to square one: Saba was once again face-to-face with his tormentor. Stan and Saba would interact uneventfully most of the time, until Stan decided to be a feline Don Quixote and start tilting at windmills.

After consulting my vet, I decided to install a professional, roomy heavy-duty outdoor dog kennel in my backyard as a safe place for Stanley to spend the daytime, when I could not supervise him near me on the sofa, barring inclement weather.

I dropped off the baby gate at the nearest thrift store, then swung into my local pet store and purchased a larger-sized dog crate to replace his present sleeping crate. Now easily half my kitchen floor was taken over by a crate designed for a Saint Bernard. Stanley was delighted. Each night was now spent there, as well as times Stan was indoors when I could not monitor him directly.

Saba and Stanley, perpetually at loggerheads, would remain physically separated indefinitely.

The backyard kennel, about four-by-eight feet and with an enclosed den portion and an outdoor area, proved to be a reasonable compromise.

I had confessed to my vet my initial reluctance to place my cat outside. "But he's a companion animal, not livestock."

She reassured me that Stanley would actually enjoy being out in "Stanleyland."

In the days that followed, I was thankful to see she had been right. My cat, who was not common livestock, nevertheless adjusted readily to his somewhat unorthodox accommodations.

And Saba very much enjoyed Stanley being away in Stanleyland.

***

As the days went by, I mulled over all my frenetic efforts to "fix" the aggression issue.

In Africa, but perhaps no longer living, was the so-called nun who once had her own incorrigible cat, Fire. I shared her trait of stubborn determination to give my cat every chance at living a full, long and good life.

Had Stanley and I still been back in Africa, our options would have been limited to just one veterinarian at best, along with any *babu* I chose to summon. A witch doctor would have readily appeared, with his magical powders of ground-up tree bark or pulverized pastes from various roots, ready to be of service. He might have carried a rod with a wildebeest tail. These traditional healers used any number of banana leaves spread with assorted dried and preserved animal entrails, or different powders mixed together in a cow horn, or gourd, or calabash. Their chanting and recitation of spells, occasionally interspersed with the tinkling of a special bell, were widely regarded by many as wielding great power over spirits. When powders were not used, certain fluids were needed, and goat's blood might be mixed with cow's milk. The African witch doctors carried considerable clout in their villages and far beyond.

To my knowledge, however, America had no witch doctors.

But they did have plenty of pet psychics.

Hey, Stanley. Do you suppose . . . ?

Opening my laptop computer, I hesitated. *Psychics are useless, aren't they?* Why should I bother to consider hiring a psychic for Stanley when all those board-certified veterinarians couldn't help him? The salient fact remained, however: Stanley was still the bane of Saba's existence.

I soon found myself doing an online search for pet psychics. The worst-case scenario would be that I would have wasted time and money and would emerge embarrassed. On a Venn diagram of a psychic and me, our two lives would have never otherwise overlapped.

And yet.

It would give me peace of mind, I reasoned to myself, that I had tried everything possible to stop his fighting.

The pet psychic I spoke with was warm and gracious about my skepticism. She preferred to be called an "animal communicator" and explained that her job involved communicating with the pet, then relaying that information back to the pet owner. Hunching my phone to my ear, I grabbed another trusty index card to make myself a reminder: *Animal Communicator, not psychic.*

The animals' electromagnetic signals convert into telepathic messages, she told me. "I'll just say what I'm getting, even when it doesn't make sense to me, because it might make sense to the client. I just have to speak it out."

So this wonky cat, who wore mongoose-like stripes in his tabby fur, whose flanks I would nuzzle, would communicate to her?

By now, Doctor Dolittle was floating through my mind. That charming fictional character who would grunt and squeak and squawk with the animals, and the animals in turn would then grunt and squeak and squawk with him. Doctor Dolittle did not deal with the reading of energy fields or animal auras or otherworldly frequencies or indeed any telepathy at all. At this point, an African *babu,* complete with handheld wildebeest tail, would have handily trounced Dolittle.

This pet psychic I had hired took pains to remind me that she could offer no guarantees of success, but I had found her warm tone of voice to be comforting, and she asked me for only my cat's name and age. We agreed ahead of time that I could withhold from her certain pieces of information, and so I specifically stayed silent on Stanley's African origins. If she was worth her salt, I reasoned, she would hear about Tanzania from Stanley himself within the first few minutes. She listened to my description of his brain damage and reassured me that I could ply him with his normal medications on the day of her visit, and that his heavily fogged brain would not hinder any telepathic communications.

A few days later, a tall, thin woman arrived at my door. I had known not to expect someone flying in on a broom with a crystal ball tucked under one arm, wafting incense and dripping with ectoplasm. But this psychic was just . . . She was just normal. Then again, back in Africa, the witch doctors, when not attired in their full regalia, looked pretty ordinary too.

My one last flicker of hope was now pinned on this psychic.

Chapter 52
The Tragedy

The peculiar state is probably produced in all animals killed by carnivora; and if so, is a merciful provision by our benevolent Creator for lessening the pain of death.
—Dr. David Livingstone, Missionary Travels, 1884

Dar es Salaam, early 1970s

My parents and I lounged on our terrace after dinner one evening. The stars were out, the mosquito repellent coil was only halfway burned down, and faint bat squeaks, or perhaps slightly muffled monkey screeches, were drifting in the warm air. At Mother's feet sprawled my little dog Alice, who was reaching for the root of her tail, mincing fleas with her teeth. I was seated on the floor with her, picking out ticks from the webbing between each of her toes. The heavy dinner had left us in a slightly drowsy state, and I was only paying partial attention as Mother continued to read out loud a letter from her friend.

"*We loved our stay at the nun's lodge! Thanks for recommending it.*" The letter went on to say how nice the nun had been to our friend and all the food had been delicious. "*How sad to

A Billion Blue Wildebeest

hear about the tragedy, though," Mother read.

Tragedy? What tragedy?

Drowsiness now dispelled, Mother, Dad, and I all exchanged glances, and Mother reread the letter. Whatever the tragedy had been, no details were forthcoming.

"We'll find out eventually," Mother said in guardedly casual tones, and then far too casually strolled downstairs, where the rotary telephone was. I would not have been surprised if her finger was in the dial almost immediately.

Joan, the letter writer, was invited for coffee the next time she was in Dar, and I made certain to find an excuse to linger in earshot as the two women sipped their coffee on our terrace. Just as I had expected, Mother steered the conversation around to the cryptic letter.

"You mentioned a tragedy?" Mother said.

"Yes, wasn't it horrible?" Joan sighed, stirring her coffee. Looking up, she must have noticed Mother's blank face.

"You didn't hear? About what happened?"

Mother added a very slight shake of her head.

Joan went on, "The lion they had there?"

I crept closer.

"He got out. He killed a child."

Mother clapped a hand over her mouth.

Joan looked at Mother again, drew a deep breath, and answered the thousands of questions she saw in our eyes.

Yes, it was Fire, and yes, he had killed a child. It had been one of the Tanzanian schoolchildren on a school tour. Yes, Fire was out of his cage. A former employee, still embittered about a previous wage dispute, and just out on parole, had managed to sneak back onto the property and had deliberately opened the lion cage.

Ahmed.

Only the male lion came out of the cage. The female and the cubs remained inside. A school tour had started without anyone aware that the male was out.

"Oh, the screams . . . the screams." Joan shuddered and refocused on her tale. The lion was shot. Right then and there.

"Sister *shot* Fire?" I was unable to conceal the incredulity in my raspy voice.

"Her brother shot the lion," Joan said. "The lion lay dead right next to the dead child." The rest of the story described how Ahmed was once more clapped in irons, but the damage was done.

She went on to tell how Sister lost her wildlife license virtually overnight, and the lioness and cubs were removed from her property. The loss of revenue from the cessation of school tours was probably no small matter. The donkeys were rendered moot as well. Gone, too, was the income from the sale of hides.

"Oh, that poor child," I moaned, not noticing that I was rocking again.

Later, I padded away and crawled up into my tree house to digest this bombshell. What could Sister be thinking, after all her years of staunch loyalty to Fire?

I plucked some nearby leaves off the tree and fumbled them around in my hands. After years of *hakuna shida*, and jubilant schoolchildren safely enjoying her magnificent cats. After years of *dum spiro, spero*. And yet in the end, there was no hope, and now he was no longer breathing.

Now somewhere in Sister's neighborhood, I thought, as I absentmindedly plucked another leaf, *a Tanzanian family had to bury a small child who never had a chance to grow up*. Such a short life. Such a sudden ending. That child would never be able to pluck a leaf off a tree again.

The shock had caused me to forget to ask any clarifying questions. Who, exactly, had the child been? Had it been a girl? Did she giggle with her friends while cleaning rice like I did? I found myself wondering if she had loved her skipping rope as much as I loved mine. Had it been a boy who was killed? In my mind's eye, I could picture him happily kicking around a homemade soccer ball with his friends. That ball would have been created painstakingly from wadded-up random scraps of plastic, all tied together tightly with rope made from—of course, it was—sisal. He would have, I imagined, only reluctantly stopped playing with his soccer ball when his parents called out to him for the third time to go tend to the goats.

Had I met the child? There had been a few occasions when I had walked past one of the big cat cages and exchanged a smile with one or more of the schoolchildren who were gathered there, gazing in wonderment at their own native wild cats. The cluster of blue and white school uniforms contrasted prettily with the warm tones found in the coats of the cats, it seemed to me. The majority of the students had been little boys, since girls, often facing a future of only domestic duties, usually did not continue past primary school. The children were all unfailingly polite, always respectfully keeping their voices at a low volume, but their undeniable excitement leaked through nonetheless. The cats were undeniably splendid, and the children's expressions were always the same: awestruck.

Had we met, that Tanzanian youngster would have likely addressed me as "my sister" as a matter of course.

My own memories of when Fire had charged at me came back, reminding me of the peculiar dissociative state that my brain had slipped into at the time.

Please, God, I hope the child had slipped into that exact same trance, that peculiar state, instead of any pain or fear.

A child had been killed.

A child who had likely been right around my age, killed by a man-eater.

Because that was what Fire was, truly. That was now irrefutable.

But was that schoolchild Fire's first and only victim, or was it his sixth, after years as a man-eater? And if this was Fire's sixth victim, then that made him a man-eater who was inexplicably allowed to live after his first victim. And his second. And third . . . If Fire had just been shot like all man-eaters are shot, like Boy was shot, all those people might still be alive.

Was I grieving more for this child than for Stanley Murithii because I personally knew the lion in question? Somehow the death of this child felt more personal for me, perhaps since the child and I were similar ages and, yes, because I had known this lion personally. And he had made an attempt on my life.

Boy and Fire will always be linked in my mind due to their commonalities. Both had been magnificent, massive resplendent males, both involved in *Born Free*. Both were shot to death within seconds of killing a human being. George Adamson had asked to be buried near Boy. I never learned where Fire was buried, but had Sister arranged for her site to be next to his, I would not have been in the least surprised.

I never learned where the child was buried, but their current location seems certain to me.

That child now stands amongst the ancestors.

In the following week, the tragedy tended to come up in my dreams. I would gape, horror-struck at the body of a small boy crumpled on the ground. For whatever reason, the murdered child never appeared as a girl in my dreams. The corpse of the young boy, instead, had lain there with limbs awkwardly askew and copious blood soaking the meticulously clean blue and white school uniform that would have cost his parents easily a month's wages. One foot was still clad in his sandal, meticulously created from the rubber of car tires. The other sandal had flown off his foot, and landed only God knows where, during his panicked—and futile—flight from the lion.

The youngster's small body was removed effortlessly after the police had finished their assessment. The search for his missing sandal was fruitless and eventually abandoned. It took four men instead, with a lot of effort, over several attempts, to remove the corpse of Fire. Dead weight, literally, and over three hundred pounds of it, was finally heaved into the open-bed truck. As the truck drove away, the little missing sandal then came to light, crushed and lying upside-down on the ground. It had been hidden underneath the lion's body the entire time.

These dreams always ended with me sitting bolt upright in bed, panting.

Mother, to her credit, never once said, "I told you so." She never quibbled over six victims or one victim. She just hugged me gently that day, and together we mourned the innocent Tanzanian child.

Chapter 53
The Basking Platform

There wasn't a tabloid press in Tanzania. I bet the story didn't get more than a newspaper paragraph or two. And it happened half a century ago.

—Craig

Tanzania, February 2017

Perhaps if a psychiatrist had assessed me at that time, they might have diagnosed me with survivors' guilt, but I'll never know. All I knew was that I had been devastated, during my childhood in Tanzania, to learn that a child my age had been murdered in a place where I'd been often, by an animal with whom I was well familiar.

After some hesitation, I decided to revisit the site of the killing.

"The child who stands amongst the ancestors," as I'd dubbed them in my mind, was still in my thoughts.

Fire, the lion who had made such an indelible impression on me, had spent hours glowering at all passersby from the stone basking platform inside his cage. Until the day he was let out. His rampage lasted only minutes before a visiting

Tanzanian youngster lay dead on the ground.

Over the following years, the tragedy would resurface in my mind each time I thought of this lodge in northern Tanzania. My mother had spent untold hours with her arms around me as I tried to process the swirling emotions. Grief, yes, but some mixed feelings about Fire and his owner too. That lion, that thundercloud incarnate, had been given every *possible* chance. His owner had hyperextended herself to give him a good life. Just like George Adamson had hyperextended himself for Boy. And yet in the end, tragedy.

Perhaps a wildlife expert would have told me to chalk this up to yet another example of why wild animals should never be pets. And *why* was the word that particularly haunted me. Why did that lion decide, in his first few seconds of freedom, that he would kill a human being? Hunger was not a factor. This was not a mother with cubs to be protected and fed. I was told man-eaters are particularly active in the first week after a full moon. Was that a factor here? The phase of the moon on the day of this killing was the furthest thing from my mind, truth to tell. The previous time he was out of his cage, I remembered, he had used his first few seconds of freedom to kill an almost defenseless cheetah. Why not simply escape into the ample bush surrounding the lodge?

This lion's behavior was predatory, not defensive.

And why kill a human? His *intent* had been to kill. A screaming, terror-stricken schoolchild fleeing for their life must have seemed easy pickings. The child's desperate flight, a natural response, would unfortunately have triggered the lion's natural instinct to chase and kill.

Over the years, the Tanzanians told me their opinion: "He was a demon. He acted under somebody else's direction."

It didn't sound entirely implausible. Belief in demons and

shape shifters was common in African magic. If the British story of King Arthur of Camelot could feature shapeshifting—the wizard Merlin changed Arthur into various animal forms—then why not in African mythology too? Was the lion weaponized by a witch doctor? Did Ahmed weaponize the cat? Had he known Fire had been a man-eater?

The thunderous incident had a ripple effect on the families involved and countless others. Was I feeling anger, perhaps? After all, a fellow human being had died, horrifically, due to a chain of events unnecessarily set in place by its owner. Was she an idealist, or simply misguided? Were these feelings of betrayal?

Thoughts ricocheted in my mind about how we had all been lied to. Would *any* school tours or lodge visitors have *ever* come had the true history of that lion been provided forthrightly to us from the very beginning? Deception galore.

This same lion's attempt to kill me had only been thwarted by the strong wire fence of his locked cage. His intent had been undeniable.

Why was my life spared from this lion? And spared multiple times in Africa from malaria, crime, snakes, and charging elephants too? My mother mused that my work on Earth was not yet done, because we are put on Earth to—

"Yes." I smiled at her as I finished her sentence in my head.

And others *do encompass animals.*

Other memories drifted back: My mother reading to me at bedtime from the memoirs of Dr. David Livingstone.[73] His own recollection of surviving a lion attack in 1843 was remarkable for its sense of detachment. Fear had not been on his mind whatsoever when the animal pounced on him. Instead, he wrote: *I was thinking, with a feeling of disinterested*

---

73   John Gready, *The Life and Explorations of David Livingstone.*

curiosity, which part of me the brute would eat first . . .

Over the years, I dared to hope that the dead child had met death with this same absence of terror.

The subject of death always left me with more questions than answers. I reflected also on my childhood stumbles when attempting to discern the difference between lies and the truth. Mother had told me the truth about Fire being a man-eater, and I hadn't believed her. She told me a lie about the magic circle, and I *had* believed her. But Fire had fooled us too. When Mother had thought the roaring cat was out of his cage, he wasn't. And when we all assumed he was safely inside his cage, he was instead outside, and killing sprees were the result.

Now, it was four decades later, and I wandered the derelict grounds deep in thought.

Flowers once bloomed here, but today there were no fragrant scents in the air. The dry grass crunched under my feet. The town had encroached on the bush, and faint traffic sounds hummed from a road some distance away.

I waded through scrub grass where the driveway once had been. The cage, too, no longer existed, not even its fence posts. My thoughts swirled as I stood where, almost half a century ago, the dead lion and slain child had lain mere feet apart. Death, holy and horrific, had been here.

Several wounds, I had been told, on the child's body contrasted with the single bullet that felled the killer. The scene of carnage had since been graciously covered by a field of waving scrub grass. The African proverb that states "The soil belongs to the ancestors" was fitting here. A nearby weaver bird launched into the first few notes of his song, then thought better of it.

The bush had crept into the interior of the cage area, and

the space was now so overgrown that it was completely erased. So overgrown that at first I didn't see it.

And then, there it was.

I stared at the stones of the basking platform.

They had fallen into a random arrangement, no longer bearing any resemblance to the former *kopje* from which the killer had glared at us all. But one stone was still fairly upright. What would it feel like, if I made my way through all that bush and reached it?

What would it feel like if I ran my hands across that stone? I continued to stare, memories flooding back.

Massive paws, the size of dinner plates, with which the cat grabbed his dinner. The jovial colloquialism of "murder mittens" had come true, grimly, in his case. I could easily picture him having readily leapt off this same platform, on his quest to kill a human being that fateful day.

On other occasions, I had seen him stretched out on his platform, giving the impression of being nothing more than an innocent, lazy, big cat. Undeniably thrilling had been the evenings of thunder, where he had stood alertly upon it, his roars sending chills down the spines of anyone nearby.

Now, it was just a pile of stones a few feet away.

My memories were real enough, I decided. No need to touch them.

Walking away from the site where two corpses had lain over forty years ago, I whispered a prayer for both of them.

Chapter 54
Baby Birds

We have lots of birds in our garden, and many varieties.

—Craig

Tanzania, early 1970s

I only wanted to get my ball back. That's all. But instead of the ball, that day involved baby birds who, unsurprisingly, aroused all my rescuing tendencies.

It was another humid morning in Dar, and I was in our backyard whacking away at some overhead bushes with a large stick. The ball I had been playing with was firmly entangled and resisted all my efforts to dislodge it, stubbornly refusing to fall to the ground. Instead, my whacks dislodged a bird's nest.

On closer inspection, I found two baby birds inside. I was immediately flooded with shame. My actions had separated these vulnerable babies from their mother. My ball abandoned, my rescue gland went into overdrive. I scooped up the nest, complete with now orphaned babies, and brought it into my room. These utterly vulnerable, incalculably fragile babies, without even feathers yet, were now facing an uphill struggle. And it was my fault. I was dead-set that these two orphans would now be recompensed. Ensconced in my happy home, they would flourish into adulthood.

While Mother's back was turned, I pinched her hot water bottle. Craig never noticed that I absconded with his eyedropper from his photography darkroom supplies.

Nobody in the entire household paid any attention as I carefully ground up pellets of dog kibble into powder. The following days consisted of me reaching my hand into the nest every two hours or so, except while I was at school, and lifting out each warm, soft, tiny nestling in turn to be fed pulverized dog kibble with the carefully cleaned eye dropper. Each baby was then tenderly replaced into the nest, with the wrapped hot water bottle next to them. And so the cycle continued, picking up each baby multiple times per day. Thompson and Thomson, as I had dubbed them (after the *Tintin* characters), cheeped loudly and ate vigorously.

It was the third day, I think, when, eyedropper at the ready in my left hand, I reached deep into the nest once again for the warm, soft bodies with my right.

Their little bodies were cold and stiff.

Hearing my anguished wails, Craig peered into my bedroom. Mother found me minutes later, where I had flung myself on my bed, still clutching the eye dropper, and in torrents of tears, dirge still in full cry. True to her nature, she lovingly stroked my hair and murmured sympathies with nary a lecture on doomed follies of inexperienced little girls who attempted to rescue orphaned baby birds. Craig reappeared, having brought Alice to me. There was now no need to gently pry the eyedropper from my fingers, because I readily surrendered it, as he probably calculated I would, as I gathered my little dog to me with both hands. I sobbed gratefully into her fur. He silently retrieved his eyedropper and quietly slipped away. Mother gave me one more kiss. Then she, too, tactfully retreated, taking with her the hot water bottle. To this day, I have no memory of who removed the nest and the corpses.

Over the coming years, the abject horror and the crippling guilt I felt over Thompson and Thomson dissipated somewhat, but it never quite left me. Perhaps the bitter lessons one learns from a rescue gone wrong eventually help the next rescue go well. I don't know. The best of intentions still do not guarantee success. Little caterpillars tenderly brought into the warm cozy bed of a five-year-old little girl in Montreal still ended up dead, and still triggered tears just as copious as those shed for two dead African nestlings.

Later in life, I found myself pondering the risk-benefit ratio of my resources when rescuing animals. Was there a point where one had to pivot from the futility of completely fixing one individual hopeless animal and instead resign oneself to stabilizing that creature and pour one's efforts into other animals? I never learned the answer. Later in life, however, this did seem to be a reasonable course of action, with certain animals.

Perhaps I never did internalize the sobering truth that one person cannot stave off death or suffering in all creatures. Not every animal can be fixed. Sometimes the death of a rescued animal is a failure, but other times it can be an inevitability. Even as an adult, I would stumble, time and time again, over the humbling reality of my own limitations.

During those few short days with the Tanzanian baby birds, I was yet unaware of how incalculably fragile these babies are. Nestlings, as I learned to my sorrow, should ideally only ever be in the care of their own parents. Failing that, a licensed wildlife rehabilitation expert. Little girls with long hours away at school, with a heart full of love and a mind brimming with good intentions are, alas, not enough. In any case, the death of the two little nestlings was a turning point in my life, so to speak.

I never again tried to keep any wild animal as a pet. I was never even tempted, for one simple reason:

I could never forget those two tiny cold, stiff little bodies.

Chapter 55
All Three Chambers

There is a belief that witch doctors could turn themselves into lions. Also a belief they can command an animal to do nefarious deeds. The belief in magic and witchcraft is widespread in Africa, also the belief in curses and evil spells.

—Craig

Virginia, circa 2017

I've actually hired a pet psychic. With a slight shake of my head, I pushed away my own incredulity as I showed the tall, smiling woman into my kitchen. I noticed, with a hidden sigh of relief, that Stanley, freshly bathed that morning, was happily asleep in his bed, on a clean pee pad, and without soiled fur. On one of our previous phone calls, I had warned the psychic there was a chance she would find him dirty, since his neurological condition often resulted in him falling down while standing in his litter box, which then resulted in soiled fur, which then resulted in yet another bath for this long-suffering cat. She laughed good-naturedly about "neuro cats" with soiled fur and reassured me that it would not hinder her session with my pet.

In preparation for her visit, I had Stan alone in the kitchen, in his bed, with his crate temporarily moved to another room and Saba locked safely away in another part of the house.

Stanley looked up, bright-eyed, when we entered. When he surmised no treats were forthcoming, he drifted back to sleep and continued to doze on and off as she and I stood a few feet away. She began to speak to him simply and softly. Perhaps she was introducing herself to him? Reading his aura? Channeling a spirit?

Unlike Doctor Dolittle, she was standing still and did not grunt or squeak or squawk.

I kept looking at Stan (impassive and still half asleep), then back to her, as she spoke softly, sometimes with eyes closed and one hand outstretched toward my apathetic cat. Was she reciting incantations over him or prayers? I decided it was prayers. I noticed no electromagnetic signals. Indeed I wasn't even sure if the remaining portion of his brain *could* emit electromagnetic signals? Had it been too heavily fogged with his medications?

Nonetheless, her apparent telepathic conversation with my cat continued like a gently babbling brook, until she opened her eyes and turned to me, inviting me to pose any questions I might have for my cat.

"Stanley, darling, are you in any pain? Do you know I love you deeply?" I asked my cat, immediately followed by a feeling of sheepishness.

I cannot believe I am expecting an answer from a cat.

She relayed my questions to him, then seemed to come back to my frequency and reassured me that he was indeed pain free at the moment, happily ensconced in my love, and invited more dialogue.

"So, darling," I said, feeling slightly emboldened as I

addressed the indifferent cat directly, "we call you Stanley, but please tell me, what name do you call yourself?" Now would be a reasonable time for an African cat to mention a Kiswahili name.

The psychic came back with an American name, and I rocked back on my heels slightly. An *American* name?

Okay, let's try another question.

"Stanley." I looked steadily into his bright eyes. "Talk about where you came from. Where were you living before you came to live with me?"

Another softly murmured monologue from the psychic, again interspersed with occasional spells of silence as she, too, gazed at Stanley, who remained serenely unimpressed with her, before she turned to me with an apologetic shrug.

"I'm not getting anything, Mom," she said, then went on to ask if I wanted to bring up anything we discussed on the phone.

Oh, yes, I did.

"Stanley." Now my tone was pleading. "The aggression. The aggression is just too, too bad. Can you *please* stop attacking Saba? Why do you *do* this?"

"What I'm getting," the psychic said to me after another few seconds of silence, "is that he was in a fear state and . . ." She paused, listening intently, then relayed back to me that my cat wanted to apologize to me.

"Mom," she said, apparently speaking on his behalf, "I'm trying so hard, Mom. I am. But it's explosive. I can't control this."

I turned and stared out the window, biting my lip and collecting my thoughts.

So has it really come to this? I wondered. *The rages can't be controlled?* And what was more, there had been not a single mention of Africa during this entire session. None. Apparently when my cat "talked" to her, his entire kittenhood, the first year and a half of his life, when his identity had been formed, just didn't happen to come up. Not a single Kiswahili word had been uttered. Apparently when my cat communicated with her, his entire conversation was in English. This from a cat who had only recently arrived in America. My skepticism was steadily ratcheting up while my hopes continued their steady nosedive.

My expressionless cat and the tall, thin woman continued their session. The self-proclaimed psychic continued to describe to me what she said he was communicating telepathically to her.

No mention that his previous name had been Bajaji. No mention of Stanley having suffered thirty grueling hours of traveling with me on two different planes.

My skepticism only ossified as the moments went by, and every word that the "Animal Communicator" reported back to me was information that I already knew, or could have come from any person who was well read or was a keen observer of cats.

"What I'm getting is, his aggression is fear-based."

I took slight comfort in the fact that she wasn't claiming to have any supernatural revelations about my time in Africa or about Stanley that could have been easily found by a simple search through my social media or a look around my living room, where she was surrounded by Africa-related books and artwork.

Several more minutes went by of her murmuring whatever it was that she was murmuring to my cat and my silent cat continuing to ignore her.

And then:

A Billion Blue Wildebeest

"Stanley? What did you just say?" She straightened up, very surprised and was now staring at the still silent, still impassive Stanley. "Can you repeat that, sweetie? I don't think I understood what you said."

I had abruptly straightened up too. *Aha! Now comes the Swahili!* And now both of us were paying rapt attention to my soundless brown tabby.

I clasped my hands together tightly. "What did he say? What did he say?" I was so excited, I only remembered just in time not to add "Was it in English?"

"Stanley, sweetie," she went on, peering intently at him, "what you just said doesn't make any sense to me." A pause, then, "Okay, sweetie, I'll tell Mom what you said, but it still doesn't make any sense to me."

"What did he say? What did he say?"

"What I'm getting is, he says to tell you that someone smacked him with a broom when he was very little." Then she turned back to Stanley. "A broom? Did I get that right? Okay." Then back to me. "Well, I think what I'm getting is a broom, but"—and this point clearly puzzled her—"there is no long handle on it."

A broom? That's it? Nothing about Africa? Nothing in Kiswahili? I stared at her, agape, then wordlessly gathered up my unconcerned cat in my arms and trudged into the living room.

I felt her eyes follow me as I left the room and sat down heavily on the sofa, cat in my arms under my slumped shoulders.

My heavy sigh did not escape her notice, and she quietly came and sat with me. The two of us stroked Stanley, who settled down on the sofa between us. I continued to stare at the floor and rumpled my face.

"I'm sorry," she said softly. "It's just . . . It's just I never know ahead of time what I'm going to be getting from the spirit plane. Or not getting." She seemed to know full well that I was deeply disappointed with the session. She continued in a somewhat self-conscious tone of voice, "That bit about the broom didn't make any sense to me either, but I always have to say whatever it is the pet is saying, just in case it does make sense to the client." She went on, hesitation entering her voice. "What I was getting was, *maybe* a broom? It looked like a bundle of reeds tied together."

"I'm not disputing the broom," I replied, still staring at the floor. "The broom is entirely plausible. I haven't the least doubt that he could have been struck with a broom."

"But I wasn't sure if it even *was* a broom, because it didn't have a long handle."

"It wouldn't have."

She gazed at me, looking somewhat puzzled.

"It wouldn't have had a long handle," I repeated dully, "because in Africa it would have likely been just that, a bundle of reeds tied up together."

I met her eyes. Her eyebrows had risen slightly at this very first mention of Africa. I sighed, got to my feet and went to fetch Stanley's export certificate, which I laid in front of her.

The eyebrows stayed up.

"Do you remember," I said, "how on the phone you and I discussed that I would withhold certain pieces of information? This is the part I withheld from you. Stanley is not from America."

"Tan . . . zan . . ." she intoned, reading the certificate, before raising her head to stare at me again. One hand reached out to touch Stanley with as much wonderment as one might touch the Crown Jewels of England.

"I brought Stanley home from overseas, from Tanzania."
She remained silent, listening respectfully.

"For all I know, his rage could be PTSD from that broom," I mused. Then, turning to her with my own incredulity, "Are you *sure* he only spoke English to you?" *Assuming that my cat ever spoke to you at all.*

Her reply was kind. Gentle, even. "What I was getting wasn't any particular language, actually. Telepathy just doesn't come across in . . . Well, I mean, it's . . . it's telepathy," she said, shrugging hopelessly.

I sank farther into the sofa and spoke quietly and frankly about how happy I had been, preparing for the trip to Tanzania. The preparation for this trip had gone more smoothly than I had dared hope. The "Africa vaccines" I had needed for overseas travel this time had been fewer than I had endured in that Montreal clinic at age seven, and the malaria pills—oh, thank you, God—were now coated. I had "chair-danced" in the car singing "Pata Pata" and other African songs the whole way to the airport. Then, learning how profoundly disabled this cat was, his cascading imperfections, my profound despair, and my desperate search for a cure, to overturn every stone so that nothing remained, to gnaw at my conscience. I had wondered, during the first horror of Stan going rogue and fighting with Saba, did Sister Maria feel this same horror when Fire went rogue against her other cats? The similarities between the two cats had impressed me. Both Tanzanian cats, rescued with the best of intentions, but then—an unexpected outcome.

With growing frustration, I found myself blinking back tears that stubbornly began to blur my vision. "You see," I said, my voice was already cracking slightly as I gathered my cat back into my arms, "What I was saying is, I've already taken him to—I mean—he has been to a great many veterinarians. And I mean, board-certified veterinarians. And some veterinary specialists too." Despite my attempts at a stoic demeanor, I could feel my facade of competence was crumbling. Tears were slipping down my face, which was now stretching into the same grimace I would get during sit-ups at the gym.

She brought little tissue packets out from her purse and handed me one of them with practiced ease.

I had hoped I would not cry.

I cried.

Having completely broken down, I continued to tell her how I had lugged this cat from vet to vet on my "who can fix my cubbie?" tour, and all the problems that beset him.

"I don't know why he fights. And the fights are so terrible, so terrible, and the intervals are every ten weeks, and"—I blew my nose—"and I even checked the phases of the moon but that's not the full moon."

"That's right. That's not the interval for a full moon." She went on, speaking softly to me, saying how she empathized with my Sisyphean task. She listened compassionately as I had bawled to her that I had been named after two great-aunts who had been rescuers. I bawled about how I was dealing with a cat who has brain damage, who has an aggression issue, who can't be helped neurologically. A cat who had a titubar, staggering gait, and who, it was now confirmed, could not see very well. He had unconfirmed occasional focal seizures too, to my understanding.

"But I'm not going to cut the Gordian Knot and euthanize him. I just don't know what else to do. I mean, if we lived in France, I would have hauled him all the way over to Lourdes and bathed him in the grottoes."

"I know."

More quiet sobbing (from me) punctuated by one slight surprised squeak (from Stanley) nestled in my arms, whom I had not realized I had been squeezing.

"I've just . . . I've just taken this cat to so many people . . ." I continued to weep. "And nobody can fix his . . ." I pointed to the back of Stanley's head, where I assumed his malformed cerebellum was. "Nobody can fix this dain bramage." I was still crying heavily, and making good use of the tissues.

"I'm sorry." She spoke in obvious sympathy and tactfully refrained from correcting my "dain bramage" spoonerism.

"And he's not a turd!" I finished, wailing miserably.

"A *turd?*" She promptly and staunchly rose to the defense of my darling cat. "He most certainly is *not*! Who ever said that? I wasn't getting that *at all*." She stroked my cat gently, the cat I had so cooed over, then turning to me, admonished me firmly, albeit warmly. "Just forget you ever heard that word. Stanley is a *good* cat."

"I know he is," I said, taking a deep breath. Regaining control, I went on to tell her, more calmly now, how I had called her because I had wanted to circumvent the brain and perhaps reach him spiritually. "If that's possible?"

I took another deep breath. "But I also called you because . . . because he is from Africa and Africa has quite a bit of witchcraft and black magic there."

The eyebrows went back up again.

"I suppose I had been hoping that perhaps you could assess if magic is, perhaps, a component here?" I carefully left unsaid, "You're my last hope."

"Ah, you mean like *juju?*"

"No, it wouldn't be *juju*." *How does she know about juju?* I wondered. "It's *uganga* or *ulogaji*, I think." I rose to my feet and settled Stanley back into his basket in the kitchen. "Or maybe it's *uchawi*," I said to her, as I came back into the living room. "I'm not really sure. But anyway, *juju* is from West Africa and Stan is from East Africa."

A contemplative look crossed her face now, and she got to her feet. She went to talk to Stanley once more, and my cat gazed back at her with his eyes now dull. She murmured more words over my unmoved cat, with an outstretched hand. Stanley remained deadpan and did nothing. *An African witch doctor might have brought out their magic tinkling bell by now*, I found myself thinking.

Another pause as the two of them gazed at one another. Then she quietly came back to join me in the living room. I sighed, inwardly berating myself, and dropped my gaze. I heard her sigh also.

There was nothing more to be done.

I wrote out a check for her services, and soon the two of us were standing at my door exchanging polite farewells. The psychic could see I was completely disappointed with the session, but the two of us remained courteous and respectful to one another, even sharing a laugh as Stanley lurched out of his bed and wobbled his way around the kitchen floor.

And then he began to defecate.

"Stanley! You have a perfectly good, clean litter box, mere inches from you!" I called out reproachfully to my cat. "Neuro cat, you know?" I turned to the psychic with a weak, embarrassed half-laugh.

"Silly little kitty!" The psychic smiled kindly over at my cat. She seemed resolved to set aside the trifling matter of Stanley's brain damage and to help me save face instead. "Oh, *lots* of neuro cats do this. And normal cats do too."

My neuro cat blithely ignored my reprimand.

I watched, shamefaced, as big, pungent fecal pellets continued to be strewn across my kitchen floor. "Umm, Stan? I could do *without* all this right now." The sewage deposits kept coming and coming, intensifying the awkwardness of the moment.

"This is weird," I muttered to her, keeping my eyes on my cat.

And then Stanley's mouth arched wide open, like an African egg-eating snake. He staggered a few steps away from his little mountain of fecal matter and proceeded to spew vomit. It just kept coming and coming and coming. The sheer amount of it, still cascading, was as unprecedented as the amount of excreta had been.

I wasn't laughing anymore. Weakly or otherwise.

"Stan?" I abandoned my guest now and hurried to my retching, spewing cat. "Cubbie? Are you okay?" I knelt beside him, stroking him and watching him with sharp concern. All bewilderment had now vanished.

"Wh-what is going on with my cat?"

The psychic had immediately joined me on her knees on my soiled kitchen floor. If she heard the quaver in my voice, she tactfully ignored it, and the two of us continued our crouched vigil next to my still retching cat, our hands on his convulsing fur. She was staring at him, as shocked as I was.

"He never ever empties two chambers at the same time," I told her.

"I feel an energy shift," she said.

I didn't get a chance to ask what she meant, because to my relief, Stanley finally stopped spewing.

Instead, as my cat stared vacantly off into the middle distance, as a vast pool—a veritable flood—of urine steadily poured out from underneath him and began to seep across my kitchen floor.

Feces *and* vomit *and* urine? And this much? And all at once? Still on all fours beside him, utterly thunderstruck, I began stroking my cat as soothingly as I could, softly crooning "*Salaam, salaam . . . tulia*" to him.

And then in English to the psychic, "Why is my cat emptying all three chambers at the same time? Why such huge amounts? Is this supernatural? What on Earth is happening to my cat!" My alarmed voice, progressively shriller with every passing second, rose in pitch, contrasting with the shiver going down my spine. "What is *happening?*"

She said she didn't know. I shot her a look that said, "Well, *this* is paranormal! *Do something!*"

She began talking to Stanley again, and I continued *salaam*ing him, completely at a loss just then as to which language would help him the most. She began repeating her previous murmured incantations, again with outstretched hand, over Stanley. For several minutes it was just the three of us in a bizarre and discordant tableau: a frantic cat owner yammering in Arabic and Kiswahili, a tall, thin murmuring woman, and a brown tabby from whom feces, vomit and urine had all come tumbling out within the space of perhaps ninety seconds.

If this had been a movie, there might have been a swelling orchestral score in the background right about now. It might have perhaps been the ominous screeching of a string section.

My cat staggered back up to his feet and proceeded to casually wobble over to his basket. He flopped down into the folds of his favorite blanket and dropped off to sleep as though nothing untoward had ever happened.

The psychic and I stared at him, then at each other.

Neither of us was able to explain what had just happened.

"A release," she said. "Some kind of a release."

I only just managed to stop myself from shooting her a withering look. *Ya think?*

There was nothing *left* to be released. She had already witnessed the complete emptying of my tear ducts, as well as the complete emptying of my cat's stomach, bowel and bladder. Almost every bodily fluid had been spilled. I was certainly in no mood to see if blood was next.

We two humans then got to our feet, and it was only then that I noticed that our clothing was saturated with the filth that now adorned my kitchen floor. She graciously brushed aside my profuse apologies and my offer to loan her clean clothes, insisting that it was no problem at all.

"Maybe that was a seizure?" she said. We looked at Stanley, contently asleep in his basket. "Maybe this is the postictal aftermath of a seizure?"

"I don't know." I gazed at my slumbering cat. Because vomiting had been present, a seizure didn't seem so likely to me. Somehow this seemed different from the typical seizures where the patient lost bladder and bowel control. A face-saving explanation to offer her then occurred to me. "Could it be," I suggested, "like one of those Bible stories of exorcisms where the demon throws his victim-host into one last spasm before the demon truly departs?"

"Yes!" she exclaimed, sounding greatly relieved and brightening up. "That is what probably happened to your cat!"

I walked her to my door a second time, only now it was two women in sodden slacks that clung coldly to our legs, each walking in shoes with soiled soles.

The summary of our "woo-woo" session together was tragically simple: Neither of us had any idea why Stanley had that episode.

Presumably to break the tension, she joked how he was a bit like those cats on that TV show. "I think it's called—"

"—*My Cat From Hell*," I finished dully.

"Oh, sorry. You get that a lot, I guess?"

She hastily took her leave. After closing the front door, I leaned my back against it for a moment, closed my eyes and took another deep breath before confronting the havoc that had been wreaked upon my kitchen. It beggared belief.

Grime compounded by sludge compounded by filth was just everywhere. The wreaker of the havoc dozed innocently.

The pool of urine had seeped in all directions by now, including under the table and chairs.

One aspect about cleaning messes is that one's brain is free to be engaged elsewhere. I gathered cleaning rags and tackled my thrice-soiled kitchen floor while my brain mulled the day's events.

Like everybody else before her, this "Animal Communicator" had found no solution for Stanley's aggression. Like everyone else before her, she wasn't sure how much of a factor the brain damage was, and she, too, mentioned the TV show, like everyone else before her. Still, *unlike* everyone else before her, the thought occurred to me as I wielded an American mop, that she might have, just perhaps, telepathically seen an African broom.

I continued cleaning. Stanley slumbered on in his basket As I cleaned, I felt—what did I feel? Grief, mixed with resignation came over me. My dream of a cure must be shelved. The melancholy truth was that my life would now pivot from "Stanley will be cured" to "Stanley cannot be cured and must remain physically separated from Saba indefinitely." At one point I was cleaning with one hand as I placed a call to Stanley's veterinarian. After hearing about the day's events, she reassured me that there was no acute need to bring the cat in, but to simply keep an eye on him. Stanley's heavy anti-aggression medications were discussed. Undrugged, Stanley's disruptive behavior was untenable. Those medications, however, were rendered moot, since Saba and Stanley would now remain physically separate. A tapering schedule was decided upon. The cat I loved so dearly would now live out the rest of his life in Stanleyland, or he would be crated or monitored when indoors. And yet, I could derive some comfort in the message emailed to me multiple times from my Tanzanian friends from whom I had adopted him, that Stanley would have eked out his remaining years in that cage back in Dar es Salaam had he not been adopted. For more comfort, I firmly decided that Stanley and I needed another dancing session tomorrow with "Pata Pata."

The floor now sorted, I roused my poopy pussycat from his slumber and proceeded to bathe him, for the second time that day. My beloved cat who cannot be fixed sat quietly while I cleaned his urine-drenched fur and fecal-encrusted legs. His bright eyes glanced unconcernedly around the room as my washcloth wiped caked vomitus from his chin and chest.

Not long afterward, a clean kitty settled into a clean cat basket, in a clean kitchen while I prepared to leave the room to head for my own shower.

I crouched down and gave him one more caress, softly waggling his tipped ear.

"That was one really bizarre episode, wasn't it, darling?"

Stan merely peered up at me with his hopeful "Is it time for treats yet?" look.

Chapter 56
Wildebeest Trophy

That was a hunting trophy? I would have thought it rather peculiar. Might as well shoot a donkey.
—Craig

Virginia, 2018

No flickering ears.

The mounted head of a blue wildebeest hung on the wall of a friend's home in America, which I was visiting less than a year after I had returned from my Tanzania trip, and I was struck by how very still he was.

Back in Africa, both ears would constantly flicker. The omnipresent flies around wildebeest herds also caused constantly swishing, swishing, swishing tails that were just as busy as those constantly flickering ears.

Who shoots a wildebeest? Who does that?

Back in Africa, during my sunlight- and sisal-infused childhood, wildebeest had been almost as docile as cattle and as common and as numerous as the grains of sand on a beach. Having this as a hunting trophy seemed as absurd as shooting a dairy cow.

A Billion Blue Wildebeest

Bagging a wildebeest was hardly any great laudatory hunting achievement. They were so vast in number and so habituated to humans that cars can frequently approach within just a few yards. Wildebeest do not carry rabies. That *would* warrant being shot on sight. Hunters are not summoned because wildebeest are an especially great threat to a farmer's crops, like elephants. Nor are they known to be particularly aggressive or deadly, like Cape buffalo. They are not a member of the antelope family who are endowed with beautiful horns, as are the oryx and impala, but most especially the greater kudu. It might be argued that wildebeest are in competition with domestic cattle for grazing. But this still did not seem to me sufficient reason for it to be shot.

I could picture an African seeing this trophy and scoffing, "*Ooohoo! Bwana mkubwa!*"[74] Later when I described this absurd trophy to Craig, he replied, "I would have had trouble not snickering."

An oft-repeated story in our family lore involved how quickly I had become bored with the sight of wildebeest after our first game drive, partly due to the sheer number of the vast herds of these antelopes. I did state that I was "fed up with wildebeest" at that time, and yet I held, for the rest of my life, the deepest affection for these familiar and comical animals, ubiquitous though they might be. Greater kudu, always held me in complete, awestruck wonder. But the "Wil-Duh-Beasties" were my buddies. During my childhood, when African soil was beneath my feet and the Southern Cross was above my head, these resilient antelope impressed me with their perseverance. I carried in my heart the lessons they taught me for the rest of my life.

This trophy was mounted just high enough to be out of

---

74 So you think you're such a big shot?

my reach, or I surely would not have been able to resist the temptation to caress the muzzle of my old friend.

Were you in Tanzania when I was there? Did I see you? Your ears would have surely been flickering then . . .

With considerable effort, I kept my thoughts to myself about what sort of person would actually hunt a wildebeest. And *why*? For all I knew, perhaps the hunter had been a kind *mzungu* who had shot it to provide fresh meat to local villagers. Perhaps the hunter then decided to keep the head and get it mounted as a—Nope. My brain still could not absorb the concept of a wildebeest head as a hunting trophy.

Nobody in the room had noticed that I had lingered, staring, in front of the wildebeest. Nobody was close enough to have heard me bid him a whispered goodbye. We soon left the room and went about our day.

Perhaps I will never get used to the sight of hunting trophies. Perhaps I will always be slightly surprised to notice that the ears are not flickering.

If anything positive can be said about taxidermy, I suppose I could have begrudgingly conceded two points: I was just as pleased to avoid encountering the odor, and the constant flies that are omnipresent around living wildebeest.

When I arrived home that evening, it was a comfort to lay eyes on my own beloved (still very much alive) little African cat.

Stanley was intently stumbling and staggering toward me, falling, crashing down at every second stride.

"What is it, *paka wangu kipenzi*?" I hastened to meet him, since his torturous treks across the floor always tore at my heart. With a heavy sigh of relief and satisfaction, my African cat collapsed at my feet, destination reached, then gazed steadily up at me with innocent big green eyes, eyes that were housed in a skull that contained only half a brain.

I met his calm, steady gaze. My cubbie was intent on trying to convey some sort of message to me, and I bent to caress him.

"What is it?"

My hand encountered the wetness an instant after my nose encountered the odor.

Oh. Right.

Pity that I never did learn the Swahili for "this cat is one big hot mess."

Epilogue

"I hold thee fast, Africa"
—Suetonius, "The Life Of Julius Caesar"

About forty years after having grown up in Africa, there came a day when I was sitting in an American library, having just found a poem that perfectly captured some of my feelings, by a South African poet named Bridget Dore: "Africa Smiled." The middle part of the poem especially caught my attention:

> *"You cannot*
> *Leave Africa,"*
> *Africa said.*

She went on to state how Africa was always with you, that it was inside one's head. This part had me nodding in recognition. During my travels, I had not come across other expatriates who had felt quite the same way about their host country as those of us feel who had once lived in Africa.

The poem captured perfectly how Africa can become such an enmeshed part of one's identity that it manifests physically, in our thumbprints, in our heartbeats, and in our souls. Her poem warranted several re-readings, during which I lapsed into reverential silence and the hand that I had initially clapped over my mouth now drifted slowly to my lap.

"We are in you," Africa said.
"You have not left us, yet."

My years in Africa were something I always regarded as an incalculable gift. It eventually amounted to ten years in total that I spent on the continent, because after Dar I also lived in West Africa and then in Egypt. Those locations never did stand out in my mind quite as vividly as the time I had spent in Tanzania, and perhaps it was largely due to the absence of any notable animals or exotic pets. Our family spent about three years in Ouagadougou, the capital of present-day Burkina Faso, when it was still Haute Volta. We went to only one game park there, in which we occasionally saw elephant, if we were lucky. There were no rescues of animals that I can recall, and our household pet was a rather prosaic but beloved dog. Never a cat, since Craig was allergic. From there we moved to Alexandria, Egypt (no game parks at all) and had a simple life with two unremarkable dogs. Somewhere along the way, I dropped saying "So, anyway, go on" but still wrestle occasionally with The Blurts, and in moments of incredulity, I've learned to replace "truth-truth?" with "Really?"

My life itself came to be divided in my mind, in direct relationship to the continent, as I found myself referring to the three parts: Before Africa, Africa, and after Africa. Another frame of reference I used to measure time was to identify a period according to which animal I had at the time. "It was after Rafiki died, but before I adopted Saba."

Not surprisingly, my African memories and medley of experiences remain indelible in my mind. A Shakespeare quote, "I speak of Africa and golden joys," (*Henry IV*) came close to describing my thoughts, but it was perhaps my mother's words in an aerogram that best captured this sentiment for me:

I will always remember these past years. They were good.

Stanley settled into American life and after the incident with the psychic, my cat never again emptied all three chambers simultaneously. The reason for his aggression remained a mystery locked away in one very small, impaired brain.

Time passed, and eventually I moved through my mourning period, accepting that Stanley could never be cured, only managed. I no longer flogged the issue. Stanley's just-is-ness was embraced instead.

Some friends of mine, concerned about my mourning, very firmly decided that I needed another CH cat. Equally firmly, I declined.

Their own rescue glands were as overdeveloped as mine, however, so they continued to approach me with poignant, plaintive and pitiful tales of various CH cats they knew languishing in shelters, each one a picture of pathos and all forlornly awaiting adoption. They knew perfectly well my veritable Pavlovian response to an animal in need of rescue.

"No more cats," I said.

"But not all CH cats are aggressive like Stanley," said one friend.

"Your cat is an anomaly," said another.

"CH cats are sweet," said a third.

"No more cats," I replied, unyielding.

My second CH cat, Mpenzi,[75] came from a local rescue, and did indeed turn out to be the archetypal good-natured neuro cat. Her brain damage and clumsiness were far milder than Stanley's. And she had zero aggression.

---

75 Beloved

"See?" my friend said triumphantly. "They're not all like Stanley."

"Yes." My tone, which began as a reluctant mumble became firmer. "But no more CH cats."

Zulu, my third CH cat, was sweeter than even Mpenzi.

All three had some gradation of the CH "loose caboose" in their hind legs and the dominant personality. They stumbled and staggered. They crashed and careened into one another. Three ridiculously lovable CH faces gazed up at me with varying degrees of head tremor. All three cats cuddled together and groomed one another.

And yes, with his periodic aggressive periods, my beloved Stanley remains an anomaly amongst CH cats.

In later life, I found that my mother's philosophy of being placed on Earth to help others was not only widespread but also echoed in the writings of my beloved tabby's namesake, Sir Henry Morton Stanley:

> *When I have quitted this world, it will matter nothing to me what people say of me. Up to the moment of death, we should strive to leave something behind us. Something which can either Comfort, Amuse, Instruct or Benefit the living; and though I cannot do either, except in a small degree, even that little should be given.*

Sometimes I go online and click on TAWESO's Facebook page, and scroll to April of 2022. There's a video clip of Stanley there, and he doesn't look whatsoever like "one big hot mess." In that footage, my darling cubbie is innocently cleaning his paws.

Catherine MacLaine

A Billion Blue Wildebeest

Above photo courtesy of Dr. Thomas Kahema

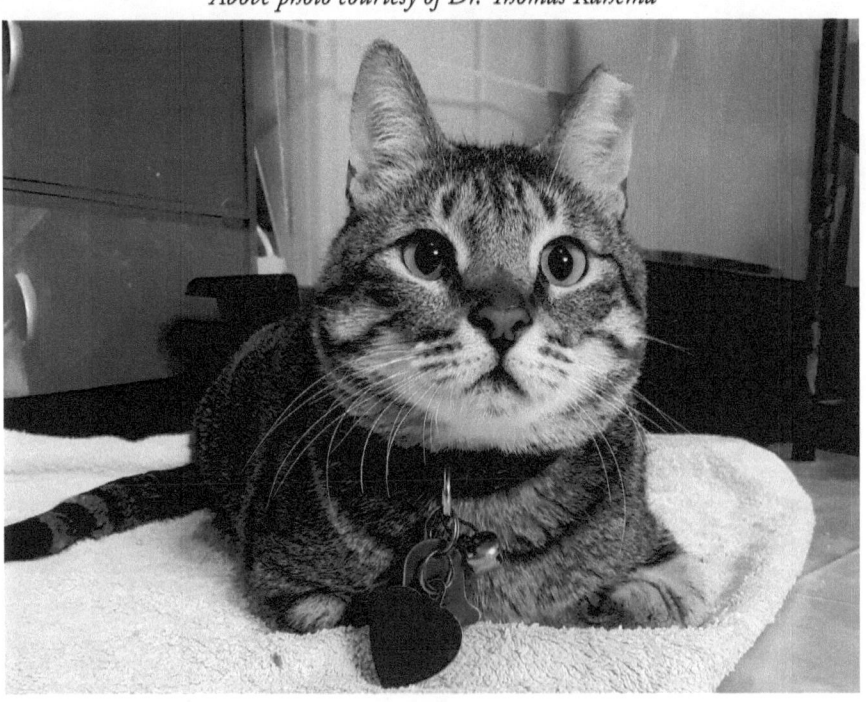

About the Author

Photo courtesy of Craig MacLaine   *Photo courtesy of Lorraine Cormier*

Catherine MacLaine has visited or lived in multiple African countries including Senegal, Ghana, Kenya, Uganda, Egypt, Burkina Faso, and Tanzania, in solo trips or with family. Her four decades of extensive travel also include Canda, the USA, the UK and Europe. Her lifetime of rescuing animals began in childhood and continued over the decades involving too many animals to count, both wild and domestic, healthy, or disabled. Among her earliest volunteer or paid jobs included animal shelters, stables, and dog grooming shops. She earned her Bachelor's degree from the Corcoran School of the George Washington University of Washington DC. She has been employed as a Medical Coder and a Coding Quality Analyst and when she is not writing, she can often be found enjoying Beatles music while cleaning out far too many cat litterboxes. She is a member of the Staunton Writers Group and has published in the Welcome Home newsletter. Catherine presently lives in Virginia with her husband and their disabled rescue cats.

A Note from the Author

If you enjoyed this book, I would be very grateful if you could write a review and publish it at your point of purchase. Your review, even a brief one, will help other readers to decide whether they'll enjoy my work.

If you want to be notified of new releases from myself and other Alkira Publishing authors, please sign up to the Alkira Publishing email list. In return you'll get a free ebook of short stories and book excerpts by Alkira Publishing authors. You'll find the sign-up button on the right-hand side under the photo at www.alkirapublishing.com. Of course, your information will never be shared, and the publisher won't inundate you with emails, just let you know of new releases.

Acknowledgments

Profuse thanks to my brother, Craig MacLaine, without whom this book would not have been possible. So many of our "remember when" conversations ended up in this book, and he very kindly shared his photographs and allowed me to quote from his correspondence and aerograms.

And to Mother, whose bedtime stories, dinner table stories, aerograms, and home videos provided some of the most vivid portions of the book.

I am humbled and grateful to have had two loving father figures: my stepfather who brought me to Africa, and my biological father who brought me figuratively back to Africa when he kept all my childhood aerograms, on which so much of this book is based.

Deep thanks to my husband and children, at whose urging this book was birthed. A very warm thanks to my daughter, who lovingly searched for a zoo that contained an exhibit of East African banded mongooses and took considerable effort to bring me there.

Much gratitude to Dr. Thomas W. Kahema, executive director of TAWESO, for bringing Stanley into my life, for his kind permission to use his words, and for educating me on the donkey hide global trade.

To the family of Dr. A Von Nagy, at Mount Meru Game

Lodge and Sanctuary near Arusha, Northern Tanzania, and especially Diana Cardoso Nagy and Zummi Cardoso, for their kindness to me in days of thunder and in halcyon days. My thanks to my Tanzanian friends who served as sensitivity readers and did proofreading and accuracy checks, including Johnny K, Nick Cashin, and Mr. Kainne, who added to my Tingatinga knowledge.

Many thanks to my editors, some of whom tied on her butchers' apron, picked up her meat cleaver and hacked away at this manuscript until we finally came in at a manageable word count, especially Christina Frey from Page Two Editorial and Katherine Kirk from Gecko Edits for copy edits. My profuse thanks always to the Alkira Publishing team and all their excellent work on this book.

I am indebted to my DeRege and Malingri relatives from Manta and Bagnolo, Piedmonte, Northern Italy. My profuse thanks to you all for your encouragement, accuracy checks and proofreading family lore.

I am grateful for the kindness shown to me by individuals throughout the book who are portrayed with pseudonyms, especially everyone connected with the man-eater saga. This one lion was perhaps amongst the strongest initial inspiring forces for me to write this book.

Much gratitude to my various beta readers, critique readers and fact-checkers, including R J Smith, Elaine D., Amy J., David W., George G. and all my friends at the gym who I annoyed by mentioning this book too often.

My deepest gratitude to the Tanzanian schoolchild. I cannot shake the feeling that somehow you might have reached down from the realm of the ancestors and blessed me by helping me with this book.

Last, I wish to thank Stanley for being patient when I

was late with his treats while immersed in the writing of "our" book.

***

If you have enjoyed this book, I encourage you to take a closer look at the animal shelter from which I adopted Stanley and consider sending a donation of any size.

A portion of the proceeds from the sale of this book will be going to TAWESO.

Tanzania Animal Welfare Society (TAWESO)
PO Box 10268
Dar es Salaam
Tanzania, Africa
Telephone +255 713 322 796
https://taweso.org
Facebook: Tanzania Animal Welfare Society (TAWESO)

The Tanzania Animal Welfare Society (TAWESO) is a registered non-government organization (NGO) that works to improve the welfare of all animals in Tanzania. Opened officially on March 1st, 2015, by Dr. Thomas Kahema and world-renowned primatologist, Dr. Jane Goodall, it is run mostly on a volunteer basis, with few employed staff members. Their goal is to raise awareness of animal welfare, especially since the Tanzanian Animal Welfare Act of 2008 is not well enforced. Dogs, cats and donkeys are, arguably, the most neglected animals in Tanzania with respect to vaccinations and veterinary care. Rabies is therefore endemic and the brutal abuse and killing of dogs and cats is common.

Donkey welfare is a particular focus for TAWESO, since these animals are often overworked, overloaded and often found pulling carts while wearing ill-fitting oxen yokes.

They are frequently beaten and abused while serving as pack animals, carrying water, working in the fields or brick kilns, or hauling logs or gold ore. Not surprisingly, this results in a shortened lifespan. The lifespan of a Tanzanian donkey can also be brought to a cruel end by those who steal and kill them for their donkey hide and for meat trade. In rural areas, the loss of a plow animal and beast of burden can then result in the ruination of the farmer. The ripple effects can extend to the then-impoverished families being torn apart as children and adults are then forced to find other means by which to make a livelihood.

If you feel moved to join me in supporting TAWESO, their contact donation information is as follows:

gofundme.com/tanzania-animal-welfare-society-taweso

Donations can also be sent using wire transfer.

Account name:	Tanzania Animal Welfare Society
Account number:	01J1095890700
Bank name:	CRDB Bank, Mlimani City Branch
Bank address:	PO Box 35407, Dar es Salaam, Tanzania
Swift code:	CORUTZTZ
Sort code:	3390

www.ingramcontent.com/pod-product-compliance
Lightning Source LLC
Chambersburg PA
CBHW030302080526
44584CB00012B/410